# This Old House

Little, Brown and Company
Boston   Toronto

First Edition

Vila, Bob.
   This old house.
   Bibliography: p.
   Includes index.
   1. Dwellings — Remodeling. I. Davison, Jane,
joint author. II. Title.
TH4816.V54    690'.837'0286    80-36745
ISBN 0-316-17704-0
ISBN 0-316-17702-4 (pbk.)


WAK

*Published simultaneously in Canada
by Little, Brown & Company (Canada)
Limited*

Printed in the United States of America

## Acknowledgments

All during the winter and spring that we were hard at work on our old house, photographer Bill Schwob was on hand to document every stage with thousands of stills, the comprehensive record supplementing the videotapes, which cannot be reproduced in print. Jane Davison and consultant Peter Steffian AIA worked on converting the story of the rehabbing into the written word, while Chris Pullman and designers Doug Scott and Lorraine Ferguson of WGBH–TV assembled both words and pictures to make a book. Betsy Pitha, the copy editor, kept track of all the thousands of details, and Peter Carr and Rachel Bunker supervised the manufacturing process. Overseeing the whole construction project was the foreman, editor Bill Phillips of Little, Brown and Company. Like the rehabbing itself, the building of the book that grew out of "This Old House" depended on many dedicated craftsmen, all of whom I'd like to thank.

Bob Vila

# Preface

The idea of fixing up an old house for television has always been an appealing one here at WGBH and has been around for about fifteen years; for one reason or another, however, nothing was ever done about it until recently. My own personal interest and background in the rehabilitation of old houses go back twenty years to when I and my poor, suffering family began to cope with an elderly wood frame cottage. Being slow learners, we next took on the termite-infested, rotting ruin of a farmhouse in which we now reside. It's not quite finished, but maybe someday. . . .

Coming to work every day covered with plaster dust earned me the reputation of resident home handyman. Fellow employees would spend their lunch hours with me discussing their own home projects. I had been lucky in that my father was a carpenter, and lots of what I knew came from him. While other kids played baseball, my brother and I painted, shingled, dug trenches, plumbed, wired, and plastered. After all those years of asking questions, at last I was in the position of passing along the information to others. Eventually the idea of sharing these trade secrets with a television audience was born.

I thought that the same viewers who lapped up sophisticated programming on subjects from microbiology to international diplomacy were often panicked by the simplest problems in the workings of ordinary houses. For practical reasons this same audience now needed to know something about home renovation and repair, as the costs of prime housing — perfectly designed, equipped, and maintained — rose out of reach. They were ready to begin at the beginning and learn.

Our notion was to provide an extended vicarious experience, not of isolated projects and specific skills but of the total rehabbing process from start to finish.

This would not be stagy or hooked up, but as close to reality as we could make it. We'd tackle a real house, in real time, with real workmen who would explain just what they were actually doing and why.

We hoped we could give viewers a sense of duration and process, and show within that large frame how the stages of a rehabbing overlapped and dovetailed as work proceeded.

Once we were off and running with plans for the show, we soon settled on a weekly format comparable to grand rounds in a hospital, when the great doctor takes his staff on a guided tour of inspection. Builder-designer-developer Bob Vila came on board as our energetic and knowledgeable host. ▼ He would represent the man in charge. He would be both *us* and *you*, the house's hypothetical owner. We even settled on a theme song that seemed suitably old-time and cheerful, Fats Waller's "Louisiana Fairytale."

But finding just the right house to rehab, the right ugly duckling to turn into a swan, was a stumbling block. I started scouting in the inner ring of Boston's suburbs,

but the places we could afford always seemed to defy rehabilitation. The market appeared to have suddenly gone dry.

One day, following a lead from Robert Fichter, then director of Boston's Parkman Center for Urban Affairs, I drove out to the section of the city known as Dorchester, which had been founded as an independent town in 1630 but was annexed in 1870. The house he recommended to me was in the historic neighborhood called Meeting House Hill, which was showing signs of life after a decade or so of neglect and flight. ▼

My first view of 6 Percival Street was from a distance, as I rounded a corner by the white-spired meetinghouse, and saw across an open park the shabby but elegant building I'd been looking for, situated high on the ledgy side of the hill, partially masked by a hideous brick garage. That's it, I blurted (much to the delight of the real estate broker). I knew nothing I was to discover on closer examination would change my mind.

The price was right, the location exciting, and the old house itself certainly offered us the chance to demonstrate a wide range of rehabbing techniques. Though impressively rundown and somewhat altered from the original plan, it still had character and a fantastic location. I hadn't come across a more deserving candidate for transformation in weeks of searching.

We began tapings. Once a week our mobile unit would roll up the hill, and the television crew would

join forces with the rehabbers. ▲ Our foray into what I call guerrilla television demanded a lot of everybody. We had only one working day to tape each half-hour show, only six to eight technicians to do all the work. The rehabbers had to compensate for our interruption of their breakneck schedule as well as perform on camera. Pressure mounted when we had shots that we had just one chance to get. A wall comes down only once.

Guerrilla television does sometimes feel like jungle warfare — with some casualties. On location the perfect conditions of the studio seemed much farther away than the station only a few miles north. Our small disasters defied the law of averages. One time every single radio microphone we had with us failed simultaneously. We just had to sit tight until replacements arrived, and then hustle to make up the lost hour. Not once but twice, cherry pickers rented for the day bled hydraulic fluid and halted with arms raised. There was no way we were going to get the aerial views we'd counted on. We had to get cracking and improvise. Fortunately, we never got really rained on, but everything else that could happen did.

We didn't have the filmmaker's advantage of shooting in short takes, with lots of extra footage that could be edited at leisure. We used a demanding television technique in which we switched back and forth between two cameras without cutting until we had to. ◀

The length of the scenes was often hard on our cameramen, who were really great, especially considering their working conditions. Sometimes they shot with plastic garbage bags shielding the camera from drizzle and snow, and Dick Holden, a cameraman of considerable skill, shot from ladders and on rooftops, and took his chances with cherry pickers. ▼ Our long-

suffering sound engineers had to deal with the sirens of passing fire trucks (that part of Dorchester is home to the busiest fire station in the city), jets roaring overhead, whining power saws. Bruce Bordett, our stage manager, had to cue Bob Vila while shooing off a pack of curious dogs. We didn't stop for much. We didn't have the time.

Long scenes were also hard on our instant stars, all those men and women experienced in various aspects of rehabbing who made their television debuts when they talked on camera with Bob. I'd encountered some skepticism about the risks of depending on interviews with people who'd never been on television before. We discovered that when someone really knows his business, he can usually talk about it coherently, even if he is shaking in his boots. Our experts were good sports, and some, I think, even discovered that they had a little bit of the ham in them.

As the programs first aired, we were delighted to find out how much wider our audience was than the usual one for public television. The constituency we'd expected did respond, but so did viewers who had previously found our programming unrelated to their interests and their daily lives. Letters and telephone calls came in, many from people who had no idea of ever rehabbing a house of their own but who found the pace, the race-against-time side of the show, to be like a sports event. Others thought of the series as dramatic entertainment, with Bob, Norm Abram (the chief carpenter), and the men as characters in a tale of suspense with a happy ending.

Would-be sidewalk superintendents rallied around their television sets. Instead of having to spy through knotholes in a barricade around a building site, they could be right there on the job with us while sitting comfortably at home.

Fans began to appear in person out at the old house itself. They came as tourists, or with suggestions or historical information, and once in a while simple self-interest brought them. During one particularly hectic taping, I became aware of a presence dogging my steps. With a certain impatience I turned to a small gnarled old gentleman. Seizing his chance, he began in a heavy brogue, "Last week on the program Bob said that he was going to get rid of those old cast-iron radiators, and I was just wondering if. . . ."

At the beginning of the series Bob referred often to the hypothetical family that would eventually live in the house. Its future occupants grew increasingly abstract as we got more involved in the project and began unconsciously to think of it as *our* house. I'm afraid I went one step farther and really got quite possessive, angrily waving trucks away so they wouldn't back into the new fence, staying after hours to paint woodwork, dropping by frequently to talk things over with Norm.

As we came down to the finish, with the showing and sale of the completed house only a few weeks away, Bob finally said, "Russ, it's absolutely clear. You're going to have to move into the house yourself."

I didn't, but some fortunate new owners did. We hope they are enjoying living in the place as much as we enjoyed working on it.

Among the many who contributed to the successful outcome of "This Old House" as a television production, all of whom I'd like to thank, some individuals should be singled out. First I think of Robert Fichter of the Parkman Center for Urban Affairs, who provided inspiration and directed us to Dorchester, and of our bankers and enthusiastic friends Robert Spiller, president of The Boston Five; and Herbert Gray, president of the Suffolk Franklin Savings Bank. John Carver, development officer at WGBH, found the money we needed as well as many donations from the community, while the late Mark Stevens, formerly program manager, believed in our idea and gave us good air time. The WGBH television crew was tops, and I'm grateful as well to both Bob Vila and Bonnie Hammer, associate producer of the show. I also want to thank Montgomery Ward & Company, whose generosity made "This Old House" available to the Public Broadcasting System. Finally, my thanks to Norm Abram, head carpenter, without whom we never would have done such a wonderful job.

Russ Morash
Producer-Director
"This Old House"

# Contents

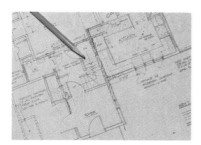

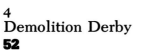

# 1
# Breaking Ground

The construction of a house used to start when the first shovel of earth was turned and the excavation for the foundation begun. Today the official beginning of a project of similar scope may be marked by the demolition of an existing wall. Sledgehammer replaces shovel, as rehabilitation comes into its own, and new homes rise out of old houses.

Open land in suburbs and cities is scarce and expensive. The costs of totally new construction are escalating in terrible leaps, and recently built houses in good condition are priced out of the reach of most prospective owners. The housing squeeze is on in earnest.

Structures that may have deteriorated, or may not be in the most sought-after neighborhoods or in the architectural styles that have recently been most popular, suddenly have a new appeal. Ten years ago an old Victorian house like the one we adopted seemed to have a bleak future ahead of it, but today buyers are taking a fresh look at residential real estate they once would have dismissed as hopeless.

The worse the condition of a house, the bigger the bargain it is likely to be but the greater the commitment to extensive work. Rehabbing projects like ours are not just a matter of a few Saturday mornings spent painting and patching, or a short visit from the electrician. The investment of time and money required is closer to that of new construction than to that of the limited fix-it jobs in the old tradition of do-it-yourself.

Lots of people have energy and imagination, but few have the skills or experience to undertake really major rehabilitations on their own, any more than they would plan to build a house from the ground up. The scale of the jobs demands help, and lots of it.

Many excellent home improvement and how-to books are now on the market, and we will recommend some of the best. These teach the reader how to do specific tasks himself, and to replace shingles or repair electrical outlets or lay tiles. In their illustrations the worker who is nailing or wiring is often an abstraction, sometimes just disembodied hands performing with hammer and pliers. All his work simply happens to assorted parts of some anonymous structure. A job begins and is completed, just one in an anthology of separate and unrelated lessons. Organization of the tasks and their cumulative effect is not the issue.

But the inexperienced owner who confronts a house that needs a major overhaul faces scores of projects that are interrelated in a crucial way. He's probably uncertain in what order to advance with them. He's unlikely to have either the time or the ability to tackle many of them himself.

He needs to understand not only what has to be done but also how to organize its doing. Though there are some details he can handle himself, he must face the fact that his role is essentially supervisory. He is literally an overseer. He needs to be able to see the broad view, the whole picture.

Breaking some ground of our own, we come in here. Unlike any other book we know of, this one provides an overview of the entire forest of separate projects. Our goal is to give the general reader, the inexperienced old-home renovator, that broad picture, so that he will have the understanding and the confidence to set off to make his own way through the trees. And, as Russ Morash has said, we have done this in a real house, in real time, and with real people at work, to provide a vicarious experience as close to reality as possible.

Our story aims to be deeply encouraging. As we describe our work, we are simply saying: this is how *we* did it. But we go on to add: this is how *you* might think about getting on with the job you have ahead of you. It's not so hard, so mysterious a procedure as you might once have thought.

Sometimes, as in reality, we made mistakes, to our loss but your profit. Our case history is supposed to give you distant early warnings about dangers ahead in order to prevent the horror show that can unnerve the unsuspecting, the inexperienced. We also chart the highs and the lows in a long job, the satisfactions and the occasional panics, the lulls when nothing seems to be moving forward, and the wonderful moments when everything falls into place. We want to show how a whole rehabbing is done technically but also what it's like to live through it — to include the human factor.

The book is also a down-to-earth introduction to the vocabulary and the methods of the building trades. You may not learn exactly how to install a plumbing system yourself, but you will learn how to talk intelligently to the professionals who can. You will learn the sequence in which the various stages of a large-scale rehabilitation proceed and how these stages interrelate to form one continuous process.

Working with still pictures and the written word, we have slowed down the fast-breaking story of the television series on which the book is based, taking advantage of a more leisurely pace to amplify and organize the material covered in the thirteen weekly shows. Each of the thirteen chapters falls into two parts, in effect show and tell.

In the first sections, we *show* you what we actually did. As if in a journal, I describe the progress made during the prceding week. The point here is to show exactly how the process moved ahead in its stages, at what rate, and in what order. (Essentially these journal entries are the scenarios of the television shows.) Then I go on to draw from the whole experience, organizing the information by subject, such as planning, demolition, or framing.

In the second sections of each chapter, we *tell* you about alternatives, give suggestions and warnings, and dispense homely wisdom. We turn from our actual experience to your potential one. In both sections of the chapters we've put the new or unfamiliar words of the building trade vocabulary into italics when they're first used and defined. When small floor plans supplement the photographs, an orienting arrow shows the position from which the photograph was taken.

Now that I've broken the ice, if not also the ground, let's go back to that first week on the job, when we weren't at all sure we hadn't tangled with the wrong house.

# 2
# Facing Facts

**Week 1**  This morning we made a hard, cold reappraisal of the old house we'd just bought. The excitement and the euphoria of the actual transaction were all over for the moment. When we returned for a second, perhaps more rational look at the place, we took with us an experienced real estate appraiser to double-check our original

estimate of the possibilities and the problems ahead. As a representative of one of the two banks that, in effect, held our mortgage, he had of course already cased the house himself. To get an appraisal *after*, not *before*, buying a marginal house like ours would have been really foolish on our part, and it certainly isn't the way banks operate.

We had had a few uneasy second thoughts. Had we adopted a white elephant just big and stubborn enough to wear us down? Would our rehabbing necessarily be so large in scope that we'd end up simply discouraging our viewers and bankrupting ourselves? Such sobering questions are typical of the morning-after malaise that hits most new homeowners but afflicts prospective rehabbers with a special intensity.

Together the voluble appraiser John Hewitt and I toured the barren grounds, sizing up the exterior of the house. ▶ We started from the south and moved in a counterclockwise route. John first sent me up on a ladder to check for rot, while he very sensibly stayed firmly on the bedrock of Dorchester, taking notes on what I found.

By the time we had made the great-circle tour I had had a pretty strong dose of the dismal. Our eaves on all four sides were in obvious trouble with rot, ▶ and the roof looked highly suspect. Rot had also eaten into the front porch. Besides its roof and floor, its Victorian ornamental posts ▼ were, in John's phrase, "all shot." So were the cellar door and the attached shed we called a mud room, which leaned wearily against the one-story kitchen wing. The paint everywhere was eroded, blistered, cracked, or peeling, and clearly there had been a long-standing problem with moisture creeping down from leaky gutters through the clapboard siding.

In addition a major remodeling forty years ago had left the old house with symptoms of split personality. Out-of-period elements that had been added stuck out like the proverbial sore thumbs: a Colonial-type entrance ◀ (with a red paneled door and flanking carriage lamps) into a vestibule on the street side; small-paned windows in the kitchen; a stark concrete patio north of the mud room, whose pitched roof was a handyman's classic of corrugated fiberglass panels. "Oh boy," John cracked, "that sure doesn't go with a nineteenth-century house. That's gotta go, Bob." I agreed.

When we turned from the patio to inspect the two-car garage, a 1940 number, we noted that its woodwork — large and small doors, and windows — was a mess, but that the brick construction was solid. The garage could be spruced up, refitted, painted to match the house, but that meant more work, more money.

My second thoughts were getting gloomier and gloomier. John tried to cheer me up by saying that at least he found no signs of termite infestation in the foundation area, but that we ought to get a professional inspection to be sure. I managed a smile.

Our exterior tour completed, we mounted the brick steps of the street-side entrance. We were glad to get inside where it was warm. A stroll around a hilltop quarter acre in early February is stimulating but a little brisk for comfort.

After passing through the small vestibule, we entered a narrow living room, whose axis ran north and south. ▼ A south window overlooked the bare and frozen little front yard and driveway, while one on the west faced the pudding-stone walls of St. Peter's Church across Percival Street.

Both the living room and the adjacent back parlor had worn and grimy oak flooring, which John spotted as veneer that might not survive further sanding. Though the rooms had leaky old cast-iron radiators and sagging ceilings, they were sunny and essentially cheerful.

In such a straightforward and unpretentious house as ours, with its plain woodwork and four-square plan, the back parlor stood out as the fanciest room in the house. ▲ It boasted two terrific features, in John's estimation: a bright bay of three windows overlooking the small park to the north; and a pretty, though dis-colored, little Victorian marble fireplace, with a coal-burning grate.

In the rest of the first floor, we confronted a floor plan that had been remodeled into a maze — or at least a puzzle. Its redundant doorways into the stair hall were original; some partitions, however, were the aftermath of various subsequent improvisations.

The former dining room was a case in point. A door-sized arched niche on the west wall contained a flimsy china closet, featuring ox-eye plastic panels, a

**9**

handyman's special that John advised us to eliminate. A much wider but similar arched space yawned opposite, on the wall between dining room and kitchen. ▲

The kitchen provoked some of John's harshest words. ▶ He didn't spare "those punky little windows, crummy old cabinets," though he did counter with an upbeat appraisal of the room as "good space, which is important today."

The last room on the first floor was the weirdo of the house. We couldn't even give it a name. Years ago it had been a consulting room in a medical suite, we were to discover, but it had subsequently been improvised upon, though certainly not improved, when the suite had been converted into an apartment of sorts. ▼

Now it was just a mishmash, with assorted paint colors turning the woodwork into patchwork, and encumbered with a confusion of kitchen appliances. A par-

tition intruded on the triple window that faced south onto the front porch, trapping one unit in a slot of a lavatory that had been inserted between the kitchenlike room and the living room to the west of it. John could see no alternative but to "rip everything out."

As we climbed up to the second floor, John commented on the unusual little double-hung window ▶ that hid behind the diagonal of the rising staircase, only half visible from either floor. After we examined the four bedrooms opening off the key hall, John was positively merry: "You have good fir floors and at least two good large bedrooms up here. Closet space is pretty good too." ◀

Then we stared into the only bathroom on the floor. What a depressing sight. It was just old enough to be obsolete, not old enough to be quaint. ▼

"Oh Bob," John said, as if offering his condolences. "Oh, Bob." Even he was at a loss for words. He knew, and I knew, that this bathroom was going to need some expensive attention.

On the third floor we visited four neat, square rooms whose walls sloped in slightly because of the angle of the roof. Dormer windows let in a lot of light and air; these rooms weren't dark and gloomy garrets. ◀ A resident caretaker was to live up here for a while, so we had installed a temporary partition at the top of the stairs for privacy.

After we had made our way down to the basement, a shadowy place lit by dangling bare light bulbs, and John had had a chance to look around, he pronounced it sound: "It's dry and lofty, the concrete floor is in good shape, and so is the stone foundation." ▶ Then he zeroed in on the ancient furnace, "an old coal-burning, one-pipe steam job," converted to oil. We agreed that its days were numbered.

When John examined our fuse board, he shook his head. At only 30-ampere service, our wiring was totally inadequate. We should have at least 100 amps to conform to modern electrical standards. But our plumbing lines, judging from those he could see running across the basement ceiling, didn't look too bad to him, though they were an assortment of copper, brass, and cast iron. While gazing upward, we noticed that the joists and the subfloor of the first story looked good, with solid 2 x 10s and some 5 x 10s supported on brick piers.

After all of John's alternating good and bad news, I wasn't quite sure what to think. Bad news seemed to be in the majority, and my fears substantiated. We had a broken-down house on our hands, which would require total rehabbing inside and major work outside.

In an earlier conversation with the real estate broker who sold us the house, he said he thought we could afford to put $30,000 into fixing up the place, considering the low purchase price of $17,000. We'd then have a fighting chance of getting our investment back when it came time to sell. At $47,000 we'd probably not have priced ourselves out of the market. On the other hand, no house in the neighborhood had *ever* sold for anywhere near that amount.

I asked John what he thought we'd paid for the house. His guess was $16,000 to $17,000, which was a relief. At least we hadn't invested too much initially. But then he added that of course we'd have to put $60,000 into the rehabbing. When I started to splutter, he put his hand on my shoulder, and I realized he was kidding. Little did either of us know that his figure would be far closer to the reality than mine.

"This house has got a good solid foundation," he

said, "and a great location. Bob, you've got a good old house."

I certainly hoped he was right. Surely with enough energy and the $30,000 we'd allocated, we would be able to do the job. Notice that I said *we*. This race was scheduled to finish in a little more than three months, and would demand steady collaboration among a lot of people with a lot of different skills. It would be an endurance contest at times — but everyone should know that a major rehabbing is a demanding process that often boils down to a matter of simply hanging in there.

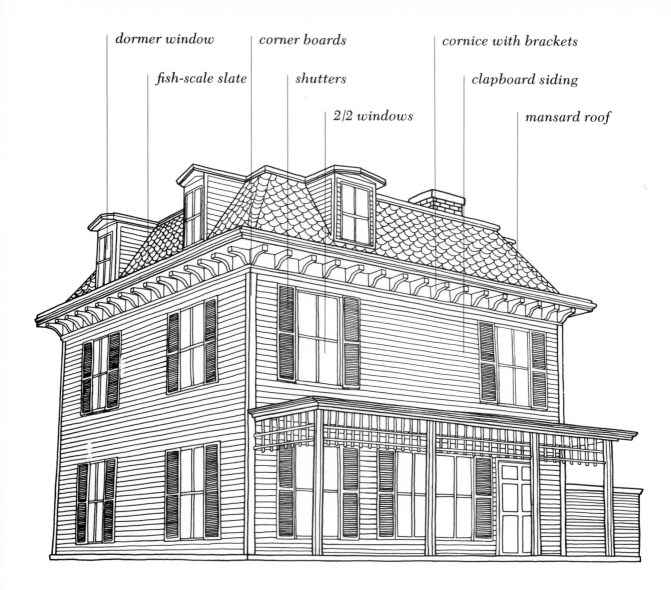

dormer window     corner boards     cornice with brackets

fish-scale slate     shutters     clapboard siding

2/2 windows     mansard roof

**O**ur early 1860s house was never a high-fashion model or a trend-setter. It was always homey, a family place. As architectural critic Ada Louise Huxtable wrote of it, "This is the kind of house that has meant home to many generations of Americans . . . a solidly and plainly carpenter-built dwelling in a mix of vernacular styles." ▲

A vernacular house has not been designed to order by an architect. It's "the house next door" that looks like the one on the next block, or in the next town, erected by a builder who usually reflected the popular taste of the period, having selected ideas from examples he saw around him.

Today many house buyers, particularly younger

ones, have a new appreciation of certain historical styles of ordinary domestic architecture that have been unfashionable for a long time. Our house was one of those described by the catchall term, Victorian, until recently a dirty word of sorts, a Halloween joke. Twenty-five years ago, the stained glass, intricate dark woodwork, or other ornamental details of such a house would have been stripped off or painted over. Now Victorian houses are prizes, and their characteristic details are lovingly restored, polished. The new wave of rehabbers understands that the recently old is beautiful, or can be.

Our house has most of the earmarks of a typical nineteenth-century house, as defined by the National Trust for Historic Preservation:

1. Dormer windows on the top floor
2. Mansard roof
3. Cornice with decorative brackets
4. Shutters
5. "Two over two" window sashes (sometimes written 2/2, indicating there are two panes in each sash of a double-hung window)
6. Clapboard siding
7. Corner boards
8. Fish-scale slates on the roof (ours were replaced with composition shingles in 1921, but the house next door has retained its original fish scales)

Our builder had a lingering taste for the Greek Revival style of the 1840s and 1850s, as exemplified by the proportions of the front porch, but he also chose elements of a slightly later fashion, the Italianate, which rose to popularity in the late 1850s and flourished in the 1860s. Our house featured such Italianate details as the decorative brackets on the cornice, an American translation into wood of Renaissance stone prototypes. ▶

The dominant feature of our Victorian house was its imposing mansard roof, curved high above the rocky site three stories below. The mansard roof was another American adaptation of a European style, the seventeenth-century French innovation of François Mansart. In the mansard style, the pitch of the roof is broken into slopes with more or less vertical sides and a horizontal top. The top of our roof was almost flat, while the sides (a cross between roof and wall) sloped steeply but with some degree of curve. Headroom under a mansard roof is of course greater than under a gabled roof, and the dormer windows that are also characteristic of this style admit a lot of light.

We wondered what the house had been like when it was new, one hundred and twenty years ago, before alterations, before improvisations, before the original intent of the builder had been blurred by changes made to suit different needs and tastes. As our work proceeded, we found clues here and there that enabled us to make a guess about the plan of the house as it was in 1860s.

Looking backward can be addictive: it's hard to stop once you get started. It all begins with simple curiosity. For example, as we started working we asked ourselves who had added the unaccompanied south dormer, which didn't seem to be original, or why there were two competing "front doors," with part of the porch taken up by the south end of the living room. Once the *whos* and *whys* start, any rehabber can turn into an architectural historian. That's how we found ourselves hustling off to dig in public archives.

We came up with a basic outline of the history of the house. The site was first privately owned in 1818; by 1864 the house was built, the owner Eliza T. Clapp;

and then a succession of prosperous and respectable Boston types moved in and out over the years. Until comparatively recently Meeting House Hill in Dorchester was prime real estate, and 6 Percival Street an address to be proud of. But, like so many older residential areas ringing major American cities, it slumped when the post–World War II flight to the suburbs siphoned off so many of the families who were its economic base.

The depressed condition of our house in midwinter reflected a nationwide phenomenon, just as the rehabilitation completed in the spring was to represent another, more hopeful trend. Many intrinsically good neighborhoods like Meeting House Hill, having touched bottom, are rebounding, and houses in them are still bargains.

Our research into the history of the house gave us some basic facts but not much life and color and detail. But because our project was before the public we had an extraordinary advantage. Neighbors and viewers would write in or come over with their photographs, documents, and memories. One former resident returned to tell us that "Mad Jack" Percival, for whom the street was named but whose identity escaped us, was a flamboyant nineteenth-century naval hero who in 1855 had retired to a house across the street from ours, having previously persuaded the admirals not to junk but to rehab the historic ship *Constitution*.

Who was the dour woman in the oval portrait found in the basement, dusted off, and initially rehung in the dining room? Moved around, project by project, sternly inspecting progress, she became a kind of conscience figure. A neighbor identified her as one Mary McGinty, whose family once owned our house. By the time of her sudden demise one morning in the great flu epidemic of 1917 she was residing in the twin house opposite ours. That evening the duplicate front porch was draped in black crape.

Our greatest windfall of both color and facts about the house came unexpectedly in the mail from Maine, sent us by Mrs. Georgia Glidden Packard, whose family had lived at 6 Percival Street from 1922 to 1938. She and her two sisters had a perfectly preserved set of photographs of both exterior and interior, which they generously shared with us, along with their vivid reminiscences. They introduced us to the house when it was alive and lived in. We could see a blaze in the marble fireplace, a cat curled up on a nearby rocker.

We learned that the living room once had floor-

to-ceiling windows that opened onto the front porch, a lost feature whose existence we had never before suspected. We had known that the single dormer on the south was added in 1932, but now we found out why: a widowed aunt had come to live, and she needed more ventilation in her room.

We heard of parties, when the young people danced right around the first floor, from front parlor to back, into the hall, and around to where they began, while jazzy music blared from a handwound Victrola set on one of the cast-iron radiators. Afterward the girls and their mother would have a late-night debriefing up in the large bath-dressing room, then in the northeast corner of the second floor. Those were the proverbial good old days, when Persian lilacs and syringa bloomed in the yard, and a grapevine covered a trellis right across the porch eaves.

Now we had personal testimony of a past mood, as well as some firm facts to flesh out the structural biography of the house.

In 1938 the house changed hands, bought by Arthur T. Ronan, a prominent surgeon who was apparently one of those legendary doctors beloved by his patients and still remembered in the neighborhood. In order to practice at home, Dr. Ronan had to make certain changes in the house. In 1939, according to building permits issued to him, he altered the first floor to provide a separate street entrance for his patients and a medical suite — waiting room, consulting room, and lavatory — that could be shut off from his family quarters. He also moved the upstairs bathroom from the northeast corner to the other side of the house. Outside he added the patio, and the next year he built the garage.

What was sacrificed in making these changes was a certain intrinsic logic and clarity of floor plan inside, and of symmetry and consistency on the outside, where choices in exterior decoration added Colonial ornaments to the Victorian mixture.

In 1965 the house once again was sold. The house we found spoke for itself of thirteen subsequent years of wear and tear, of many children in good moods (poster-painting bright flowers on a bedroom wall) ▼ and in bad (scribbling dark threats on another), of repairs postponed and danger signals ignored, of "home improvement" projects slapped together. How fast a house can slip into depression! Worn out, abandoned, at first glance the place seemed hopeless, until we began to *see the possibilities,* a phrase that sometimes falls into the category of famous last words.

etermining what is worth saving in an old house is an essential part of the initial appraisal of it. An unfinished basement like ours is the place where evidence of the present state of an old structure merges with that of its past, and where investigation of both past and present suggests logical ways to plan for its future. We might well have started our own appraisal down in our basement, rather than ending there.

What can you learn by looking around in a basement? First, you can get a sense of the original floor plan of the upper stories. Not many people drastically remodel old basements, and even if part of it has been

finished off for a playroom or some other use, enough original structural members usually remain out in the open to give you the inside story. Even in a finished area you can usually poke up through holes around pipes and measure the *joists*, timbers that support the floor above. ▲ Masonry or steel major supports, like the brick piers in our basement or Lally columns in other houses, will probably have remained untouched over the years, even if the walls upstairs they once supported have been removed. Often basement partitions remain as a clue to former counterparts above. The existence of doubled joists also suggests that a partition above them may once have existed.

The relation of walls upstairs to supports down under helps you to deduce the original floor plan and load-bearing structure of the house, and so indicates exactly how much remodeling has been done, and where.

When you're doing a rehabbing, most often the sensible general procedure (aside from any particular interest in restoration) is to return the house to the way it was. It would be silly, for example, to devise a floor plan that called for a new living room six inches wider than the original had been, when a support system designed for the original dimensions still existed. Research into the precise structural history of a house clearly has a practical purpose.

A realistic rule of thumb is that most remodeling of old houses has not been done with the care of the original construction. Often it has been amateur work that doesn't measure up to professional standards. This is particularly true of a house in a neighborhood that has gone down. Though it may be on the way up now, during the depressed years repairs probably were done on the cheap. When appraising the effects of previous remodelings, you should particularly note all the junctions where old and new meet. These may well be trouble spots.

In the basement the fact that so much of the inner workings of the house is exposed to view makes further inspection easy. You can check out more major structural members, not simply as clues to the plan of the house, but for their intrinsic condition. Do beams sag? Are there signs of rot or insect damage? How about the *sills*, the wooden base attached to the foundation on which the whole frame of the house rests? They might look all right from the outside, but you can get at their inner secrets by reaching up inside the basement and testing them. Stick a sharp tool like a screwdriver or ice pick into any exposed wood to see if it's suspiciously soft or spongy.

You can see how large the joists are and how closely spaced. You can check out the exposed plumbing pipes and electrical wiring for variations in material, and you can note the way they are notched or attached to the joists. In this way you may find clues to additions to the systems or reroutings incurred in past remodelings. You can examine the furnace and hot water heater. You can look for signs of water leaking into the basement from outside.

There are certain key faults that almost automatically disqualify a house from further consideration. These are:

### Excessive settlement

The foundation has settled unevenly, and the house is askew. Cracks in the foundation are one indication; sloping floors, gaping joints, shaky stairways, doors that won't close because of uneven frames, are some other signs. There are borderline cases of settlement, whose symptoms can be lived with, but the problem cannot be ignored. Listen to professional opinions. The scale of remedying both the major problem and the multitude of minor problems that reverberate from settlement, even when it's partial or arrested, is usually too great to be undertaken on an ordinary domestic level.

### Termite damage

If there is extensive damage to major structural members, abandon all hope. The house is basically unsound. If you see signs of sawdust during your initial inspection, be wary, but before automatically ruling out the house, call in an exterminator, or licensed pest control inspector, who will be able to tell you if there are active termites or some lesser infestation, such as carpenter ants or powderpost beetles. He can also determine how much damage has actually been inflicted and what can be done to get rid of the pests. The situation may not be as bad as you suspect. Remember that the seller is responsible for providing an official certification of "termite clearance."

### Sills in need of replacement

Whether the cause is insect damage or rot, if most of its sills are decayed and undermined, a house is not worth considering. Replacing sills is a major structural job that under ordinary circumstances no one should undertake. The whole house has to be jacked up and the faulty sills replaced piecemeal, a very expensive proposition. By the time you're finished dealing with the sills, you're only back to where most rehabbers start. ▶

Though the house you're considering may have none of these basic disqualifying problems, you may find that so many minor

deficiencies may have accumulated that you won't want to commit yourself to paying for fixing them. The assortment of needs that our old house presented would probably frighten most prospective buyers off (as apparently it did, until we came along).

When you're looking around a house yourself there are certain things you should keep a weather eye out for. Though no one of them is in itself disqualifying, here are some we think are important, in capsule form:

### Heating system

The age of the system is important, even if the furnace and its means of distribution seem to be sound. Older heating plants, especially converted coal burners, eat up lots of fuel. Hot air systems are drafty but often cheap to run. Forced hot water is what you want.

Today the cost of operation is as much an issue as the mere fact that a system is in operating condition. An old oil burner may be working as well as it ever did, but if it has always wasted oil, that's no help. Anyone considering a house with an older heating plant might do well to price a new furnace and hot water heater that contain energy-saving improvements and figure those costs into his calculations.

### Plumbing

In the patch-on systems common in old houses the combination of different kinds of pipes can present a major problem. You often have to count on starting again from scratch.

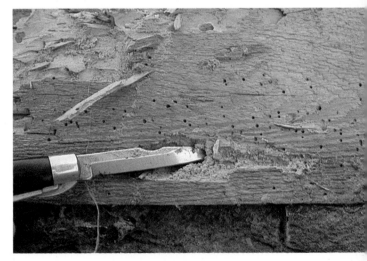

Be sure to check out water pressure. The difficulty usually arises between the street main and the house, in an old underground pipe, one clogged with sediment or damaged by tree roots or in some other way. Inside the house, similar mineral buildup may also further diminish pressure. Turn on faucets throughout the house, some simultaneously, to gauge the service. When the water in the kitchen is running full blast, do you get only a trickle in the basin in the third-floor bathroom? How much new work would be required to get the pressure up to an acceptable level?

### Electrical system

First go right to headquarters and look over the electrical board in the basement. If you find only fuses, you will know that the system is pretty old. ▼ A board that has both fuses and circuit breakers is newer, one with nothing but circuit breakers is newest.

The number of fuses or circuit breakers tells you how many circuits you have. By examining them you can tell if you have at least one 220/230-volt circuit as well as the standard 110/115-volt circuits. You should have at least 100-ampere service coming into the panel. This should be adequate enough to serve a house of moderate size, like ours, especially one that doesn't have air conditioning. Since the trend will undoubtedly continue to be toward energy-saving or transistorized appliances, 100 amps should take care of future needs. Two-hundred-amp service costs a great deal more to install than 100,

and might provide twice the power you'd actually need. We chose to install it, but we could have gone the other way.

Again, especially if you have a patch-on system, you should have a professional engineer or electrician tell you what you have and what you may need in additional circuits. Remember, however, that there is a difference between a dangerously under-wired system, and one that is only mildly inconvenient because of too few outlets. You may be able to live with the latter, if you have other priorities. Electrical code requirements apply if you make major renovations in old systems.

### Stairways

Check your stairwell if you have one. Many old cantilevered staircases with turns like ours tend to sag away from the wall toward the center of the well. If yours doesn't, so much the better. A serious sag may require reconstruction. A less serious one is something you can learn to live with.

### Paint

Besides the obvious matters of wear and tear on interior surfaces, and peeling, checking, and blistering outside, look out for paint buildup on window frames. Sometimes windows are sealed shut with an accumulation of paint and can't be opened again without damage to the frame itself. A time-consuming restoration job is the result. In any case, stripping down frames so they can operate properly is at best a great deal of work.

### Bathrooms

Just because a fixture is old doesn't mean it should summarily be condemned. Why bother to substitute something else for a superb old claw-and-ball bathtub in good condition? On the other hand, many old fixtures are irreparably stained and must be replaced.

Water damage to the bathroom floor itself, such as loose and curling composition tiles, has probably resulted from surface water, from splashing children or dripping shower curtains. Serious plumbing leaks occur under the surface and will show up on the ceiling of the room below.

When ceramic tiles are loose or missing, water from underneath or behind is usually responsible, and in this case the source

will have to be found and fixed. In general you have to count on taking up a whole tile installation, because it usually can't be patched. Ceramic tile sizes have changed over the years, and a match is practically impossible.

### Chimneys and fireplaces

Most problems with chimneys are caused by deteriorated mortar and soot buildup. ▲ Outdoors, look up at the chimney for missing mortar or problems with a cement cap. Focus on the *flashing*, the metal strips around the base of the chimney that seal the joint between masonry and roof. Black gunk on the flashing is a sign that tar has been used to try to correct leakage problems that may still be unsolved.

Binoculars are a useful tool in appraising areas you can't get to, like chimney, roof, or gutter, so don't be afraid to look like a birdwatcher. We might well have used a pair when we checked our own roof and eaves.

Perhaps we would have made a more realistic appraisal than we did with the naked eye.

Inside, check to see if there is a damper and make sure it operates. Look for signs of smoke on the mantelpiece, a mark of a poor draft. If the chimney passes through an attic, go up there and check to see if any soot is coming through the joints between bricks. In many cases leaks can be remedied by the insertion of a flue liner (by a professional). Try to check around the chimney to see if there is any charred wood abutting it. As a fire precaution, framing should clear the masonry by 2 inches for interior chimneys and ½ inch for exterior ones. If it doesn't, you should figure on some rebuilding to isolate the wood.

### Roof

Many an old house still has its original slate roof. There's no better roof, but it does present a continuing maintenance problem. **25**

Roofers who can repair and replace missing slates still do exist, but their work is not cheap. Often a homeowner will be talked into redoing his whole roof with modern composition shingles on the grounds that it would cost very little more than a small slate repair job. He should resist the sales pitch and stick with slate.

Some more experienced or naturally independent buyers feel they are capable of doing the entire house appraisal themselves. They would probably do well to organize their findings by following a checklist. Ours is only one example. You can devise your own or adapt other more detailed ones from reference books like George Hoffman's *How to Inspect a House*. A formal checklist keeps you from overlooking any steps in your investigation, and also prevents you from ignoring practical problems you might prefer to gloss over because you've fallen in love with the house in question. Often your pocket calculator will tell you something your heart doesn't want to hear. But both feeling and fact are important. Buying a house is not, after all, like buying a factory.

Even if you're determined to conduct your own inspection, you might still do well to get outside evaluations about specific technical aspects from plumbers, electricians, or other members of the building trades. These people can tell you if what you have is adequate or inadequate, and what you would have to do to bring it up to minimal standards. Old houses usually have electrical and plumbing systems that have been patched onto over the years, and these are very hard for an amateur to evaluate.

A specific evaluation of this sort is well worth the fifty dollars or so it might cost. Bear in mind that you are not asking for a detailed estimate, but just for an opinion. Even so, it should be a real report, in writing, and not just a casual telephone conversation.

After poking and peering, you may find that you have gathered a lot of evidence but can reach no general final conclusion of your own. Now is the time to seek professional help. A familiar cliché is that buying a house is probably the largest single investment most people make. It could also be the single most costly mistake. This is no time to be proud. If you feel you need counsel, by all means get it, from any of several sources: a real estate appraiser, an architect, or an engineer. Any of these professionals can give you a general overall appraisal, but each has a special perspective.

**A real estate appraiser** will give you an overview in the terms in which a bank thinks, and therefore may be a bit conservative. What is the present worth of the building in real terms? How much will you probably have to put into it? Will the finished rehabilitation produce a house that can return the investment? What is the nature of the local real estate market? Is it on the rise or on the decline? What of the immediate neighborhood? Even though you are not buying as a speculator, are you really up to having the most expensive house on the block? Could you live with the possibility that if you had to sell you might not get your money back?

**An architect** is interested in design, in spaces. He is future-oriented and will see what you *can* do. He will tend to evaluate electrical and mechanical systems on a strictly visual basis, unless he has some special interest or experience. Architects are notoriously bad at estimating costs unless they are particularly experienced in home remodeling.

**An engineer** is present-oriented, compared with an architect. He is trained to size up mechanical/electrical systems in a house and can also estimate accurately the present value of such elements as insulation and structure. He is also familiar with the costs of compensating for various lacks in a building. Professional *house inspectors* are usually registered engineers.

A prospective buyer will tend to gravitate through a kind of natural selection to the sort of adviser — appraiser, architect, or engineer — who will give him information on the aspect of the house that interests him most. Someone concerned with the feasibility of restoring or preserving historical architectural details, or in possible rearrangements of the floor plan that won't destroy the original intent, would quite naturally turn to an architect for advice. A no-nonsense person who wants his house to function efficiently according to the latest technical standards would do best to consult an engineer. A speculative type, primarily concerned about making a good deal, might well seek help from a real estate appraiser.

Any of these consultants can aid you in determining whether a basically sound old house is feasible for you, given your tastes, goals, and finances.

For anyone new to the old house game, the language used in it is sometimes confusing. So many words begin with the prefix *re-*, and seem to be interchangeable, but they aren't. What is the difference between them and a term like *preservation*?

**Preservation** calls for the prevention of any further deterioration, without major changes or extensive rebuilding. Preservation holds the line against time by rendering the structure stable but essentially frozen in the present.

**Restoration** looks backward and attempts to restore a building to the state it was in at some specific point in the past. Turning back the clock to a certain hour requires that any later features be removed and all earlier ones be replaced if they are missing.

**Reconstruction** aims to replace exactly, using new materials, a construction that no longer exists. Reconstruction starts all over again from scratch, but follows an old plan.

**Rehabilitation** is a practical compromise that often involves the use of the other three techniques. The object of rehabbing is to make an old building inhabitable once again. This may involve change — rebuilding or remodeling — and the standards are those of the present, of useful daily life today. When it can, rehabilitation preserves or restores significant historical architectural features. It tries to remain true to the spirit if not the letter of the law laid down in the past, if it can do so without sacrificing utility.

From our first brainstormings, we knew that we wanted to rehabilitate — not preserve, restore, or reconstruct — 6 Percival Street. But as we worked on, we found that what we were actually doing was *restoring the exterior* to a semblance of its original nineteenth-century appearance, while we were *rehabbing the interior* for modern family life.

Sometimes the distinctions were unclear. For example, we might take down an offending wall in the course of rehabbing, but that same wall would have come down if we had been doing a restoration. Sometimes we started out to restore, but found we had to reconstruct. If this proved to be too expensive, we settled for remodeling.

Our exterior restoration was not absolutely pure. We chose to retain some previous alterations (the triple window in the doctor's suite, the added dormer) for reasons that were more practical than theoretical. We weren't aware that we were reflecting new thinking among preservationists until much later in the game when our preservation consultant lectured us. She pointed out that current attitudes encourage keeping some historical changes, and directed us to the U.S. Department of Housing and Urban Development's *Guidelines for Rehabilitating Old Buildings*, which says, "Many changes to buildings and environments which have taken place in the course of time are evidence of the history of the building and the neighborhood. These changes may have developed significance in their own right, and this significance should be recognized and respected."

With *remodeling*, which is renovation without historical self-consciousness, a homeowner faces certain temptations and dangers. Because he is introducing new elements into an old building, he can easily make wrong choices and incorporate shoddy goods that ruin the appearance and reduce the value, historical and monetary, of his house. Whoever inserted the "punky little windows" into our kitchen made a mistake, because they were out of scale and out of period. They simply looked wrong, and always would.

Aluminum or vinyl siding is a prime example of a "cure" for deteriorated clapboards like ours that remodelers often find irresistible. Installing it usually involves stripping off or covering up most architectural detail. Because it forms a shell that doesn't breathe, condensation may form between it and the old siding, thereby producing rot. And after about fifteen years, it may itself need painting, and you're back where you started.

We took on the sanding, scraping, repairing, priming, caulking, and painting of our exterior walls in full knowledge of what we were getting into. But we also knew that when we were through we would have made a real and lasting improvement. Aluminum siding would have dealt with one problem by avoiding it, while introducing other difficulties; it would have substituted a second-rate cover-up for a first-rate restoration. Many so-called home improvement schemes are appealing because they're quick and easy, but their sort of "modernization" usually looks ersatz, dates rapidly, and ends up by being no improvement at all.

The single most important advice to remember as a rehabber is: *don't make any irreversible changes* if you can help it. Paint, for example, is a reversible change, since even the most unfortunate choice of color can be painted over. But junking an original 1869 front door with irreplaceable etched glass panels is a mistake you may well regret later. It may have been the most important detail in your old house, but once lost, nothing can ever bring that particular door back to life.

When all is said and done, appraising a house is a matter of facing reality. If you assume unconsciously that you are going to be able to take an old house and turn it into a new one, then you are in for a lot of work and expense, and eventual disappointment. If you don't want to live with the quirks of an old house, you really shouldn't buy one. Little eccentricities will always remain that you'll have to live with and learn to love. Probably you'll never get certain walls absolutely plumb, but as long as your doors can open without the screech of a haunted house, and they look as though they fit, why be unhappy?

A basic axiom is that if you don't *have* to tear things out then you probably shouldn't. This is especially true in any sweat equity job in which you're investing your own hard labor. You won't want to waste your physical resources and your time on projects that in the best of all possible worlds you might ideally undertake.

A sense of proportion has to be cultivated. Not everything in your house has to be done in the grand manner. All walls with cracks don't have to be stripped down to the lath. Patching can work miracles, and camouflaging imperfections with a rough-surfaced wall covering like grass cloth is not dishonorable. Absolute perfection is not a realistic goal.

Another thing to remember is that no matter how well organized you are, and how painstaking your appraisal, you are not going to be able to predict every eventuality. Once you get into the job there will be surprises, but as long as you have protected yourself against getting into something you can't finish, then you're reasonably safe. Biting off more than you can chew may mean that you run out of money and/or energy.

As we worked backward, as one does during the early weeks of a rehabbing, we were like archaeologists digging through layers of wallpaper ▶ and plaster, down to the bones. ◀ When landscaping later, we actually did excavate and came up with real bones buried by some long-forgotten dog, plus assorted household artifacts. As work progressed inside, we uncovered other treasures, like the walnut of a banister long hidden under white paint. We also found booby traps, surprises, and catastrophes that made us worry.

People vary in just how much they're willing and able to take, not only financially but emotionally. An honest estimate of how much mess, uncertainty, dislocation, and confusion you and your family can endure is essential. Unfortunately no professional can be called in to help with this sort of assessment. You're on your own. Don't forget to figure in attrition, the effect of wear and tear on the spirit. Ask yourself how fast your initial optimism will decline, especially if you're planning to do much of the work yourself. A realistic self-appraisal is as crucial to the ultimate success of a rehabbing as any evaluation of the old house itself.

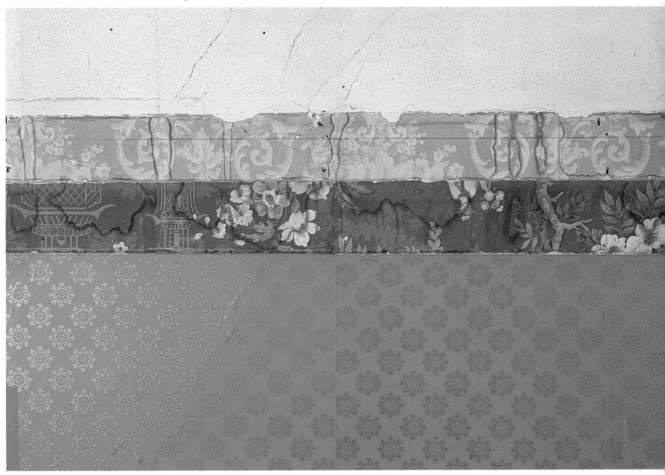

# 3
# The Best-Laid Plans

The outside of our old house underwent a temporary transformation during the past week. Rented scaffolding went up on its south and east sides, and Norm Abram, our master carpenter, and his associate Greg Boyd got a high platform to stand on, to move easily along as they dealt with the eaves. ▶ The planks ordinarily used are narrow, and less experienced carpenters would always have to be on guard against stepping back to admire their work. But scaffolding is essential for such a major job. Working from ladders, which have to be moved back and forth, is neither efficient nor safe.

First Norm carefully removed the decorative brackets from the cornice boards they were attached to.  ◀ The brackets never supported the eaves, nor were they designed to, but because they were characteristically Victorian ornaments, we decided to restore, and eventually replace, them.

Next, Norm took off the long *cornice boards* that enclosed the eaves: the vertical *fascia* and horizontal *soffits*. With these removed, he could then look inside at the framing of the roof itself. When he did, he found — disaster! The decay up there went beyond the surface, beyond the rafter ends, and far deeper into the structure of the roof itself than we had been able to diagnose when we appraised its condition from below and outside. We suspected that the rot caused by water seepage might extend up some rafters, but now we learned that it had also eaten into some of the boards that made up the sheathing hidden under two layers of old shingles.

Our cause had not been helped by our animal friends. Over the years, squirrels had been gnawing away up there, according to Norm, and nesting pigeons had also done their bit.

That was one sick old roof, at least around its edges. We steeled ourselves for a serious and realistic reestimation of the amount of time and money we were going to have to set aside for it.

We also hadn't calculated on abnormal weather conditions. Everyone expects a little cold weather in midwinter in New England, but day after day the temperature hovered around zero, and all records were broken for the length of such a freeze. Like molasses in February we slowed down on outside work and had to readjust our schedule further. In our original timetable we had probably figured in too much good luck.

The site of the house, perched high up on what amounts to a promontory, exposed it to big winds sweeping down from the north. We experienced the full force of the Montreal Express, which whistled right through

the north side of the house and out again without meeting much resistance.

During the week a corps of trainee energy auditors swarmed through the house, checking out our heating plant and tracking down cracks and crevices where the wind came in and heat leaked out. Today their supervisor, energy consultant Ross Donald, said we couldn't have found a less energy-efficient house if we'd tried. We were apparently the owners of a structure that could boast about a 90% loss in efficiency. You can't do much worse than that.

In order to mull over the implication of that and the other news of the week, we stayed inside, where we could enjoy the simple pleasure of sitting on our radiators, which were inefficient but still warm enough for that. We combined creature comfort with heavy thinking as we reviewed progress and reassessed our plans.

The mud room or shed had been torn down the week before, ▼ leaving behind it one solid section of concrete patio, and another of scrap wood and rubble, with some abandoned concrete steps that led to nothing.

We thought we would build a wooden deck over the whole area, one as deep as the kitchen wing and as wide as the old patio, which we would convert into a partial foundation. Then we'd move the back door from its original position near the front of the east wall of the kitchen (which ran the length of the deck area) toward

the back of it, to the spot where a little window was. Changing the doorway would give us uninterrupted wall space inside the south end of the kitchen.

We could visualize ourselves walking directly through the kitchen, without intruding into the work area, and out onto the deck. By spring, we thought, we should have a pleasant place to sit and enjoy the breeze and the view. Dreams like this are a part of planning. They're a kind of fuel for the brain.

Work inside had also been proceeding at a good clip during the week. The kitchen cabinets were all down and out, and the ceiling had been stripped right

down to the substructure. Also gone was the partition that filled in the back of the larger arched niche in the old dining room (to become our family room). ▲

Now we had an open archway, six feet wide, linking two related rooms, kitchen and family room. When there's a change as dramatic as this to take in, I find I have to stand still a moment to reorient myself.

With the wide arch opened up, I could look east from a pivotal position in the family room and see straight through the kitchen to the window that would be replaced by the back door. Then if I turned 90 degrees to the south I could glimpse, through the hall doorways, both the original front door and the kitchen windows that opened onto the front yard.

Moving into the kitchen and facing west, I could look back through the arch from the other side and see that the other, smaller niche on the west wall of the family room had been emptied of its homemade shelving and plastic-paneled doors.

I could hardly wait to get my hands on that par-

tition at the back of the niche. ▲ If that little wall had been down, I'd have been able to walk right from the kitchen through the large arch into the family room and then continue on through a smaller arch and into the old back parlor, which we planned to use as a formal dining room.

But before I allowed myself the treat of that comparatively easy job, I had some harder demolition work to do. Later that afternoon I began wielding my sledgehammer on the intrusive partitions of the doctor's suite.

**I**n our preplanning for the house as a whole, we had established early in the game that within limits we wanted to achieve the following basic goals.

### Design

We wanted to turn the orientation of the exterior of the house firmly back around to the south, reestablishing the original front door as the *only* front door, removing almost all traces of the 1939 additions, and returning the front porch to its original dimensions. Inside, we wanted to clear out the clutter in the plan of the ground floor, and, by opening things up, to improve the flow between rooms.

### Technology

We wanted to bring the technical features of the house up to contemporary standards. Redoing heating, plumbing, wiring, and installing new fixtures and appliances would mean a major remodeling of the kitchen and to a lesser degree (we thought then) of the second-floor bathroom. We proposed to add a lavatory on the first floor. We also saw as a priority the installation of various energy-saving features, particularly insulation.

### Maintenance

We were determined to counteract the ravages of time and what is euphemistically known as "deferred maintenance." We were prepared to repair or replace wherever necessary to bring back the structure and appearance of both interior and exterior of house and grounds. (This turned out to be one of our more open-ended commitments.)

We found that we needed to have at the start plans of only the first and second floors. We chose to have one perspective drawing made, one that projected the way the finished house would look. Our motives may have been the same as those of the cart driver who dangles a carrot in front of his horse. We needed something to look forward to.

Our stripped-down preliminary plans tell a lot but certainly not everything. They don't say anything about all the technical jobs we were to undertake that had nothing to do with design: roofing, plumbing, heating, wiring, insulation, painting, and so on. We planned these separately with our various subcontractors.

Throughout the whole process of rehabbing our old house I tried, in peaceful moments, to be philosophical and to remind myself, ahead of any specific crisis, that the best-laid plans of mice and men often go astray. No rehabbing is totally predictable, or as clean and precise as our measured architectural renderings. A series of interlocking jobs that depend on one another requires of a supervisor that he must plan to be flexible and willing to compromise and ready to listen to informed advice. Many times we had to give our experienced workers the leeway to use their best on-the-job judgment, particularly in an emergency. We had to be prepared to abandon our plans and wing it.

**E**ven a glance at our various floor plans ▶ makes it clear that our main priorities centered on the first rather than the second floor, and that a good part of our remodeling there was to take place in the kitchen, the single room most often done over in American houses today. But no other room, except perhaps the bathroom, demands such careful preplanning. Nothing can be left to chance. A number of essential details must be checked and double-checked, because a specific sequence of work has to be followed, unless, for example, you want to discover that you've gone ahead and closed up your walls before the last plumbing and wiring have been roughed into them. That's a much more serious, and expensive, miscalculation than painting yourself into a corner.

Since 1922, the year when Georgia Packard's family moved into our old house, mass production and modern technology have gradually transformed the appear-

**House as we found it**

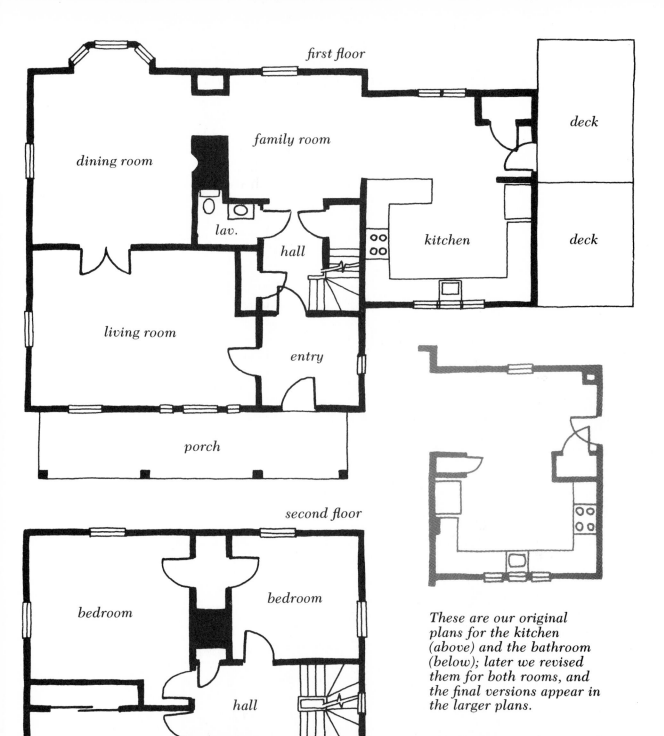

first floor

dining room

family room

deck

lav.

kitchen

deck

hall

living room

entry

porch

second floor

bedroom

bedroom

bedroom

hall

master bedroom

bath

master bath

These are our original plans for the kitchen (above) and the bathroom (below); later we revised them for both rooms, and the final versions appear in the larger plans.

**37**

ance of the American kitchen, constantly adding new and better appliances, as well as producing standardized cabinets and fixtures, and new materials (like laminated plastic, for example) that keep stimulating the urge to "do over" — and over again.

Our kitchen had kept pace with progress for a while. Hadn't the soapstone sink and the old iron stove disappeared long ago? But then it bogged down, and stopped where it was. When we arrived on the scene, the room was ready for a great push forward.

The "dream kitchen" we imagined would be light, efficient, fully equipped with the latest appliances, with a work area out of the back-and-forth traffic pattern of the rest of "the family."

Sometimes our imaginary family had two children, sometimes it had six, but we consistently planned for a group of both parents and children, some of whom worked in the kitchen, while others didn't. Our original kitchen plan reflected our ideas for reorganizing the space into a coherent, semi-segregated work area. ◀

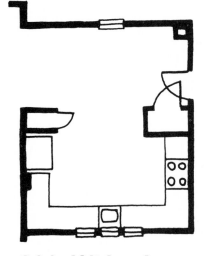

**Original kitchen plan**

The key lay in moving the kitchen door from the front to the back of the east wall. That single alteration (1) enabled us to adopt the most efficient kitchen layout, the U-shape, (2) thus increasing counter space and (3) increasing storage space, as well as separating the work area from the general traffic pattern to and from the back door. The nonworking members of the family could pass by without intruding, but had easy access, as they wouldn't have had if they were walled into a hall.

No sooner had we presented our plans than we got some feedback about the location of the refrigerator: "It's too far from the back door! You're not thinking of the person who has to carry bags of groceries clear across the room from the back door." This objection seemed reasonable, we reconsidered, and then we simply swapped the position of stove and refrigerator.

We had also toyed with the idea of having a work island smack in the middle of the U, with a skylight overhead. We discarded the island as being in the way, but we did retain the skylight. Later, when we unexpectedly ran into acute structural difficulties with the arched opening between kitchen and family room, we changed the kitchen's geography once again. For our lost island we substituted a new peninsula. We ended up with a very useful surface (with storage underneath) that was a snack bar, serving counter, and an unloading area as handy to the refrigerator as anybody could ask. We redrew the plan, pleased that a change forced upon us by a fate and some poor construction in the past had turned out for the better.

In our revised plan the kitchen work area was organized to proceed clockwise function by function, wall by wall. It beautifully illustrated the principles of sound kitchen planning. ▼

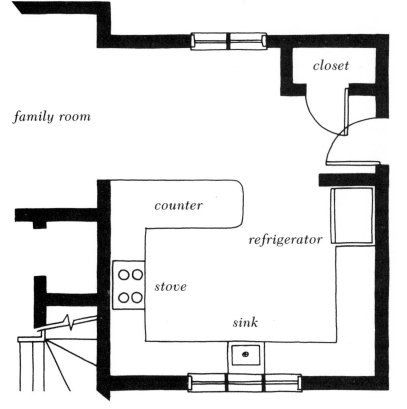

**Final kitchen plan**

### The east wall

This was where major food storage was to take place, as well as mixing and assembling. The refrigerator was, as it should be, at the end of the counter. There it didn't interrupt the span, which was much longer than the minimum of 36–42 inches recommended for mixing space.

We have to admit, though, that we didn't think absolutely everything out. When we changed the position of the refrigerator we forgot to revise our order for a door that hinged on the right to one that hinged on the left. In its final resting place the refrigerator had a door that swung toward the counter and formed an obstacle between the cook and her butter and eggs. Kitchen planning does offer all sorts of opportunities for small miscalculations like this.

### The south wall

Experts say that 46% of kitchen work time is spent at the sink. We made sure that our worker would have plenty of light and air from the new casement window. (The room was cross-ventilated but not air-conditioned.)

We allocated more than the suggested 30 inches of counter on either side of the sink, with the dishwasher no farther than 12 inches from it, and storage for dishes, utensils, and so on nearby. Much of the preparation of raw food — fruit, vegetables — would occur here, near water and garbage disposal.

### The west wall

The stove established this as the cooking area, and where there's cooking, there's serving. Our peninsula was right there, as the spot for serving and eating informal meals, as a snack bar. On more formal occasions, it could function as the pickup counter for food en route to the dining room nearby. Here the two-dimensional plan is deceptive: it was only a few steps more from peninsula to dining room than from peninsula to sink.

The circuit around the kitchen followed a single clear progression of space and function. In addition, the natural traffic pattern among the three focal points of refrigerator, sink, and stove formed the magic triangle recommended by kitchen planning experts for maximum step-saving and efficiency.

The only real disadvantage of the U-shaped kitchen is that with both counter and storage space maximized, and with the need for special lazy-Susan corner cabinets, costs are higher than for the other orthodox kitchen arrangements: the L-shaped, the galley (or corridor), or the one-wall. This was dramatized for us when we got estimates on kitchen cabinets and on plastic laminate counters.

When we arrived at the stage of actually ordering our kitchen cabinets, our supplier provided a detailed layout. He used only standard stock units (we were not into custom cabinetry, an expensive proposition and unnecessary when such a range of stock styles and prices exists).

Working out a coherent whole when there are so many givens presents a challenge. Our layout was an ingenious combination of base cabinets and wall cabinets in the various widths available. Standard heights and depths have also to be worked into the puzzle, but that's a simpler proposition.

After the kitchen, the next most often remodeled room in American homes is the bathroom. The one in our house had been where we found it only for a mere forty years. Perhaps when the house was built it had had no bathroom as such (the room as we know it today is a fairly recent development). Perhaps all four rooms on the second floor were bedrooms, each featuring a washbasin and water pitcher set on a piece of furniture known as a commode, which also discreetly stored, behind closed doors, a chamber pot. ▶ Downstairs, a privy may once have lurked inside a closet in the unheated shed we called the mud room.

At some point, perhaps in the 1880s or 1890s, the northeast bedroom had been "modernized" into a full-scale bathroom, with a built-in tub, a marble-top vanity with sink and storage space, and a thunder-box toilet with pull chain.

In 1939 the bathroom migrated across the hall, and there it stayed until we came along. At first we thought we'd simply refurbish and redecorate. Then we started thinking about the fact that one bathroom might have to serve the occupants of, potentially, eight bedrooms on two floors. We began to revise our thinking, and our second plan took shape, as shown in the small floor plan on page 37.

This new scheme retained, essentially unchanged, the 1939 master bath, but converted the southeast bedroom, which was almost unusably small, into an ample combination of laundry and second (or children's) bath. We proceeded to strip off wall surfaces and pull up floors, all in preparation for the plumber.

Structural problems intervened again. The framing of the walls turned out to be shaky and inadequate, as was the existing plumbing. Also the supporting floor joists had been weakened in 1939 by an excess of notching to make space for new pipes to pass through.

We had to admit that our second scheme was doomed. Though it was hard to let go of it, we didn't have time to mourn. The plumbers had been scheduled to arrive shortly, and we didn't want to have to postpone them. We had to think fast, willing pet preconceptions out of our minds.

So we went back to the drawing board, only this time it was a piece of scrap plywood. Right there in the peeled-down bathroom we sketched a new plan, which called for us to leave only a vestige of the old north-south wall between bath and bedroom, and to swing the axis of the main partition between the proposed two bathrooms around to east-west. This gave us two long narrow rooms of about the same size. The master bath still had all its features, including a door directly into the master bedroom. But now we could eliminate the little off-center window added in 1939, since the original south window would be a source of daylight and venti-

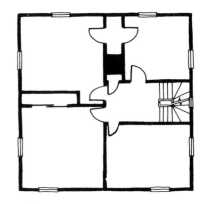

*1860s*

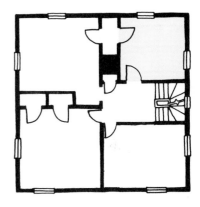

*1880s*

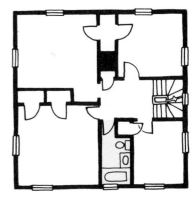

*1939*

**41**

lation. The second bath retained the laundry area as we had originally planned it in our second scheme. ▼

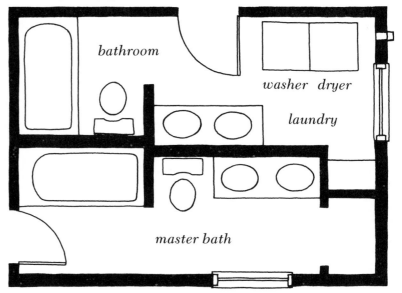

We asked Ron Trethewey, our plumbing contractor, to come advise us on the technical feasibility of our final plan. After a look around, he approved, saying, "This new plan is a good one. Especially because the plumbing serves both bathrooms on an inside wall." Frozen pipes wouldn't be a problem with this setup and we'd economize by having a back-to-back arrangement. He suggested that we add a floor drain by the washer as a safety precaution in case of overflow. Finally he added, "I'm so happy these changes were made *before* we started roughing in the pipes."

Obviously it is better to make changes on paper in advance than after the fact. We'd had a narrow escape, but we had managed to save the situation and to avoid disrupting the work sequence. We hadn't had to postpone our date with the plumbers, or backtrack, or settle for something we didn't want. Our kitchen crisis and our bathroom dilemma had both turned out to have happy endings, mainly because we'd managed to stay loose, and open to a change in direction. Flexibility and a willingness to improvise often light up those dark hours when paper plans seems to have crumbled and it's hard to see the way ahead.

Our original blueprints of the old house couldn't record the hours of preplanning we spent, those long sessions on site mulling over alternatives. Many a "what if?" had to be resolved before formal plans could be drawn. Impracticalities had to be culled out ruthlessly, and sound ideas allowed time to emerge.

**P**replanning should follow a certain logical sequence, according to a descending order of importance. You as a prospective rehabber should focus first on your broadest objectives and then gradually zero in on details. Unless you want to get hopelessly bogged down in minutiae, all of which can under stress seem to be equally urgent, you have to establish firmly in your own mind (1) what you want to accomplish overall, (2) the various steps you must take along the way to do so, and (3) the priorities among them. This kind of forearming may seem to be simpleminded common sense, but cross-purposes can quickly blur ordinary good judgment. The small can seem big, the big small, and the combination overwhelming.

Do you envision a major rehabilitation like ours, with most of the work done by pros and nothing postponed? Or would it be more practical for you to consider a long-term project divided into stages, a kind of domestic Five Year Plan, in which you gradually do much of the work yourself? How would either of these alternatives suit the realities of your finances, your skills, your temperament? These elemental questions shouldn't be sidestepped.

Just because you are planning to hire either an architect or a general contractor, don't indulge in the mistaken illusion that you can give a sigh of relief and abdicate all responsibility. You are the owner of the house, and as such it is up to you to make certain broad choices early in the process of a rehabbing project. The period of preplanning allows maximum flexibility for testing ideas according to your own standards. Only you can determine what you want, what you do and don't like.

Many first-time rehabbers assume that their inexperience disqualifies them from major decision-making. They are wrong. You don't have to be a veteran plumber to be able to say firmly that you want a lavatory on the first floor and that you'd like it off the center hall. A plumber may then tell you that, for technical reasons, you can't have it there, but that's a different matter. You don't have to hold the Gold Medal of the American Institute of Architects to appraise the style of your family's life and opt for both a separate dining room and an informal eating area in the kitchen.

Do you want someone to dictate to you how you should live? Of course not, so don't tempt those who are supposed to be working with and for you to do just that. Express yourself. Don't be intimidated. Architects and general contractors aren't mind readers. Clients should have their objectives and limits almost as firmly in mind as if they were entirely on their own, and should clearly and firmly communicate their wants. Human nature abhors a vacuum, and professionals dealing with wishy-washy clients, who don't know or won't say what they want, will naturally tend to supply their own ideas. Too late you may discover that you have surrendered your own standards of taste or quality to someone else's.

Use the preplanning period for independent research. Look around suppliers' showrooms. One organized approach is to assemble a collection of clippings, idea sheets, notes, and paint chips. You're in much better shape with specific material in hand, rather than with just a head full of vague ideas. It's a starting point for further discussion and development or refinement. For example, you can refer to details of a picture in a big book on bathrooms or kitchens and take it from there.

You don't have to be a great innovator and produce totally original schemes that are the ultimate statement of your identity. It's all right to be selective, even derivative, but you must start out *somewhere* and with a clear vision of what you're aiming to achieve.

Whether you're doing it yourself or you're not, you should always try to inform yourself about what *it* entails. How else will you be able to tell whether or not *it* is being done right? Even if you've delegated responsibility to a supervisor, you should still be able to talk intelligently to workmen on the job. Learn the symbolic language as well, so that you can read building documents with understanding. (We'll do our best to instruct you in the elementals as we go along.) Mastering the idiom is obviously essential if you plan to go it all alone and be your own general contractor, but it's always best to know how to speak the language.

From the beginning our basic premise was that we would be our own designer/contractor. But ours was a group enterprise, with a pool of professional and advanced amateur experience among us to draw upon. If you are an average homeowner with no one to depend on but yourself, and you have a rehabbing job approaching the magnitude of ours — a budget originally projected as $30,000 — you might justifiably be nervous about going it alone. You might well want, and need, help in planning and managing the project.

You can seek a lot of help or a little. In a spectrum from the least self-reliance to the most, you have various options:

1. You can share a major portion of the responsibility for the work on your house with an *architect,* or you can use his services more sparingly.

2. You can choose not to consult an architect at all but to deal directly with a *general contractor.*

3. You may decide to act as *your own contractor.*

4. You can undertake to *do everything yourself.* This extreme may be feasible for a small job with no deadline but is hardly practical for a project like ours.

### Working with an architect

If you are inexperienced and are embarking on a major investment, you should give some consideration to hiring an architect to work with you. His service can be used in a big way, or in a number of smaller ways. Even if your job is comparatively minor, you might profit from a few consultations. A young architectural student or someone just starting out might be eager to take on a limited assignment like helping you draw up your own plans.

Whoever you hire should have some experience and a special interest in the problems of old houses. You should see examples of work he has done for other clients, and get frank references from them before formalizing your relationship. Find out how cost-conscious he is, and whether he tends to ride roughshod over clients in matters of design.

You may have such a large job that you will decide you want an architect to oversee it for you from the beginning to end. You should realize the scope of his responsibility. He will undertake far more than the "creative" work of providing ideas of his own and/or translating yours. He will also serve as administrator of the whole project, putting the job out for bids once plans are firm, advising on the choice of general contractor, whose performance he will monitor as your representative. He will keep tabs on the construction schedule, standards of workmanship and quality of materials, costs and budget, and will warn you when any of these seem to be going wrong. The contractor is, however, ultimately responsible for his company's performance.

Various options exist for paying an architect. Perhaps the least attractive way is to determine a percentage of final construction costs, ranging between 10% and 15%, as the architect's fee. This approach is in fact open-ended, and can lead to hard feelings on the part of the client when a job runs over the original estimates and he has to pay more than he planned not only to the builder but also to the architect. On the other hand, the architect might grow to resent the fact that the client felt all too free to extract more time from him than the fee justified, because that commitment was also open-ended.

An alternative but related method of payment is based also on a percentage, but of estimated costs rather than actual ones, and this is translated into a fixed fee agreed upon in advance.

But probably the best arrangement in a rehabbing is to arrange for an architect to work for you on an hourly basis, at a set rate plus expenses, his total fee not to exceed an agreed-upon maximum. The theory here is that a client will be encouraged to use the architect's time judiciously and will enter the relationship with eyes wide open, knowing in advance that the job *could* cost as much as X dollars, but could also cost somewhat less.

Whatever arrangement you make, however flexible, should be spelled out in a letter of agreement, with all expectations clearly stated. The client should know what the architect is going to do for him; the architect should know how and when he is going to be paid.

## Working with a general contractor

Perhaps you will decide to do without an architect and will negotiate directly with your own choice of a general contractor. You should know what to expect of him. He will earn his fee by assuming the responsibility for hiring all subcontractors, coordinating and scheduling their work, and seeing that the whole job is satisfactorily finished on the date agreed upon and at the price contracted for. The contractor also absorbs most of the risks that someone doing his own subcontracting runs, and it is he who assumes an employer's liability for his workers.

The selection of a contractor can be a crucial step, and anybody choosing one without an architect's counsel should be sure to inform himself thoroughly beforehand. There are many good guys and a number of bad eggs in the business, as in any other. References are essential.

Talk to your friends who have worked with the contractors you are considering and get their opinions — if you can. You will find that some people will never admit to having been taken, while others obviously would never have been satisfied with *any* performance. You must seek out those regular folks who will be candid about their experiences.

Contractors vary in their competence and willingness to assume an informal role as designer-builder. Find out where the one you are investigating stands. The answer may help you make your choice. You may want someone who is more than a technical supervisor.

Find out from your references if their contractor completely finished all aspects of the job, no matter how small, to their satisfaction. Some general contractors have a tendency to leave as much as 10% of the work incomplete, preferring to sacrifice final payments of a few hundred dollars in order to get on to another job. Persuading a departed contractor to come back and attend to unfinished niggling details can become a major life work.

In your contract, you would be wise not only to describe exactly what you want done, according to what schedule of performance and payment, but also to specify that from each installment of your payment you will hold out a *retainage* of 10% as a guarantee, to be paid when the job is completed. It is not so easy to skip off and leave ten percent of the whole shebang behind.

The normal method of payment, incidentally, is either monthly against invoices, or at certain prearranged stages of the job. Beware of a proposal that calls for a lot of money up front. Your contractor is understandably interested in how you are going to pay him. If you have a mortgage or a nest egg of cash that will cover your expenses, tell him so. His peace of mind will serve your own best interests.

Three principles to remember when dealing with your contractor are:

1. Be precise and explicit about details. Don't allow any fuzziness to linger. For example, in your financial dealings, be extremely clear and businesslike. It is useful to develop a set form, which you include with each check, that accounts for running totals of money paid and money retained.

2. Don't change your mind and your plans, if you can help it, after your contract is signed. The terms of the original agreement get muddled, and tacked-on costs usually seem larger than they should.

3. Be open with your contractor. If something seems to you to be going wrong, query. Don't be timid about making suggestions about choices of subcontractors. You might want him to use local plumbers and electricians, who may be more expensive than his regulars but who would be available to you for repair service in the future. Therefore incurring a little extra expense would still be worthwhile to you in the long run, and you should tell your contractor so.

Also, if you are planning to save money by doing some of the unskilled work yourself, you should spell out your responsibility exactly and beforehand.

## Working as your own contractor

If you decide to assume the role of contractor, remember that your job is going to be very time-consuming, and the project as a whole will probably take longer to finish. You will have to have maximum flexibility in your own schedule, because you will have to be constantly available to supervise, coordi-

1                              2                              3

nate, receive deliveries, and rise to general emergencies. You will earn the 10–20% over costs you would otherwise pay a general contractor.

One practical alternative when you can't always be around is to hire a carpenter who will act as a constant presence, a coordinator, and a de facto supervisor of your subcontractors. This is what Norm Abram did on our job, and he didn't miss a day. Your carpenter will probably have enough to do to keep him busy when you're not around, and when you are, you can work along with him. Two men working together accomplish more than twice as much as one man working alone can in double the time.

Otherwise you must act as the foreman, which may be feasible only if you are living on the job, in the house, and do not have overriding responsibilities elsewhere from 9 to 5.

Getting your own detailed estimates of costs involves a lot of legwork, making the rounds of lumberyards and other suppliers, but comparison shopping pays off. So does intelligent questioning of salesmen. They are usually happy to help, unless you make the mistake, for example, of trying to consult with them on a crowded Saturday morning at some cut-rate, high-volume outlet. To make sure you don't omit anything vital from your estimates, you might work out a personal version of a standard estimating form.

When you are getting bids from tradesmen for an ordinarily complicated job, you probably won't need a precise set of plans before you talk to them. For example, when we were dealing with Ron, our plumbing and heating contractor, we simply walked around the house with him, picked his brains about what was needed, and had him give us an estimate based on our discussion. Code re-

quirements often provide the basic outline, with whatever else you want taking off from that point. The procedure is less theoretical than practical: in electrical work, for example, there are a certain number of outlets and an amount of service you just have to have, and you add to that minimum.

You should get several bids for each job (the classic number is three). Settle on a firm price with the subcontractor you choose. He is obliged to stick by that figure, even if the job goes over his estimate, unless — and this is crucial — you subsequently make changes and additions to the work he has agreed to do. Change equals cost, and even minor switches mount up. Before you have second thoughts and casually ask him to do something extra, find out exactly how much your new idea will cost. You may decide you don't want to do it after all. Even if you go ahead with the change, at least you will be informed before you are billed for additional work and find that your original budget bears little relation to reality.

Even if you are scrupulously careful about sticking to your original plans, you should still add 10–20% of the total of all your estimates and hold it in reserve for contingencies. We reserved 20%, which as it happened wasn't nearly enough.

Scheduling the subcontractors you hire is complicated. You have to plan their appearances according to a certain scenario based on the sequence in which interior work always proceeds.

1. Demolition comes first.
2. Carpenters then do the rough framing for new walls, straighten the floors and ceilings.
3. Insulation goes in while the walls are still open or unfinished.

4  5  6

4. Electricians and plumbers rough in wiring and pipes, including the heating system, before the walls are closed up. The plumber has the right of way, because he relies on the pitch of his pipes to make his system work. The heating system, though it does have to contend with gravity, is not quite so constricted by it. Bathtubs are installed before walls are finished.

5. With the installation of wallboard, the rough stage of construction ends, and the finish work begins. Roughed-in mechanical and electrical systems are now enclosed.

6. Plasterers come next.

7. Electricians and plumbers return to do their finish work: installing fixtures, surface outlets and switches, radiators, appliances.

8. Carpenters proceed with their finish work: moldings, baseboards, doors, cabinetry. New floors are laid.

9. Painters begin to work on finished walls and woodwork.

10. Floor refinishing comes last.

In the meantime, any exterior work has been proceeding at its own pace, in its own, somewhat more flexible, order. Roof and gutter work is usually completed first. Insulation is installed before siding is repaired. Painting comes last.

As we continue to narrate the saga of our old house, you will see this timetable in action, and you will grow to appreciate the interdependence of the various trades, with their arrivals and departures necessarily dovetailed. One major delay can result in multiple postponements.

Before you come up against your own crisis, get your subcontractors together to talk about relating their tasks. The electrician, who will be providing power and some actual

7

8

9

10

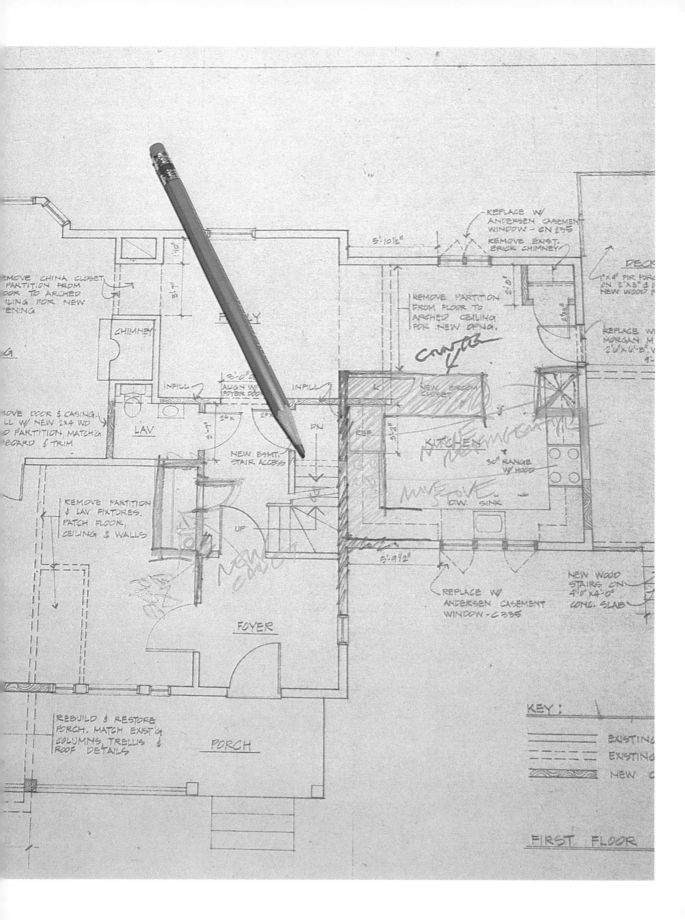

wiring for oil burner or pump or control systems, will find it useful to talk to the heating man, who will be installing the heating pipes. He will in turn want to chat with the plumber, who will run the cold water supply piping to the boiler. The installer of an alarm system may have to coordinate his needs for outlets with the electrician. All these people are going to have to work together, and it's up to you to facilitate communication. Experienced tradesmen know what they want of each other, and once they get going they will be able to deal with one another without your acting as a courier among them. What is a big deal for you is standard operating procedure for them. They are used to interrelating their work.

Remember that tradesmen like to complete their stage of the work in one uninterrupted block of time. They don't like to stop and start, or shuttle between jobs. If your plumber has to halt in the middle because of some scheduling snafu, you may find you have trouble getting him back when you need him.

To operate as a successful contractor, when you have little experience and those working for you have a lot, demands organization, flexibility (as always in rehabbing), forthrightness, and above all, tact. Your job is to be on the scene to answer questions and say *what* you want. Your job is not to tell the professionals *how*. A distinction does exist between being bossy and being the boss. Ignore that reality, and no matter how well you have planned ahead, your initiation as a general contractor may be an experience you and those who worked for you will want to forget.

Sometime before work actually starts, you will have to draw up some working plans. Obviously the paperwork required for the rehabilitation of an existing structure need not be as detailed as for a completely new construction, but it should spell out *everything* your workmen need to know.

◀ We felt our plans didn't need to give every dimension or present views from every angle. In general we gave precise measurements only for new work, and we listed any specifications for materials right on the plans themselves. Our plans, which were only of the first and second floors and of the site, represented a middle-of-the-road degree of coverage; a full-scale treatment would have given more specs, more detailed drawings, as in this full roster.

**Plan views** are two-dimensional, as seen from above, and show the arrangement of rooms and walls and windows and doors on each floor of the building. In plan views the interior is spread out like a map.

**Elevation views** show each of the four sides of the house in exact detail from foundation to rooftop. While plans give a horizontal view of the interior, elevations present a vertical view of the exterior.

**Sections** are large-scale cutaway views of particular parts of the construction.

**Details** are similar and focus even more closely on exact methods of joining different materials together.

**Mechanical and electrical drawings** specifically detail the plumbing, heating, and electrical work.

**Survey and plot plans** show the lot and the placement of the house in it in the manner of an aerial map, which is expanded to specify planting in a **landscaping plan.** A survey is useful to have, and a plot plan is essential when applying for building permits for additions or new outbuildings like a garage.

**Written specifications** amplify the drawings listed above. They set forth instructions for procedure and materials and standards in an orderly fashion by category and should be detailed and explicit. The point is to have every aspect of the project documented, so that everyone concerned knows what is expected.

**T**he mere prospect of getting building permits often strikes terror into the heart of the novice, but unnecessarily. Building departments are not out to intimidate applicants. Obtaining a permit is often simply a matter of filling out an application form, and sometimes the people in the building department will even help you do that. Go tell them what you're doing. If you have problems, they will answer questions — but only if you ask them. You may have to make a few trips, but the procedure is not intrinsically mysterious.

If you are planning additions and ex-

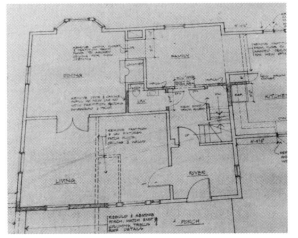

*plan view*

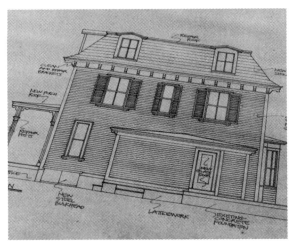

*elevation view*

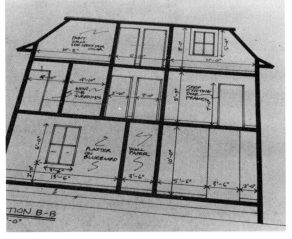

*section*

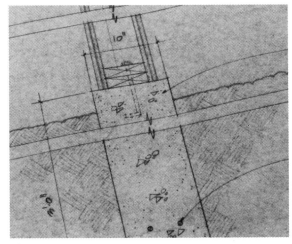

*detail*

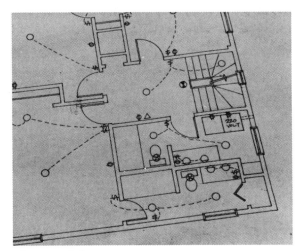

*electrical drawing*

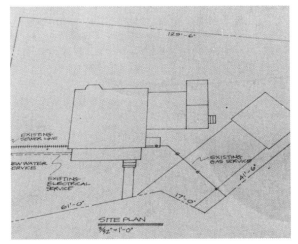

*plot plan*

tensions that will change the dimensions of your house, you will be asked for your plot plan before a permit is granted. This is to make sure that your work will not infringe zoning regulations in such matters as setback from the street or distance from your lot lines.

If you are going to make major structural changes inside the house, you will probably need to present a plan that has been stamped by an architect or engineer.

If you are going to have major new work done on your mechanical/ electrical/ heating systems, you will need a permit, and you will usually need to have licensed tradesmen working for you, in the interests of safety. They will usually, as a matter of course, pull their own permits and arrange the required inspections themselves.

Once you have your permit, you will have to display it prominently. Ours went in a front window. The law says it must be posted in full view on the premises, and anyway we were pretty proud of ours.

Long before permits are an issue, when you begin to contemplate a crash program on the scale of ours, one major question immediately arises: where do you plan to live during the blitzkrieg? The answer depends on whether your house has or can be provided with a basic support system in working order: some running water and a functioning toilet, some heat and electricity. If temporary utilities can be rigged up and the building is reasonably tight and secure, then you might well consider camping out, particularly if you can segregate a temporary headquarters from the chaos elsewhere in an arrangement similar to our third-floor apartment, where we were able to provide a clean place to sleep and some basic amenities. Any such makeshift setup demands of its inhabitants the same hearty spirit as camping out does, sus-

tained good sportsmanship by all parties concerned. Remember that few normal adults are equipped, emotionally and physically, to live in a wilderness for more than a couple of months at a stretch.

When a tight and separate living area is not a practical possibility, even though utilities may be functioning throughout your house, you should probably beware of trying to move in until after any major dirty work is all done. The plaster dust and dirt of demolition, which sifts throughout the house, is the classic deterrent to living on site.

Of course the ideal situation, as far as personal comfort is concerned, is to be able to live somewhere else entirely for the duration, but few can afford the luxury of double residences. And there are positive advantages to living in the midst of a job. You are on hand to keep tabs on progress by those working for you, or you can work along at your own rate on whatever it is you are doing yourself. Living where the rehabbing is going on makes it easier to be more deeply involved in the whole process. That may be exactly what you think you don't want, but especially if you are acting as your own general contractor, your life will actually be simplified if you are right on the job at all times and don't have to be summoned like an absentee landlord.

Even earlier in the process, there are other advantages to living in the house while you are still in the preplanning stage. You can slowly get a feel of the space and the way you want to use it, a sense of what you can live with and what you can't. Your decisions may turn out to be less conventional and doctrinaire, more practical and personal. After all, it is *your* house — not the architect's, the contractor's, or the subcontractor's. As useful as their services are, you are the boss.

# 4
# Demolition
# Derby

**Week 3**   Today we were excited about the break in the weather. The Great Freeze seemed to be over, the sun was out, the temperature up, and we could really get on with the work.

During the past week Norm and colleagues continued their labors up on the cold windy scaffolding on the front of our house, working away at the eaves and roof in spite of the Siberian weather. What sent a special chill through us all was that the roof rot we first encountered a week ago has proved to be really widespread, and the job even bigger than we had thought then.

It was hard, bone-chilling work, but the crew almost finished restoring the eaves and reshingling the roof on the south side of the house, and that included priming and preparing all new wood for the final painting. But there were still three more sides to go.

We encountered some other problems, surprises we could also have done without. During the depth of the freeze, the water pipe into the house from the city main buried under Percival Street did just what the Water Department reported many such pipes all over the city were doing. It froze to a halt.

It was a lead oldie, probably already partially clogged up by years of mineral deposits that had significantly reduced its inside diameter. With the combination of low temperatures and low water pressure, the tiny mainstream iced up. All flow of water into the house and its old plumbing system stopped cold. The furnace, with no water to heat and circulate, was of course out of commission.

We'd grown used to shivering outside the house, but shaking just as much inside it was much tougher to take. Luckily we were able to set up an auxiliary gas space heater in the basement, with one duct to the third floor, to cope with the emergency (which was acute for the caretaker upstairs). Whenever we'd have a moment we'd retreat downstairs for a quick warm-up session.

Because the ground was frozen hard, there was nothing we could do but be patient until there was a real thaw. Then we could dig down to see what was what with the pipe. I was sure we'd have to replace it (and I was right).

Earlier in the week, when we had removed the interior surface of the south wall of the kitchen wing as we prepared to install our new triple casement window, we exposed a checkerboard of weird and unorthodox framing inside, the mark of some previous, probably amateur remodeling.

Rather than waste time and money, we decided to junk the whole jerry-built wall ▲ and to start fresh with new and competent framing. Again and again as work proceeded in the house, when we found that either the original construction or some past remodeling was inadequate, we as rehabbers had to face hard choices. To prop up or to pull down, that was the question.

When it was simply a matter of replacing ordinary

walls or floors, we usually reached the same conclusion: demolish and replace. But when the choice was between either restoring or losing some authentic period detail, like our Victorian porch posts or cornice brackets, we went to some lengths to save the originals. We were trying not to lose or distort the antique spirit of the house, particularly on the exterior.

Because our demolition promised to produce a great deal of trash, we rented those large portable containers known as dumpsters. ◄ The system worked like this. The parent company supplied us with an empty dumpster, we filled it up, and the company regularly

returned to leave an empty one and cart off the full one. We were charged for the removal of each dumpster we filled. Ours cost somewhat less than $200 for each large 30-cubic-yard container, and half as much for a junior Son of Dumpster, which could hold only 12–15 cubic yards, a size that was more than large enough when our rate of demolition slowed.

Getting rid of the old mud room had been our first major job of demolition. In the two weeks since then we had filled six dumpsters with debris of various kinds. This kind of count may seem to be a strange way to measure progress in the demolition business, but it's a practical index.

After disposing of the mud room, we had attacked that eccentric, expendable south wall of the kitchen wing. We removed the old window and eliminated one small section of wall. Then the carpenters sawed almost all the way around the perimeter of the remaining part with their *reciprocating saw*, which is a power tool with a blade similar to but longer than a saber saw's. When the wall was pushed from the inside, it fell outward with a great crash and a low cloud of dust. The pusher suddenly had a room with a view, an unobstructed vista of our twin house across the driveway, our own slightly ◄ distorted mirror image.

Now the east wall of the kitchen bit the dust ► in the same way and for the same reasons as the south one, whose sturdy new framing and triple window were already finished when we started work that morning. Before the day was out the reframed east wall was up, and we had started demolishing some interior partitions, consigning whole rooms to history, the greatest dumpster of them all.

**I**n our particular old house, we undertook demolition projects for three reasons:

first, to clear the decks for necessary rebuilding, that is, for structural rehabilitation, as in the case of the kitchen walls;

second, to remodel the design of the house, either for function or for appearance's sake;

third, to restore to an earlier or original state.

The 1939 remodeling had radically changed the house to suit the needs of a home medical practice, considerations that were irrelevant to the patterns of ordinary family life. Forty years later we were undoing these changes, returning the space to general use. Our demolition was the 1939 remodeling in reverse and began with the bathroom in the medical suite. That was our prime target because it was just plain ugly, and it also intruded right into the middle of what had originally been the largest, most open room in the house.

When I first slammed into that bathroom wall from outside, I got a special kick. With each blow the corny old multicolor tiles that lined the shower stall inside clattered to the floor. A sound like that is as satisfying to the ears of a man with a sledgehammer as the crash of stock cars is to fans at a demolition derby.

In all the excitement of that first assault we set a bad example: we forgot a prime safety consideration and bashed into a wall containing electrical wires that were still live. ◄ We were lucky, and nothing happened, but before we started any interior demolition we should have made sure that the electricity was shut off, at least in the circuit that served the area we were dealing with.

As we had found in the kitchen's south wall and were to discover again and again, old walls often conceal surprises within them. A careful researching of the plumbing and wiring routes up from the basement, as well as on-site observation of various outlets and switches at hand, could have told us a lot, but not everything. In any old house inspection and deduction will take you only so far, but intuition is even less dependable. Don't rely on it.

In dealing with the problem of the second-floor bathroom, we uncovered hidden intricacies in stages. First we got rid of all the yellow and black tile, the floral wallpaper, the fixtures no longer the last word, the midget radiator. In short, we gutted the room. ▶ When we began work on the wall, papered over with a swarm of blue ballerinas, that divided the southeast bedroom from the bathroom, we found all sorts of pipes. First, in an emergency, we dug holes to find and fix some leaks; later we systematically took down all the plaster and lath. For a while a Rube Goldberg plumbing job stood alone like a screen where the wall had been.

**N**ot only were we concerned with what was inside the walls we demolished, we were also necessarily wary about what they held up. When we approached a load-bearing wall with a sledgehammer, we had to be sure we knew what we were doing. Nonbearing partitions were not such a worry.

One minor remodeling job on the second floor demonstrated the precautions necessary when working on a bearing wall, in this case the north wall of the master bedroom. When the doctor added a pair of closets there, to replace those he sacrificed to make his new family bathroom, he cut into the existing wall to make two door openings that were so small that structurally nothing was weakened. Also, he added a new and parallel wall as the back of the new closets, and that also assumed some of the load of the third story above.

When we remodeled the siamese-twin closets into a single large one with a 5-foot-wide opening (to

accommodate sliding doors), we had to be careful to provide extra structural strength to replace the support we removed. We added a doubled horizontal member, known as a *header*, that stretched across to form the top of the new door frame. It was held up at either end by two new, equally sturdy vertical members, each also doubled.

Support was also an issue in removing that 1939 extension on the south end of the living room. We had first to find out what, if any, structural support had been added where the chunk of the original bearing wall had been subtracted. We staged a little exploratory operation, and our probing revealed, to everyone's relief, that the previous remodeling had installed as reinforcement a steel I-beam, which was concealed inside the ceiling. This long beam absorbed the redistributed stress from above. With it in place, we knew that we could remove the addition without worrying about having to supply complicated temporary bracing along the front wall of the house.

We had an unfortunate lesson in what can happen when any wall is meddled with so that it doesn't provide sufficient support for weight from above.

The wall between the family room and the kitchen wing was structurally an exterior wall, but not a bearing one. When we removed the partition that filled in the broad arch there, we easily produced a sense of flow from one room to the other. We also removed any feeble support that partition, in itself an alteration of the original floor plan, had contributed. Moreover, at some point, probably during the 1939 changes, a boxed ceiling beam had also been removed. It had run parallel to the arch and had actually supported much of the weight from above that the arch pretended to carry. To compound matters, we found that a corner post on the north side of the arch was mysteriously floating a foot or so off the floor. This conspiracy of structural oddities caused problems.

Incidentally, we had uncovered elsewhere another example of the strange orthopedic disease that afflicted the corner post. In the east wall of the kitchen several studs failed to give much support to the roof of the wing, because they weren't even touching base on floor level. They were simply levitating.

The missing beam in the family room ceiling and the floating corner post combined to make that section of the house a shaky proposition. As we worked to strengthen both the horizontal and the vertical there, we managed to lose the broad, open arch we had had, however briefly. The unsupported plasterwork at the top of it simply gave up and collapsed under the strain.

We had much better luck with a smaller but similar span, when we removed the back of the china closet in our family room, in order to provide the new entrance into the dining room. ▼ Because the closet had been improvised out of an original doorway (in a nonbearing wall) between the two rooms, sawing around the rim of the added partition and then pushing it down like a drawbridge was an easy job, no more hazardous than removing a screen or a curtain. Because there was no unsupported stress from above, the arch remained intact. Sometimes the old place did seem as easy to rearrange as a house of cards.

Beginners are wise not even to consider messing with the removal of part or all of a bearing wall by themselves. Our carpenters were veterans. For example, they knew exactly what they were doing when they took out the exterior walls of the kitchen. They knew how to build temporary supports and where to put them. Besides, the kitchen wing was only one story high, and its

walls bore only a roof that was, comparatively, as light as a lid.

When one by one each of our kitchen walls departed, the weight of the roof was carried temporarily by A-frames, simple homemade supports of two 2 x 4s wedged against each other to form an isosceles triangle. To raise up the roofbeam, the bases of the A-frames were brought closer together, and to lower it the reverse. A brace nailed from leg to leg, parallel to the floor, held a frame in position. ◄

Cleaning up after a major demolition project like the living room clearance was rather less exciting than knocking down the walls. But cleanup does go surprisingly quickly, we found, and newly opened-up space looked more promising sooner than we had expected. When the last of the rubble had been carted out of the house for disposal — perhaps through the very door the raw materials had entered forty, seventy, a hundred years before — and when the floor had been swept, ► then we felt at last that we had reached the beginning of our real work, construction, not destruction.

By the time the last interior demolition was over, hardly a surface in the house had escaped a touch of the crowbar or hammer. The oak veneer strip flooring in the living room came up; so, eventually, did other floors in the family room and stair hall. Many, many ceiling and wall surfaces went down. Partitions departed from both bedrooms on the south, and from the family room. Of course the kitchen had surgery of the most major kind. At one point the inside of the house seemed skinned down to a skeleton, a ghost of its former self.

We wreaked havoc inside the house, and outside as well, though we would happily have skipped some of that dubious pleasure.

We had counted on just making some repairs to the front porch after removing the 1939 extension onto it, not on rebuilding it. What happened in reality was that we ended up pulling down the whole creaky business in a series of installments. It was like yanking out a tooth slowly. Anyway, we had to start over again, practically from scratch, as we had with the kitchen walls, and rebuild the whole porch.

Our heaviest exterior demolition project also began small and grew and grew. We had originally planned that we'd demolish the brick steps that led up to the doctor's entrance after we'd gotten rid of it. A minor undertaking, we thought.

Then came the freeze, and we had to plan on a major excavation to replace the water main from the street. Unfortunately the main was buried six feet deep, and its route lay right under the steps to the vestibule, a cement walk, and another flight of brick steps, which led down from the lawn to the sidewalk, with massive stone retaining walls on either side. All the brick and cement and some of the stonework had to come up.

We had to wait until spring finally came and the ground thawed before we could begin. Even then it took more than strength and a sledgehammer to get through those heavy masonry obstacles. We had to hire a back-hoe and expert operator to do the job. Sometimes even the most independent rehabber has to admit that hiring a big gas-guzzling machine to work for him saves time, money, and his back.

**I**f you decide to do your own demolition, you may have to begin by nerving yourself up for the job. Gary Paulsen, a veteran renovator, has written: "For some obscure reason . . . many people assume that a wall is somehow inviolate. The truth is that with a light sledgehammer it is possible to remove every wall in the house in a single morning."

Demolition may not be all *that* easy, but for those who aren't intimidated by the sacredness of walls, creative destruction can be very satisfying, one of the most rewarding and dramatic stages of the whole renovation process. Great changes are accomplished quickly, for instant gratification. Though you do need a certain physical stamina, you don't have to have great skill or experience. You can also vent aggressions and save money at the same time, a combination hard to find in other pursuits.

Some people, instead of being intimidated, suffer from the opposite problem. They are overstimulated and tend to run amok. A few words of caution. Be careful to remember what your goal is, to be sure that you have in your preplanning considered thoroughly what you actually hope to achieve by removing that tempting wall. Don't give way to impulse and take it down just because it's there.

You should ask yourself if you will really be happy with the resulting space. Will its look and feel be pleasing or suitable? Bigger isn't automatically better, and some people find that once they have produced a room that looks like a parking lot and are rattling around in it, they remember the two or three smaller spaces they've lost as having been warm and cozy, even intimate.

If you are tempted by the idea of a hypothetical morning spent removing every interior wall in the house, never lose sight of the fact that some walls are load-bearing, and some are not. The distinction is crucial.

What, in theory, is the difference between the two kinds of walls? *Load-bearing walls* are structurally essential because they hold up the house, bear its weight. *Nonbearing walls* enclose space, but are not structurally essential. Some exterior walls are load-

bearing; some are not. Some interior walls are load-bearing; some are not.

How, in practice, can you tell which wall is which? The clue lies in the *joists*, the horizontal members in wood frame construction that support floors and roof, and from which ceilings are hung. ▼ These timbers

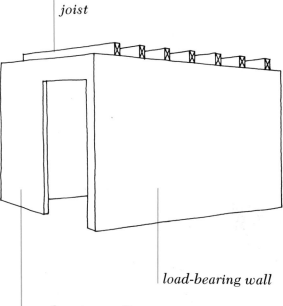

*joist*

*load-bearing wall*

*nonbearing wall*

generally go from one side of the house to the opposite side and run in the same direction on every floor. Their ends are supported by the foundation and, above, by facing exterior walls; in between, the spans are supported by the interior walls they intersect. The walls, exterior and interior, on which they rest are by definition load-bearing. So joists run perpendicular to bearing walls — and that is the handy index, the clue that enables even a novice to distinguish between the two kinds of walls.

The easiest place to determine in which way joists run is an unfinished area like a basement or attic. In our old house we simply went down into the basement and looked up at the exposed joists supporting the first floor. They ran north and south, at a right angle to the front of the house. This simple observation told us that our bearing walls ran east and west. Therefore, among our bearing walls were the front (south) wall of the house, where we removed the doctor's extension, and the interior wall between the **63** master and guest bedrooms, where we enlarged the closet opening.

There's one other identifying characteristic of bearing walls to remember. They are usually stacked on top of each other floor by floor, one supporting the next one above. If you are investigating in your basement,

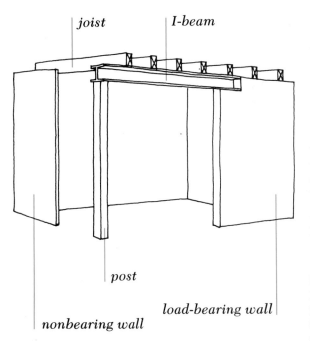

joist     I-beam

post

load-bearing wall

nonbearing wall

note the location of walls, piers, or other structural supports down there. Consider what is above them. If it's a wall, you can assume that it too is structurally essential, and is transferring weight down through the basement construction to the ultimate support, the ground itself.

No bearing wall or significant section of it can be removed, even temporarily, without providing some alternative means of support. Something has to hold up the load at all times. You can't expect the laws of physics to suspend operation during even the briefest interval.

Temporary bracing can be comparatively modest, like the A-frames we used in the kitchen wing. Usually it has to be much more substantial, a real substitute wall made out of a frame of 2 x 4s that, when wedged firmly into place, is strong and tight enough to take over the stress from the wall scheduled for departure. The standard arrangement is to erect two such temporary relieving

walls on either side of the bearing wall to be removed *before* taking it down. There are other effective safeguards and systems, such as adjustable Lally columns inserted under a temporary beam, that you can investigate. But the principle remains the same: temporary bracing must be sufficient to assume the load.

After a bearing wall has been removed for good, as when two small rooms are combined into one large one, the permanent substitute for the departed wall has to be installed before the temporary supports can be retired. A strong new wooden ceiling beam supported by a pair of sturdy posts at either end is the usual stand-in for a bearing wall, though a steel beam is another possibility when the span to be reinforced is long and therefore the stress is great. ◀ Beams can be boxed in or otherwise disguised. They don't intrude on the floor plan. Posts, which do, present a decorating challenge but not an insoluble one.

Before you touch a load-bearing wall, get professional advice on your particular project, or better yet, consider having the professional do the job for you. Even if you think you understand the principle, think twice before going ahead without specific, practical advice about your case. There may be special engineering considerations that you never dreamed of, such as the different kind of force that wind loads exert on exterior bearing walls.

We feel that demolition that involves structural matters demands experience, and should not be entered into lightly or unadvisedly. Samson rose to an emergency with the load-bearing structure of the temple, but look what finally happened to him.

This is not meant to be a counsel of timidity but of common sense. You needn't resign yourself to an impossible floor plan because changing it would involve an alteration of bearing walls. But be aware that such a project is not comparable to the removal of a simple partition, which can be taken down like a curtain. As a rehabber, you are free to undertake radical structural changes. But you must know exactly what you're doing, or else you will get in over your head.

Even when only partitions are involved, demolition is a sport that has its ups and downs. As Jill Robinson, an energetic beginner determined to make the best of things, put it in an article titled "How to Do Anything When You Don't Know How": "Nothing is more exciting than pulling down walls, except perhaps living by candlelight until the electrician comes to put back the wiring one has inadvertently hacked away at."

Certainly you should check everything out in advance as completely as you can, but remain alert to the unpredictable, the unthinkable, the pipe that veers for no comprehensible reason right into the path of your sledgehammer, the wandering cable that lurks where you least expect to find it, and even the horizontal stud, asleep on the job.

When in real doubt, don't be shy or lazy about seeking a second opinion. We can't make this point often enough: *get help.* Consult your most reliable local expert, who is more likely to be a licensed plumber or electrician than your brother-in-law. Read up in some of the many fairly technical guides for nonprofessional rehabbers available at your library or bookstore. We have recommended several, which appear in the bibliography at the end of this book. The more you know ahead of time about what may hide inside the walls you'll attack, the better.

There is one overall principle to keep in mind in order to understand the process of demolition, or the taking apart of a house. Demolition is construction in reverse, and thus the sequence for interior demolition is logical. For example, finishing touches such as door casings and baseboards and all other applied ornamental woodwork that went on last, go off first. Then the wall surface. Then the framing that supported it.

But before your work begins, there is yet another sequence to be followed. This is how we prepared ourselves before the first blows were struck (an order of events that other practitioners might do well to follow):

1. Assemble all the tools you will be using. Our tool recommendations are listed at the end of this chapter.

2. Turn off the electricity. If your demolition project is extensive and will take days to finish, you may want to have an electrician provide a temporary alternative source of power, or the plumber rig up a temporary water system. On the other hand, you may

have a smaller job ahead of you and will feel that all that is needed is to kill the relevant electrical circuit at the board.

3. Spread drop cloths on the floor and tape them down securely. This will make cleanup easier, but probably won't save the floor finish. (Assume you'll have to refinish.) Block off open doorways with more drop cloths, so that plaster dust won't spread throughout the house. Open a window for some ventilation.

4. Put on hat, heavy work gloves, filter mask, and safety goggles. Be sure the soles of your shoes are thick enough to be nail-resistant. Now you're ready to start unbuilding.

### Unbuilding — Interior Demolition

1. Carefully remove with a flat bar any woodwork you want to save for reuse. Otherwise you can be rougher and use a crowbar (or wrecking bar). ▼

2. With a sledgehammer, crowbar, claw hammer, or any similar tool that seems to work for you, shatter and remove the wall or ceiling surface from the substructure of framing that supports it.

But before you start in, in order to make a clean job of the division between wall that will remain and wall that is going out, make a definition between the two surfaces by scoring the borderline with a utility knife or an old saw blade or a circular saw. Otherwise you're likely to overdemolish, taking jagged hunks out of the part you planned to keep intact.

The procedure used in removing either wallboard or plaster-and-lath is basically the same. Some people use a keyhole or circular saw to cut out and neatly remove large sections at a time. Wood lath poses no problem, but metal lath requires a special cutting blade. (For lath see Chapter 8.)

Ceilings present one major annoyance: everything that comes off falls down, usually right in your face.

3. When the surface of the wall or ceiling has been removed, you will have exposed the turned-off wiring. ▼ If you are discarding

the entire circuit, first disconnect the cable at the receptacle box and then trace it back to its origin, usually a junction box, and simply disconnect it there. If, on the other hand, the cable serves other outlets that you want to keep, you should probably have a talk with an electrician, who can either advise you or do the job himself.

If you plan to retain the wiring and just cover it up again, be careful to keep it safely out of your way as demolition continues around it.

4. By the time you reach this stage,

you have already stripped down to the joists of the floor above you (in the case of a ceiling) or to the vertical studs (in a wall).

If your plan calls for entirely removing the partition, you obviously have to eliminate all the exposed studs. Freestanding ones can be sawed in half, and the halves worked loose from the places where they are nailed in at top and bottom. When you get to the final vertical and horizontal boards nailed right to wall, floor, or ceiling, pry them off carefully so that you won't unintentionally damage abutting surfaces you may want to keep intact. Brace your pry bar against a piece of scrap wood so that it won't matter if your lever leaves scars.

Try to set aside and save some of the old studs you remove. You'll find them useful for blocking in open spaces — for example, doorways you're deleting — and for patching. Because of the redimensioning of modern lumber, an old 2 x 4 stud can be at least ⅛ inch larger than the nominal 2 x 4 of today. It is better to fill in old framing with recycled old studs that match exactly.

Also, old wood is necessarily well seasoned, and therefore it won't warp and will hold nails tight. It can be put to good use as a solid base onto which to fasten or hang things such as cabinets.

If it is at all feasible, assess your task and plan to try to finish all your tearing down and cleaning up in one massive effort, rather than in demoralizing small installments, with their long succession of cleanups. In this connection, remember that the cleanup is an imperative, no matter how you schedule your demolition. You can ruin perfectly good floors elsewhere in the house by neglecting your broom and shovel, and by allowing gritty, abrasive plaster to be tracked out of the wartorn zone. Besides, unrelieved dirt in the house brings on demolition depression, a gloomy feeling that chaos is a permanent state.

When you are involved in a small project, you might get away with leaving large cans and boxes or rubble out for municipal collection. We suggest that you use galvanized metal trash cans, especially for relays to the dumpster when you're into a large job. Plastic cans don't hold up well — they tend to split, we discovered — but they are cheap,

many of us already have them on hand, and they'll do in a pinch, for a while.

We did our demolition, especially in the kitchen wing, in a big way. We had the manpower, the reciprocating saw, and the incentive of showmanship urging us toward staging a spectacle in the grand manner. Relax and remember that you will be able to achieve the same end, though at a slower rate of speed, if you simply slog away on your wall with your crowbar, taking it down all right, but less dramatically. Rome need not be unbuilt in a day.

## Tools and Equipment for Demolition

Flat bar
Crowbar
Claw hammer
Hacksaw
Nail-puller (or cat's paw)
Nail punch
Sledgehammer
Pipe wrenches (2)
Keyhole saw (or hand circular saw)
Cold chisel and mallet (for masonry)
Drop cloths and masking tape
Shovel
Broom
Galvanized metal trash barrels
Electrical tape
Nose/mouth filter mask (respirator)
Goggles
Leather gloves
Hat
Work shoes, with thick soles
Eyewash

# 5
# Frame-up

This was a stage of our work on this old house that gave us a satisfying sense of progress. We might have had a few of the usual setbacks during the preceding two weeks, but they were overshadowed by all the positive action around the place: new faces, new projects under way. The working population on Percival Street had exploded. Electricians, plumbers, and insulators were hard at it now.

No longer were we mainly destructive, just carting out cans full of shattered ceilings and walls. We were deep in a new phase, actually reshaping the house according to our own vision. After all that planning and clearing out, we were into the creative part of rehabbing.

When the day started I had to climb onto the porch roof through one window in order to inspect another, or, rather, the place where one had been. This was the week Bill Gonder literally lifted out the off-center bathroom window ◄ from the south wall of the second floor, and then boarded in the gap.

But that was a minor part of the week's saga. The big news was that the walls of the 1939 addition, which filled in half the original porch, were all gone! ◄ This meant that the boxlike vestibule with the street entrance was gone too, though its brick steps lingered on.

At last the old house was back to its 1860s silhouette: a simple three-story cube, with a corner-to-corner front porch, a one-story wing to the east. There had been some casualties, however. The porch roof had only two of its original posts as support. These collaborated temporarily with 2 x 4 substitutes.

As I circled the house, I noticed that up on the east eaves, the gang had already stripped off the brackets as well as the fascia and soffits, and were repeating the renovation sequence they'd completed earlier on the south side.

But something new and strange was going on up there on the roof. I knew what it was, but a passerby might have deduced that we were vacuum-cleaning the shingles. ▼ What we were actually doing was blowing insulation into the roof cavity. Driven by my compulsion to climb ladders, no matter how creaky, I went up to the top to inspect more closely. A fluffy pulverized cellulose material was being sucked up from a supply hopper on the ground through a flexible hose, and was being forced into the curved sides of the mansard roof.

As I looked down from the heights, I could survey the gleaming wet streets that circled the park below. Fine showers, little more than mist, offered a gray pre-

view of spring. But in the interval between last week's sun and this week's drizzle we were dealt one last dirty trick when freezing weather returned briefly. In the on-again, off-again situation of our water supply, the furnace reacted with a terminal leak in its boiler, followed by a fatal crack.

We had hoped to keep it going during the remaining chilly weather, but we just couldn't manage.

That afternoon we pushed it over, the plumbers sledged it into pieces, and off it went, along with the other reminders of an earlier era in home heating, the obsolete pipes and the cast-iron radiators that had warmed us only a couple of weeks ago.

Upstairs, on both the first and second floors, structural emergencies during the past few days had forced us to improvise some quick changes in our original plans for both the kitchen and the bathrooms.

In the third week the wide arch between kitchen and family room had collapsed. Rallying from that disappointment, we realized that we were in fact liberated from the dimensions of the old arch, and we did approach the problem of working out a variation on our original plan with a certain zest. As newly framed in, the two rooms interlocked, with little suggestion of a wall between them, no vestige of the arch. We were determined to make the best of the shotgun marriage. I was sure it would be a good match. ▼

Almost simultaneously we were faced with the confrontation between the needs of weakened old floor

joists and the demands of new plumbing in the bathroom upstairs. We rapidly had to make another revision in our original scheme for the area.

This was the day when we consulted with Ron Trethewey, our plumbing contractor, and he confirmed that the new plan was practical, though it wouldn't save us any money. The $3,500 he quoted for the cost of labor alone for the third plan took me back momentarily, but I knew the expense was justified.

At the same time Ron reconfirmed our plumbing plans for the lavatory downstairs and the kitchen, which were from his point of view unchanged, except for a few details like swapping the locations of refrigerator and stove.

Last week I had announced that I wanted to save the problematical north wall of the kitchen wing. Like the gnarled tree outside its window, it was all askew, and the sill it rested on had touches of rot, but we gambled that it would be most economical to salvage it, unlike the south and east walls we'd already lost.

We removed the punky little window, opened up the space for the eventual installation of a larger casement, cross-braced the opening, and finally sealed it against the weather with a heavy polyethylene sheet. The tree outside turned into a kind of ghost.

After patching the sill and trying to make the 2 x 4 studs *plumb* (that is, return them to the perpendicular), carpenter Adam Tamsky began to rough in the new window opening, checking his work with a long level. His framing for the window was almost the same (but turned upside down) as that which he would make for the wide opening of the remodeled closet in the master bedroom. He filled in across the top with a *lintel,* or header, at the bottom with a *windowsill,* and on the sides with doubled studs. Then he filled in the open space under the sill with the short studs known as *cripples.* ▶

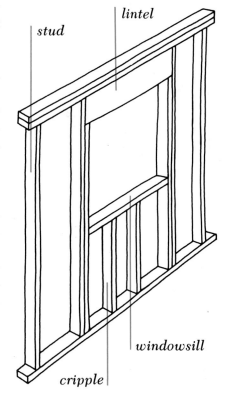

As Adam worked, we began to realize how bad the old framing still was, especially when contrasted with the new. We were still wasting time on first aid that would never restore the patient to full health. Rather than go on throwing good money after bad, we decided to go back and start all over again from the beginning. After all Adam's work, the decision was difficult.

So the third and last wall of the kitchen wing was toted off to the dumpster, and the twisted tree popped back into full view. Outside, the new, prefabricated frame waited in the wings, ready to be raised into place.

Back inside the house, in the family room, reframing of a single wall during the week had greatly simplified the floor plan. The loss of the archway into the kitchen had already opened up that space, and this further remodeling helped to clear out the fussiness of the central part of the first floor.

The first move had been to strip the old hall wall of its plaster and lath, right down to the original framing with its two door openings. When reframed the two spaces were eliminated and a single, wide, open doorway, centered, replaced them. ▼ Just beyond the doorway to the right, the new lavatory had been framed in. Its rear wall had originally contained the door into the back parlor from the hall.

Another reframing job included the west wall of the kitchen as well as the hall wall in the family room. (A post was put in as a temporary support for the ceiling,

with its exposed joists. We would eventually install a strong ceiling beam to take over the post's job.)

Walking around to the hall, we could focus in on the details of the framing above the new entrance down into the basement. ▶ Because of the slant of the stairway above, the cripples had to be cut to fit the angle. The basement door had been moved around 90 degrees to the west, so that it would open out into the hall, opposite the new lavatory. (If all this seems a confusing shuffle, you might look back at our first-floor plans in Chapter 3.)

In the living room, where the doctor's extension had been demolished and the gap in the south wall filled in with new framing, we had come face to face with one of the home truths of rehabbing an old house. A new wall will be perfectly perpendicular, but an old one may well tilt, and the place where the two meet can present problems. Ours encountered each other in a very public place.

Our old wall section was leaning in about 1½ inches, measured at the top. Norm had noticed that the rear, or north, wall of the house leaned out, on a parallel plane. He guessed that perhaps the rack might simply be the result of a hundred years of stress, or that the great winds of the famous 1938 hurricane were to blame. A force strong enough to have blown down the mighty tree once on the southwest corner of the property was bound to have had some effect on the house.

Whether a slow slump or a traumatic event had been the cause, the fact was undeniable: things were out of whack in the living room. To have started all over again here to reconstruct the whole south wall, corner to corner, would have cost a couple of thousand dollars. Surely there was something cheaper we could do to save the situation.

Standing in the living room, Norm and I discussed the possibility of working out a cosmetic treatment that would simply cover up the jog where the new wall met the old. My thought was that we might attach ¾-inch wood strips to bring one part up to the other, and then cover the surface with wallboard.

But when we viewed the gap from outside on the porch, we realized that we couldn't cover it up with clapboards, because they wouldn't cooperate. Clapboards don't bend that way.

Norm's solution was simple. He would pull the whole old section out again. The tool that made this possible was a *come-along*, ▶ a ratchet arrangement on a cable, with one end attached to an existing porch post

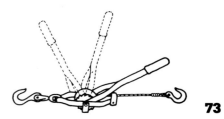

and the other to the beam running along the top of the offending section of old wall. When Greg, outside, operated the come-along ratchet, the cable tightened, and since the porch post was solid, what gave was the beam, which moved out a fraction of an inch at a time. Simultaneously, Norm, inside, slammed into the beam with his sledgehammer, providing a push to Greg's pull. After only a few pushes, the wall had moved out ⅜ inch, and soon the two sections were almost flush.

I was curious to know if there were any danger of the joists of the second floor slipping off the beam once it had been pulled out the whole 1½ inches. Norm assured me that even in the new position, there were a couple of inches of joist still resting on the beam. One other aftereffect did become apparent. A new, horizontal gap between the south wall of the master bedroom above and its floor opened up. Later, we were able to fill in and mask this gap, when the baseboard radiators were installed.

**T**he fate of our kitchen wing was a case history of the downs of demolition. The wing was also an illustration of some of the ups of framing in general. In three installments, wall by wall, it demonstrated the method of construction known as platform framing. As we gradually worked our way around the wing, from south to north, knocking down and building up, we followed pretty much the same procedure. The east wall best serves as the prototype. ◀ The sequence went like this.

After consulting the plans, Norm measured and remeasured the existing east wall, as he had the south one. Someone who may be described as slightly overzealous once said that every measurement should be made at least twelve times. Another maxim is "Measure twice, cut once."

1. The various vertical *studs* and horizontal *sole* and *top plates* were then pre-cut, all at one time, and arranged in order on a flat surface, in this case the paved driveway.

2. Next the pre-cut pieces were joined together, using a nail gun. The newly framed wall, lying on the driveway, looked like a flat of scenery ready for the school play.

After the old wall had gone down with a crash, some dust and debris were left behind. We had to sweep off the sills so that the horizontal base, or sole plate, of the new frame could slip into place smoothly.

74

3. Then everybody pitched in for the great wall-raising.

4. Gradually the prefabricated wall tilted higher and higher, a lot of the push coming from the 2 x 4s temporarily attached like shafts on a cart and called *pike posts*. These have been used for house-raisings for centuries.

A short while after the new wall had been anchored firmly in place (both top and sole plates nailed to the adjacent members of platform and roof), it was left to itself, as close to perfectly plumb as we could make it.

The view out through the newly framed wall from inside the kitchen showed the temporary A-frame braces still on duty, silhouetted in the roughed-in door opening. ▼ This view from inside out also documented the distance between the garage/driveway and the kitchen grocery-unloading area, the span we reconsidered before deciding to rearrange the refrigerator location and the counter plan. Perhaps it was a bit early in the game, but even then, standing about where the peninsula

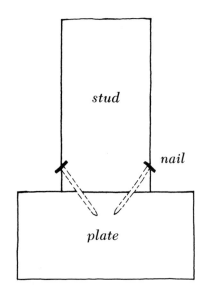

stud

nail

plate

would be, we could imagine a member of our hypothetical family, arms full of brown bags, staggering in through the back door, and thanking us. The revision had been a good idea.

One difference between framing walls for the kitchen and for the living room was that in the living room we were able to construct and install the new section *before* we demolished the old extension. Another was that instead of assembling the framing outside, we did it inside, flat on the floor. Then we raised it into place.

There was a vacancy left ready to receive the window that was still in place in the extension wall. Before it could be transferred, Adam had to finish up a few details. He toenailed in the cripples above the roughed-in window frame. ◀ *Toenailing* is a basic carpentry technique. As Adam demonstrated and Norm described, "When you toenail, you start the nail at an angle in one piece of wood, so that when it comes through, it grabs into the second piece at the same angle." The resulting joint is firm and secure. Often, as in the case of a T-intersection of a vertical stud and a horizontal sole plate already attached to the floor, the only way two members can be joined is by toenailing.

When we were stripping the second-floor bathroom right down to the bones, we uncovered a peculiar set of conditions. When the room had been squeezed into place in 1939, the existing studs and joists had been notched out (and butchered, which is unfortunately typical) to make room for the plumbing pipes. Also, a closet doorway in the master bedroom wall had been filled in with new studs. ◀ The tile floor had been installed in four inches of cement, and the tile walls were not just cemented but set in mortar (a so-called *mud job*) so thick that it in effect was holding the framing together. That bathroom was as solid as a concrete bunker. But once all the cement and mortar had been removed, the remaining structure was such a flimsy proposition that we saw no alternative but to get rid of it.

When we finally completed the new framing, according to our third bathroom plan, the view west from the laundry area (over the tub, and into the master bedroom) was so different that we could hardly remember the old scheme. A few steps to the south we had another vista to the west, this time from one end of the master bath to the other, and beyond. Still another perspective, from the master bedroom eastward, let us survey both the bathrooms, ▶ with their tubs at right angles to one another, separated by a see-through wall, and we could also catch a glimpse of every other room on the floor.

We eventually framed in a few other miscellaneous areas such as closets in kitchen and hall, and studded up the chimney walls, which had been stripped down to bare brick, in the guest room and the children's room. Then we were finished.

When a wall is framed and in place, it serves as almost the deterrent it is when wallboarded and plastered over. People instinctively hesitate to edge through the 16-inch standard space between studs. They tend to walk around to a doorway, just as if they were blockaded by a solid surface. On the other hand, airy and open walls are just what plumbers and electricians like to have in order most easily to do their roughing-in. Once our frame-up had been completed, these gentlemen arrived in force to get on with the next steps of the rehabbing process.

**E**uropean visitors to the United States are often startled by the vast number of houses they see that are made of wood. In England, France, and Italy, where wood is scarce and expensive, brick, stone, and stucco are most commonly used in building. In contrast the typical American home has wooden walls (either clapboard or shingle) and floors and trim and — most relevant to the story of this old house — is constructed upon a wooden frame. While America may be the land of opportunity and the freedom to be different, it is also overwhelmingly the land of wooden houses: 90% of the total, according to one recent estimate, have wood frames.

The tradition is a long one. Our forests have always been a great natural resource, and Colonial builders of the seventeenth and eighteenth centuries, particularly in New England, had wood to burn, and to build with, free for the taking. The design of the wood frame houses these earliest American designer-builders constructed drew on English precedents, which were gradually adapted to the new situation and the new plenty. The transplanted techniques of building made lavish use of the large hand-hewn posts and beams so readily available.

The form of construction itself is, in fact, known as *post and beam.* ▶ The basis of a house built according to this method is an extremely strong and rigid frame made of massive vertical posts and a variety of equally large horizontal beams, fitted together at their intersections in exceptionally strong joints, like a *mortise and tenon.* These joints were then pegged or pinned for extra security.

The craft of joinery, which was until recently almost a lost art, is now reviving, as "honest," vaguely countercultural; and sometimes handsome post-and-beam houses go up all over elemental places like rural Vermont, where people who want to get back to basics tend to go.

The joiner's business has always been joints, and he has perfected all sorts of ways to fuse together a collection of heavy sticks into an enduring assembly of straight lines and right angles without depending on nails.

In Colonial times nails were very expensive, because they had to be hand-forged, one by one. Carpenters used them sparingly as the luxury they were. This made the filling in of spaces between the posts with the smaller vertical members called *studs* a more painstaking task than it is today, as was the insertion of horizontal floor joists between the beams, or of minor rafters into the massive frame that supported the weight of the roof.

Our modern system of wood framing is really not unrecognizably different from the antique way of building a house, but it does use smaller, more uniform framing members, and many more nails. In the 1840s newly developed machinery made it possible to mass-produce nails and mill lumber to

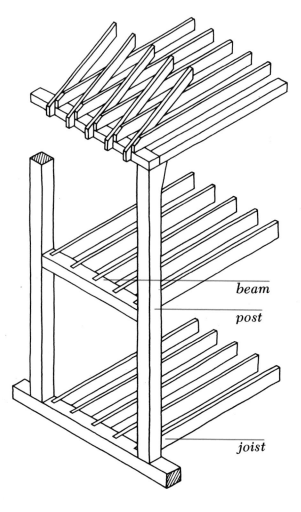

beam

post

joist

**Post-and-beam framing**

The 1860s, the period when our house was built, was a transitional stage in American home-building practices. The construction of the house reflects this: it has elements common to both balloon framing and its later development, platform framing, two variations on a single theme, as well as some large beams reminiscent of the earlier era.

In balloon framing, studs rise in a single long span from the base of the first floor to the roofline, like bars in a canary cage. Both joists and studs rest directly on the sill.

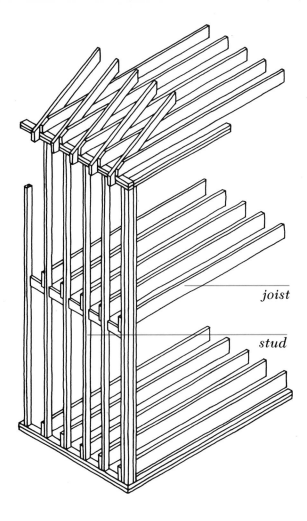

*joist*

*stud*

**Balloon framing**

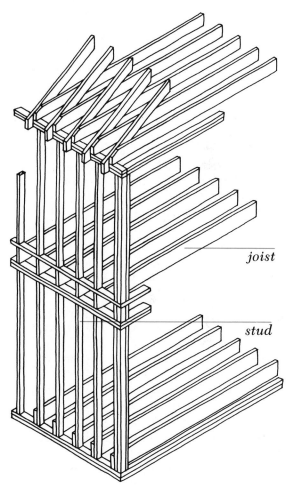

*joist*

*stud*

**Platform framing**

standard sizes. A new type of house framing came into use: *balloon framing.* ▲ The term is a little misleading. It does not refer to spherical houses.

The difference between it and the old post-and-beam construction is essentially this. The old method depended on comparatively few large, load-bearing members — a rigid skeleton of dinosaur bones, if you like — while balloon framing distributed the weight more equally among a much larger number of smaller, uniform posts, in comparison the flexible boning of a fish. The balloon to think of is not the soft rubber bag of air sold at the circus, but the carefully constructed hot-air balloon whose many seams work to define and strengthen its surface, like struts in an umbrella.

In contrast, *platform framing* ▲ produces a stack of open boxes, one on another, and each box is a single story of the house. Each box has its own bottom but no top. Separate studs for each floor rest on separate platforms.

**79**

The nineteenth- and twentieth-century carpenters who built the "new" balloon and platform frames for houses still retained much of the eighteenth-century joiners' vocabulary, which is one reason we have included the preceding bit of architectural history. The names of some of the principal posts and beams — chimney girts, summer beams, and purlins, for example — did fall out of use. But many other words and the framing members they denoted continued to thrive in the currency of language and in modern construction: *sills, plates, studs, joists,* and *braces.* ▼

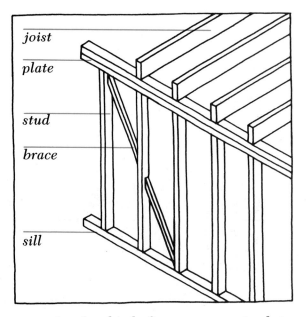

joist
plate
stud
brace
sill

Another kind of currency survived, in name only, and that was the penny, which is still the designation for the size of nails. The two-penny (2d), or smallest, common nail once cost 2¢ a hundred, while the largest, the sixty-penny nail (60 d), fetched 60¢ for the same amount. (The *d* stands for *denarius,* the Roman penny and later the old English pence.)

Like any natural product, wood comes in various sizes and grades (and prices). The *nominal* size of a piece of lumber is its dimensions when rough-cut from the log. Modern standards demand that the rough-cut piece be finished by planing, which makes it smooth but also reduces its size from the nominal measurement. Today,

a so-called 2 x 4 when it comes to you from the lumberyard is only 1½ inches thick by 3½ inches wide.

In the past, builders used more rough-cut, unplaned framing members, and the nineteenth-century 2 x 4s found in a house like ours are slightly larger than newer ones, probably about 1¾ by 3¾ inches. You can tell at a glance the difference between a darkened splintery old stud and a smooth albino modern one, which is also distinguished by its slightly rounded corners, where planing has removed the sharp edge.

When you ask for a 2 x 4 x 8, you get a stud that may be slightly less thick and wide than you specified but that is at least as long as you ordered, perhaps a bit more. Length is one dimension that is not shortened.

Incidentally, the word *board* is not one to throw around casually, at least when you're talking to carpenters. In the exact language of the trade, a board is any piece of lumber whose nominal thickness is 1 inch and whose width is 2 inches or more. *Floorboard* is an accurate usage. Whether a 1 x 2 or a 1 x 12, both extremes are still called boards. To be absolutely precise, you would have to speak of a ¾-by-1½ or a ¾-by-11½. You can see why nobody does.

In order to avoid the heartbreak of shrinking and warping, you ought to make sure that you use *kiln-dried* lumber. The process that produces it is exactly what its name suggests: green (unseasoned) lumber is heated and treated in a kiln, so that moisture is taken out to the point where the cellular structure of the wood itself has shrunk and become much more dense. Kiln-dried lumber will have its ends painted red or green, and it is often branded as well.

Unlike naturally seasoned wood, which has simply been stored until it has dried, kiln-dried lumber cannot again take on moisture, because it has permanently lost its ability to expand and reabsorb. Its minimal moisture content is guaranteed. Because it is so stable, it is better to use than its naturally seasoned counterpart. It will neither shrink nor twist. To appreciate what this means, imagine the lumpy look of a wall whose surface has been attached to green studs that have begun to distort into spirals. (Shrinkage in wood occurs in the horizontal dimension

much more than in the length.) A floorboard made of green lumber will be a squeaky one, and nails holding it down will loosen as the board itself distorts.

▲ Large plywood sheets have replaced traditional lumber in much modern building. Gone, for example, is the old diagonal corner brace made out of a 2 x 4. It had to be *let in*, that is, set into notches individually cut out of the studs it crossed. Otherwise the brace would rest on the outside of the studs and make the installation of a flush wall surface impossible. Plywood does the job quicker and better. A thin plywood rectangle can brace corners without having to be recessed.

Deteriorated or erratic framing, a phenomenon we certainly encountered, can be caused by (1) settlement or (2) rot. When a wing, for example, is added to the main body of a house, the addition may have a tendency to settle slightly, while the house itself stays solidly put. The strain on the framing of the addition is so great that it may go askew. Rot

imposes a similar strain. When a sill crumbles, the construction that rests on it is pulled out of plumb.

Wood is a forgiving kind of material and will try hard to bear its unequal burden in a case of settlement. But unlike steel or other materials, it will not take overstress for an unlimited time. Eventually it will start to go, and once it has started, it will go very quickly. Moreover, wood transfers its load erratically. You can't predict how it will resolve its problem. If settlement and torque were indeed the basic problems with our kitchen wing, probably no one could have guessed that the studs of the *east* wall would rise up off their base. It could have happened in the north or the south.

In our old house, and particularly in the kitchen wing, we perhaps did more reframing than the ordinary rehabber might think of undertaking. Even quite crazy wood framing can eventually be made to work, but it does take time, and time was what we

**82**

didn't have. If we hadn't had to keep to a tight schedule in order to meet our special sort of deadline, we might possibly have jacked up a kitchen wall, replaced a faulty sill, strengthened weakened studs by attaching, or *sistering on*, parallel supports, wedged up floating studs, and firmed up the structure to a reasonable state. We could have counted on plywood sheathing covering the outside surface to strengthen the whole.

But we happened to have carpenters standing by and ready to go. Experienced and fully equipped with efficient tools, they could reframe more rapidly than they could patch and prop up. Time is money, and they could be counted on not to waste either. Rebuilding our kitchen wing from scratch turned out to be, for us, better, quicker, and cheaper than the alternative. ▼

On the other hand, the average do-it-yourselfer, confronted with the same choice, would probably not be able to count on such speed and efficiency. A less radical or a piecemeal approach might suit his abilities better — in fact, might be all he could undertake. Besides, his labor would be free, an important practical consideration.

The moral here is that the calculations you make in a sweat equity job are different from those in a project in which you are employing professionals. If you have a carpenter working for you and he says that it would be cheaper to rebuild, you should probably trust

his judgment in that matter as you do in others.

Elsewhere in the house we also treated ourselves to a few more minor reframings than a scrupulously thrifty homeowner would have. For example, when in the master bedroom we turned two adjacent closets with two separate swinging doors into a single closet with a 5-foot-wide opening for a pair of 30-inch sliding doors, we had to reframe the new, broad opening. Though admittedly the result would have been less sleek and neat, we might well have retained the original two closets as they were, substituting bi-fold doors for the swinging ones we objected to because they took up so much space when they opened into the room. Bi-fold doors when opened wouldn't have been absolutely flush, like sliders, but they would have been an improvement by half over swinging ones, and perhaps that would have been enough. Anyway, we would only have had to hang new doors, rather than have Adam spend most of a day reframing.

Our scheduling demands may have been unusual, but so was the condition of our walls. You shouldn't count on having the bad luck we ran into. But in dealing with any old framing, you should keep alert and be ready for anything. You never know what quirks the original work or alterations through the years may have produced.

There are certain basic ways you can expect old framing to differ from new. Here are some of them:

1. It is rough-sawn.

2. Its members, such as studs, have slightly larger dimensions.

3. A wider variety of lumber occurs. You might find solid oak beams, for example.

4. Joists may vary in size and spacing.

5. Studs will usually be spaced regularly and conventionally, 16 inches from the center of one to the center of the next. Don't count on it, however, and before you try to hang a heavy object on a wall, test to make sure you really have a stud behind the spot where theoretically it ought to be.

Old framing may also be out of plumb. Either it may have been built a little erratically, or it may have settled slightly. If the problem is not severe or continuing, you

**83**

probably should try to live with it. Starting from the basement and trying to level a house is as difficult as it is expensive. You may start off a chain reaction: having restored a door frame to strict 90-degree angles, you then find that your previously undercut door no longer fits. (A sagging floor around a heavy fireplace is another matter, involving a specific, rather urgent structural problem that should be corrected.) In short, abstract perfectionism in rehabbing is admirable in principle, costly in practice, and often simply inappropriate.

Some more specific advice, of the humble sort that carpenter fathers pass on to their children, concerns on-the-job procedures.

1. Carry a pencil and rule at all times.

2. *Always* wear hard-soled shoes on the job. On one memorable occasion, when the fall of the east wall of the kitchen was being immortalized on videotape, Norm stepped on a nail, and unfortunately that day his soles weren't quite hard enough. In the great tradition of The Show Must Go On, he limped through the scene. In view of his heroism we refused to say anything like "we told you so."

3. We've said it before, but we'll say it again. Keep the job site very clean and picked up along the way. It will pay dividends.

4. Don't walk around a job with your hands in your pockets. Stumbling blocks are everywhere, and if you trip, you want to be able to catch yourself before you fall flat on your floorboards.

When we were framing in walls and parts of walls in our old house, we unself-consciously used the language of several centuries of joinery-carpentry, much of its traditional building material, and certain basic tools that had stood the test of time. We were certainly not antiquarians, however, and were happy to take advantage of new developments in hand tools and of various electric power tools for sawing, sanding, and drilling — all standard equipment. ▶

Part of an appraisal and preplanning, as we have said, is deciding what proportion of a total job you will do yourself. You must also estimate which tools you will have to have on hand to do your part. Whether or not you are going to undertake major carpentry yourself, you will want to be able to do maintenance work in years to come, and should plan on assembling a basic collection.

You don't need to buy the best in the world — the cabinetmaker's selection from the luxury supplier — but don't waste your money on bargains from the discount store in the shopping mall. Reliable lines offer serviceable tools at a moderate price that will do the job you want for years, while a cheapie screwdriver, for example, won't perform for long. It'll be less strong than screws, which will chew it to bits in no time. Buy the best tools you can reasonably afford, and you won't be sorry.

Flea markets and yard sales can be an unorthodox but good source of secondhand tools and equipment, as long as the seller doesn't think of the object as an antique and jack up the price.

You can rent a wide range of special tools that you might not need very often, particularly power tools, and rates are surprisingly inexpensive. Also, the rental people can be a great help when all you know is that you're in difficulty on the job, and you haven't a clue about what it is that might help you. Often they can pull out a tool you've never heard of that will solve your problem.

One sunny lunch hour, our carpenters — Norm, Greg, Adam, and Bill — sat on the front steps of our old house and put together a list of tools that should be in a basic collection.

## Hand Tools for Basic Carpentry

1. Hammer, heavy curved claw, with metal-and-rubber handle (20 ounces)
2. Saws
   - crosscut saw (10-point)
   - back saw
   - coping saw
   - keyhole saw
   - Optional: 8-point crosscut saw, for heavier outdoor work
3. Miter box
4. Hatchet
5. Utility knife, with replaceable blades
6. Framing squares
   - regular steel square
   - combination square

   Optional: bevel gauge
7. Levels
   - 30-inch 3-bubble aluminum level
   - plumb bob and chalk line
   - Optional: 4-foot level, for framing and door-hanging
8. Putty knives
   - 6-inch knife
   - 1½-inch knife
9. Nail apron, leather or canvas
10. Work gloves, all leather or leather-faced
11. Rules
    - tape rule, steel, 12- or 16-foot
    - folding rule, wooden, 6-foot
12. Pencils
13. Wood chisels, a selection of four (¼-inch, ½-inch, ¾-inch, and 1-inch)
14. Safety goggles or glasses
15. Nose-mouth filter mask
16. Screwdrivers
    - 2 regular (for large and small screws)
    - 1 Phillips head
17. Awl (or ice pick)
18. Nail sets, selection of three
19. Pliers
    - lineman's pliers
    - vise-grip pliers
20. Staple gun, heavy duty
21. Block plane, low-angle model, which is compact and can plane end grain easier
22. Sharpening stone, red India stone rather than Carborundum
23. Nail claw
24. Nylon line
25. Adjustable scribe
26. Clamps
    - four 6-inch clamps
    - four spring clamps
27. Stepladder, 6-foot
28. Wirecutter
29. Adjustable wrench
30. Flashlight
31. Toolbox
32. Caulking gun

Optional: to supplement or substitute for various power tools
   - hand drill
   - brace and bit

## Power Tools for Basic Carpentry

1. Portable circular saw
2. Saber saw, with at least four blades
3. Drill (⅜-inch size, rather than ¼-inch)
4. Extension cords (round wire, not flat)
5. Adapters for plugs

# 6
# This Cold House

When a rehabbing job is going well, you start to daydream — of what the house once was, what it will be again. This week nothing distracted us. Nothing broke down or went wrong. There were no major problems of the kind that keep worriers awake at night, recalculating, measuring in the mind.

By now we had gotten used to the look of the house with the 1939 additions gone and the front porch opened up. We zoomed in on the newly liberated porch to see exactly what we had when we looked closely. Only two of the original porch posts had survived; two new ones were needed to replace the temporary supports. The roof had to be redone, but that was no big deal, and certainly no more a surprise than the fact that the porch floor also had to be replaced. We were not delighted to discover that, now we could really inspect it, some of the substructure had to be rebuilt. In other words, we had a porch, but we didn't have one.

Still, our imaginations were stimulated by the relic, if that's what we had. When we squinted we could almost see the house of the 1930s, as captured in the photographs lent us by the Packards. Forty-five years ago the porch was a real old-fashioned piazza, a retreat from the full sun, dappled with shadows of the vines that ran along the trellis fixed at the roofline. The scene was really idyllic.

During the past week we'd torn away the hopelessly overgrown yews and lilacs that up to then had obscured the porch. Now we had clear access to the foundation.

As I walked around outside, I noticed that the kitchen wing was completely enclosed in plywood sheathing, except for the new windows in the south and north walls.  ◄ What had happened to our back door? The whole east wall was as blank as a shoebox. But

when I studied the seams of the pieces of plywood, I could see one door-sized section outlined in the proper place. The blank was only temporary.

The whole wing looked good and tight against the penetrating winds that made the weather seem even damper and chillier than the actual temperature. This was a particularly good day to plan on taking coffee breaks down in the basement, close by the space heater there, which was still our only source of heat. The new and compact gas furnace was in place but not yet hooked up. Still waiting in the wings was the new energy-saving hot water heater that would eventually stand beside it.

This morning Norm had just started repairing the masonry foundation for our new metal bulkhead, ▲ the replacement for the rotted wooden cellar doors that had long gone into the dumpster. He finished the job, bulkhead installation and all, by the end of the day. ▶

Scaffolding was still up on the east wall, and on the north and west walls as well. The battle of the eaves was proceeding simultaneously on several fronts (or sides).

Certainly our exterior progress had been steady and reassuring, but the interior changes were *really* encouraging. Upstairs and downstairs, new partitions had been going up with amazing speed. The sense of instant achievement is one you don't enjoy when you're working by yourself.

In the second-floor bathrooms, the new and revised walls had been framed in. On the first floor, the anxiously awaited lavatory was not only framed but actually walled in, the door hung, and a working toilet installed, at last.

In the kitchen, both the coat/utility closet by the back door and the small end wall opposite it were also framed, and structural reinforcing work in the ceiling continued. The rough frame for the skylight was finished and waiting. ◀

Between the family room and the stair hall, more new framing had already produced the centered door of our plans, simplifying the traffic pattern and the look of the room. But another new doorway, one cut into the wall between the living room and the stair hall, seemed to have appeared unannounced. It hadn't even been at the back of anyone's mind until this week when, faced with one more practical dilemma, once again we improvised.

What had happened? The plumbers working above in the bathrooms found that a 4-inch waste pipe headed down to the basement was simply too large in diameter to fit inside the hall wall, which was somewhat less than four inches thick. We had counted on being able to slip it inside the wall, but now we had no choice but to reroute it outside, either in the stair hall or in the living room. At first neither choice seemed acceptable.

We wanted a route that would involve the least new cutting into the erratic, water-damaged joists that had supported the 1939 bathroom. We had to keep in mind that they would soon be supporting not one but two 300-pound bathtubs. The most efficient *chase*, or pipeway, led down right along, but not inside, the east wall of the living room. To have, in effect, a sewer quite so prominently featured wouldn't have suited even the most let-it-all-hang-out, hi-tech taste in interior decoration. It certainly didn't suit us.

Why not box the offending waste pipe in, we asked? Answering ourselves, we had to admit that, even if we insulated against sound, a chimneylike construction that climbed the wall wouldn't be much of an improvement in appearance over an exposed pipe. We tossed the pros and cons of other alternatives around,

and ended by deciding to be bold. By midweek our solution was on display.

We had framed in a closet in space taken by eminent domain from the northeast corner of the living room. ▲ Its doorway had been cut out of the hall wall, facing the bottom of the stairs. Weeks ago we'd sacrificed the original coat closet to gain space for our lavatory, but now we had a proper replacement, with plenty of room for storage or even for a hi-fi center from which wiring could go to speakers elsewhere in the house.

Some people may think we just rationalized a design decision imposed upon us by necessity. I'd counter that we made the best of an awkward situation. There is a difference.

Five weeks ago our appraiser had warned us that the ceiling in the dining room had to go, and today it was gone, at least the plaster and lath. We were down to the joists, and it was clear that any new surface attached to that erratic framework would turn out wavy as the ocean. Today I found myself up on one of the smaller ladders in my repertoire, demonstrating how to straighten the ceiling by adding extensions to the lower edges of some of the joists. My goal was to rig up as level a base as I could for the new surface we would soon put up.

We were also doing some milder stripping nearby in the living room. The pale green vinyl damask wallpaper there had easily been pulled off, but upstairs we had a stickier job. A portable wallpaper steamer and its operator were at work in the master bedroom. ▶ In both the guest room and children's room, not only wallpaper but much of the plaster had been removed from walls, some of which were down to the bare lath, or in the case of chimney walls to bare brick. Also down and out were the last of the upstairs ceilings slated to go.

This was our final chance to walk through the electrical plan for the kitchen, the most complicated wiring job in the house. The electricians had been making rapid progress in the bedrooms, so it wasn't going to be long before they would be ready for the kitchen. I wanted to make sure we hadn't forgotten a single switch, outlet, or ceiling fixture, and I had my fingers crossed that all our preplanning had taken account of code requirements. Happily, the plan seemed to check out.

While the newly framed and sheathed exterior walls in the kitchen were open to the inside, that is, not yet covered by the wallboard due to arrive in a week or so, we had another last chance. We still had time to install a different kind of insulation from the cellulose fill that the pros outside were pumping into the roof and the finished walls.

When I unrolled the fiberglass blanket and started to measure a batt that would fit tight between a pair of studs, I couldn't help commenting that this job was not my idea of fun. Fiberglass strikes me as an unpleasantly itchy material to work with, especially in hot weather. Gloves and a long-sleeved shirt are a good idea. But this method of insulating is so easy — it's largely a matter of being able to measure accurately and to staple — that I couldn't justify hiring someone else to do it. The job is a pretty painless way to turn a profit out of a rainy day, and is another easy-to-master skill for the beginning rehabber.

**O**riginally, in terms of energy efficiency, the old place had been such a loser that we hardly knew where to begin to tighten it up. So, early in the game, we had called in Ross Donald and his energy auditors to give us their professional appraisal of exactly how

much and where our heat loss was, as well as some suggestions about the ways we could produce more heat and plug up the leaks. A tent wouldn't have had a much lower rating than our house did.

Our furnace was producing only half the heat it should have for the amount of oil it burned. A major part of the loss was in heat that went directly up the flue from the furnace, heating some of Meeting House Hill but not the house. The rest of the problem lay in the out-of-date heat distribution system, with its leaky old radiators, and a single thermostat that made temperature control an all-or-nothing proposition.

Another major problem lay, as we knew, in the various gaps in the *building envelope* — the outer shell

**Potential heat loss in average house (50% of heat produced) without retrofitting**

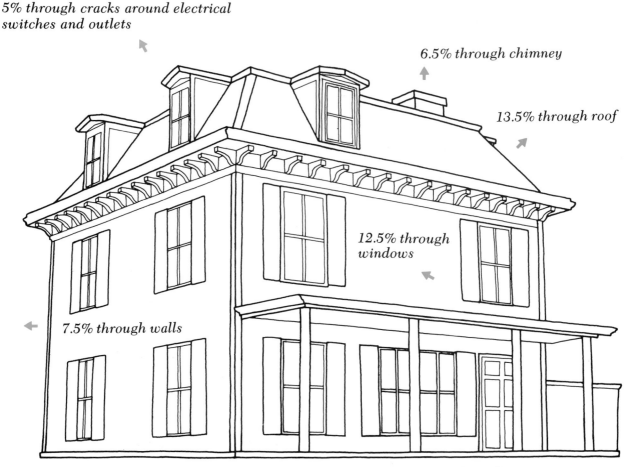

*5% through cracks around electrical switches and outlets*

*6.5% through chimney*

*13.5% through roof*

*12.5% through windows*

*7.5% through walls*

*5% through doors*

of the house. We desperately needed to give it a seal and some means of internal resistance to the cold. We had a major affliction, or two versions of it: drafts. To be very precise, the chill air blowing in from outdoors and whirling around our ankles was *infiltration*, while the heat leaking out was *exfiltration*, but the pair of problems is usually called just infiltration. Anyway, the fact was that the house was plain uncomfortable.

It would have been silly to increase our energy-producing capacity without tightening up the shell first so that we wouldn't lose what heat we did produce. So we began with conservation, and suddenly we were into the *retrofitting* business. In other words, we went back to the drawing board in order to revise the house for

## Potential heat savings in average house (percentages of total heat cost) with retrofitting

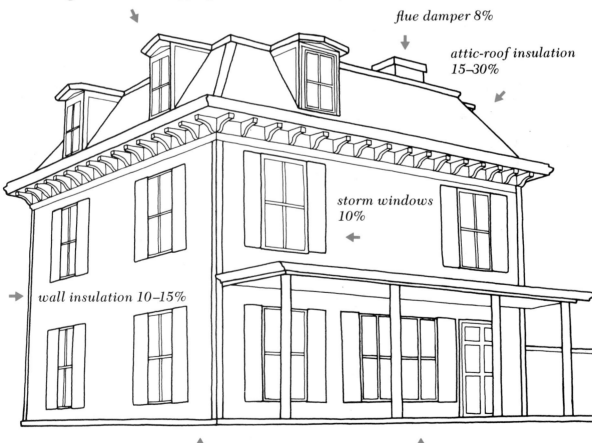

*setback thermostat 10%*

*caulking and weatherstripping 10–20%*

*flue damper 8%*

*attic-roof insulation 15–30%*

*storm windows 10%*

*wall insulation 10–15%*

*floor insulation 0–20%*

*new furnace 10%*

improved energy efficiency without making drastic alterations in it. The single word *retrofit* is a compression of two others: *retroactive fitting*.

Our first target was the arch-enemy, infiltration, and our strategy called for sealing up the chinks where drafts came in and heat escaped. We would caulk wherever exterior door and window trim met the clapboard siding; we would renovate the windows themselves, reputtying their panes, tightening the fit of the frames, replacing whole window assemblies when necessary (expensive, since our windows were no longer stock size, and new ones had to be custom-made). We planned on investing in a full set of new storm windows. There were some rickety old combination jobs already in place,

**Building envelope of This Old House showing insulating materials used in retrofitting**

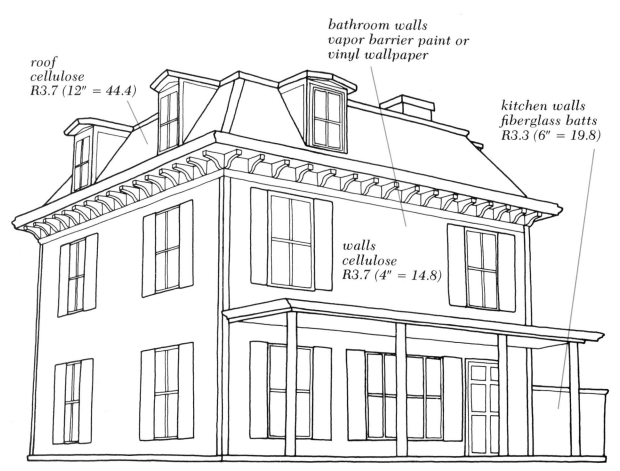

*bathroom walls*
*vapor barrier paint or*
*vinyl wallpaper*

*roof*
*cellulose*
*R3.7 (12" = 44.4)*

*kitchen walls*
*fiberglass batts*
*R3.3 (6" = 19.8)*

*walls*
*cellulose*
*R3.7 (4" = 14.8)*

*crawl space*
*fiberglass batts*
*R3.3 (6" = 19.8)*

but we had no guarantee we could bring them back into condition. Any new windows were to be double-glazed, and even our kitchen skylight would be thermal. We would of course give the exterior siding several new coats of paint, which would help the cause. There certainly wasn't any seal left in the flaky paint job we had.

So far our program fell under the heading of *passive measures*: we were making sure that the existing building was as energy-efficient as it could be without supplementary action, such as adding insulation or replacing the heating system. By combining simple conservation (examples would be turning down the heat, and servicing the furnace so that it would run most efficiently) with the passive measures against infiltration we took, a considerable amount of the estimated fuel bill could have been saved, even if we had stopped here. One generalization is that infiltration causes about 25% of the heat loss in the average older house.

Moving on to *active measures,* we had to keep reminding ourselves of the fact that whatever we did to the outside of the house should not alter the mid-Victorian appearance we were trying to reestablish. This wasn't too hard, because we had never been tempted by inappropriate storm doors with scalloped trim and embossed American eagles nor had we suffered from the illusion that aluminum siding was a solution for insulating problems.

Our major active project was insulation, and our goal was to provide a modern heat-resistant backing to the building's wooden shell, a second or inner envelope inserted within the first.

Historically, any insulation in old houses was definitely makeshift and ranged from corncobs and sawdust to crumpled newspaper wadding. One of the less orthodox but at least comparatively fire-resistant materials used for insulating was seaweed, which as Mrs. Georgia Packard remembers filled the crawl space under the kitchen wing when she lived in our house during the 1920s and 1930s.

There was a practical question about which kind of insulation we would use. It seemed a little late in the day to bring back corncobs and sawdust, though seaweed does seem to be undergoing a revival. A New Jersey architect has been conducting feasibility tests, and has already installed *Zostera marina,* or eelgrass, in his own attic. We decided, however, to stick with more conventional modern technology.

The rationale for our final insulating scheme went like this:

1. For the surfaces where we had open studs or joists, we used fiberglass batts we installed ourselves. These areas included newly framed walls and the unfinished, unheated crawl space under the kitchen.

2. For finished surface, both walls and roof, we used an insulating material that was professionally blown into the cavities under pressure, through small holes drilled into them from either the inside or the outside. ◀ The holes in the siding were plugged and eventually painted; the holes in interior walls were plugged and plastered over.

Several kinds of home insulation are now on the market that can be inserted into finished cavities and are therefore particularly suitable for retrofitting: blown-in or poured-in fiberglass or mineral wool; poured-in perlite or vermiculite; and either urethane or urea formaldehyde foam. Urea formaldehyde seems to give off noxious fumes as well as moisture; Massachusetts has recently outlawed it, and it may well go off the market. Foam has another drawback. An incompetent installer can fail to take into account its expansion rate and can so overfill a wall that it can actually blow out into a permanent bulge. Finally, there is cellulose.

We chose cellulose, which is a particular favorite among preservationists and rehabbers like us because it is thermally effective, competitively priced (the payback should take only 3 to 4 years), long-lasting, and most important, it can be compacted evenly in the irregular cavities of erratically framed old houses. With our mansard roof, whose sides and top were finished inside with plastered walls and ceilings, we had to have insulation that could be blasted from outside into the spaces between the rafters. ▶ A conventional unfinished attic would have been far simpler to deal with from inside with fiberglass batts we could have installed ourselves.

Cellulose insulation is a recycled material. "Short cellulosic wood fibers" simply means reprocessed newspaper. (There is one exotic but unconfirmed rumor around that some cellulose insulation is worn-out and ground-up paper money.) The gray fluffy stuff may look "like an old mouse nest," according to retrofitter Charles Wing, but actually rodents and other vermin choose to settle where it isn't. There's something they hate about printer's ink.

The cellulose is fireproofed with various chemicals. The best brands, and the one we chose, are treated

simply with boric acid. You should beware of any kind that is treated with substances that can combine with the moisture in the air to form sulfuric acid, hardly welcome in the home environment.

The effectiveness of the various kinds of insulation is measured in terms of their *resistance to heat loss,* or their *R factor,* which is figured by the inch. In our roof we were able to install 12 inches of cellulose fill, rated R3.7, which came to a total of R44.4, far greater than the R39 experts have recommended for roofs. ◄ On the other hand, in our old walls, which had cavities ranging from almost 4 inches to only about 2½ inches, we did the best we could, figuring that whatever we inserted would be better than nothing.

Anyone insulating a house has a double task. Obviously he wants to bar the exit of heat, but what is often not understood is that he also wants to prevent the escape of moisture. In the old days moisture inside the house wasn't much of an issue. For example, people weren't in the habit of daily showers and baths, of constantly filling bathrooms with steam.

In the winter, when warm moist air from inside a house leaks into the cavity of an outside wall, it encounters cold air from outdoors. When the two meet, the warm moist air condenses, and a dew falls within the wall.

*Before* insulation is installed, this dew can gradually evaporate in the air space and dissipate through leaks in the sheathing and siding of the wall, not likely to be perfectly tight. But *after* insulation has filled up the cavity and the outer surface has been tightened, the situation is changed. Any condensation necessarily settles into the insulating material, where it remains as if absorbed into a sponge. As moisture continues to accumulate inside the cavity, exposed wood becomes more and more waterlogged.

This encourages a dread scourge to move in. *Dry rot* is what it's called, a misnomer if ever there was one. Dry rot is really a fungus that preys on wet wood. In order to live, dry rot requires not only moist wood to eat, but also darkness and temperatures higher than 50 degrees, though it is patient and will remain dormant through the winter until warm weather arrives and activates it. The fungus is a sneaky, hungry visitor whose attention is well worth avoiding.

The tactic in dealing with water vapor — both general humidity inside a house, and the steam produced by cooking, bathing, and laundering — is to prevent it from escaping into the wall in the first place. To accomplish this, a waterproof skin, the famous *vapor barrier,* ▶ is introduced inside the wall cavity in order to keep the moisture in the house where it originated, and away from the cold air. The barrier lines the warm inner surface of the cavity, not the cold outer surface. Remember this one simple fact, and you will never be confused: whether installed horizontally or vertically, a vapor barrier always goes *against* the warm surface.

Fiberglass batt insulation comes with a vapor barrier backing attached to one side, and it also comes without one (which means that a separate sheet of polyethylene or some other barrier must be provided). The fiberglass we installed between the studs of our kitchen walls had a brown kraft-paper backing. When we put a batt in place, the kraft paper faced into the room. It was eventually concealed behind the finished wall. ▼

Fiberglass also comes with a foil backing. Aluminum foil is waterproof, less likely to deteriorate than kraft paper, and also reflects heat. A special wallboard is now manufactured that has one side papered with foil. When the wallboard is used to finish a wall, its foil

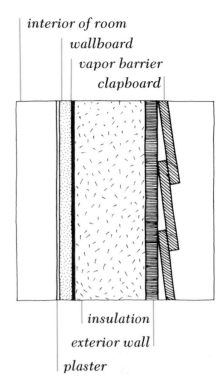

interior of room
wallboard
vapor barrier
clapboard

insulation
exterior wall
plaster

side faces toward the outside, that is, into the cavity. The closely butting panels present a vapor barrier with very few seams, an advantage when each seam is a potential leak. Another advantage is that the foil is fixed flat on a rigid surface, rather than on a soft pillow of fiberglass where it is more likely to be punctured or torn.

The cellulose blown into our finished outside walls was water-resistant, but not absolutely impervious to an overdose, either in the form of leaks from outside or as water vapor from inside. To minimize the latter, we had to provide another kind of impermeable skin, a vapor barrier applied on the interior of rooms where a lot of water vapor is produced, since we could hardly blow it inside the walls along with the cellulose.

What we did was this. In the bathrooms, where there is maximum moisture potential, we painted the walls with a special latex vapor barrier paint. Two or three coats of oil paint on wood or plaster are almost as effective as the special product, but ordinary latex paint is not. Then we provided yet another waterproof membrane by papering the walls with vinyl. In the other steamiest part of the house, the kitchen, vinyl paper also supplemented the kraft-paper barrier on the fiberglass inside the wall.

Under the kitchen in the unfinished crawl space where seaweed once served as insulation, we installed more fiberglass. Which way was the vapor barrier? The answer is up, this time facing a horizontal warm surface, the floor above. We held the batts in place with chicken wire that we stapled to the floor joists, as if to the studs of a wall. Then we covered the bare earth floor of the space with a sheet of 4 mil polyethylene plastic to keep the ground damp from rising. (Six mil would have given even better protection.) Like installing the batts in the kitchen wall, this job is one a homeowner can do for himself on a Saturday afternoon, but he should be especially sure to wear a mask as he works.

**W**hile we battled against waste as conservationists, by sealing leaks and installing insulation, we were also actively modernizing our means of production. Our dream machine was a compact, prepackaged, gas-fired furnace, complete with the latest technological marvels. About the size of two microwave ovens piled on top of one another, it was capable of heating the whole house as never before, and was potentially many times as effective as the fallen giant that had originally burned coal, had been converted to oil, and had finally precipitated its own early retirement when it stopped cold.

We did stick with the forced hot water or *hydronic* system we found, though we switched from oil to gas as fuel. We decided on gas mainly for convenience's sake. We were installing several other gas-burning appliances: hot water heater, kitchen stove, and laundry dryer. It made sense to go with gas all the way.

We were also influenced by both the compactness of the gas furnace and its clean, quiet operation, as well as by the economics of oil. In other respects, other situations, however, a modern new oil burner would have done the job perfectly well.

Our new heating system incorporated one special energy-saving device, a computer mastermind. The regulator on an ordinary furnace with no powers of decision is usually set to maintain a room temperature of 70° on a 0° day. It behaves the same way whether the temperature outside is 55° or minus 5°, telling the boiler to heat the water to a constant 160°–180°, just as if the demand for heat were the same in all kinds of weather.

But our mastermind had an outdoor sensor that fed it the latest information on the day's temperature. It then processed the data and programmed a regulator to adjust the water temperature accordingly, reducing it as low as 120° on a mild day. This constant process of readjustment and accommodation avoids unnecessary overheating, thus saving fuel.

The collaboration between an efficient heating system — the producer — and effective insulation — the conserver — was to transform our leaking sieve from an outrageous energy waster into an exemplary energy-miser. No longer would a drafty ark groan under the impossible burden of having to heat the immediate neighborhood in order minimally to heat itself. In the future the warmth produced would remain inside where it belonged, inside a ship that, unlike many of its contemporaries, was very tight.

The beauty but also the thermal weakness in the design of many old houses lies in their many ample windows and doors — elegant, distinctive, and leaky. Drafts can whisk under paneled nineteenth-century doors and through cracks in them, and they rattle the sashes of 2/2 windows that don't fit as well as they once did a century ago. A reasonable assumption might seem to be that the older the house, the less energy-efficient.

Actually, recent studies reveal that antique buildings are not the champion energy wasters, a title that belongs to houses built from 1940 to 1975. Even though infiltration was minimized in the newer houses, energy-gobbling systems of heating and air conditioning were installed as if there were no tomorrow, or at least no end-of-the-month utility bills. This was before conservation made financial sense.

Energy conservation, though it wasn't called that, was certainly an important issue in the nineteenth century. Keeping warm without making a career of it was probably no less urgent for Eliza T. Clapp in her house at 6 Percival Street in the 1860s than it was to us, rehabilitating the place in 1979. Even if cost wasn't quite the issue it is today, comfort was.

Since furnaces in nineteenth-century houses were either nonexistent or elementary, Victorian builders had to be crafty in devising ways to conserve what heat they did produce. Floor plan design played its part. Our foyer was typical. It could be closed off from the rest of the house simply by shutting two interior doors, one into the stair hall and the other into the front parlor. When a winter visitor entered the front door, the cold blast that accompanied him was trapped.

By the 1920s the door into the front parlor was gone, filed away with several companions in the mud room. It had been replaced by the thick door-curtains known as portieres. The door to the stair hall, with its frosted glass panes, remained, less in the interests of heat conservation than of privacy.

Victorians also capitalized on natural sources of energy, as had their Colonial predecessors. For example, when our house was new, it featured floor-to-ceiling windows in the front parlor. These faced, not north, east, or west, but south. In the wintertime the sun could pour in and warm the room. Ms. Clapp would never have spoken of *passive solar heat,* but that's what she enjoyed.

But what of the summer? Some early owner of our house recognized that a very large leafy shade tree on the south side of the house would shield its southern exposure from July's blazing sun, not so welcome as January's. So he planted or encouraged a maple that eventually grew to a great size and served well until it toppled in the hurricane of 1938. It and also the roofed front porch shaded the front parlor. ▶

We couldn't tell if anyone had ever planted a barrier of evergreens on the north side of the house, but the combination of deciduous shade trees on the south side of a house with evergreens as a winter windbreak on the north was another common tactic.

Because the house was perched high on a hill, it enjoyed excellent summertime cross-ventilation, at least before the 1939 partitions interrupted the free flow on the first floor. Originally a cool breeze might sweep right through from north to south, entering through the bay in the back parlor and exiting through the tall windows in the front.

That same draft was not so desirable in winter. An old-fashioned way of maximizing a house's heat retention was to paint its exterior a dark color. But there was thermal benefit in simply keeping the house well painted, whatever the color. Multiple coats provided a seal against cold winds by in effect caulking all tiny cracks and joints in clapboard siding.

Back-plastering was another way Victorian builders often used to tighten up their houses. No longer a common practice, back-plastering provided two plaster

shells, rather than one, in exterior walls. An extra grid of lath was installed between the outer edges of the studs and the sheathing of the exterior, with a thick, rough coat of plaster applied to it from inside. A second layer of lath and plaster was then applied to the inner edge of the studs and plaster was then applied to the inner edge of the studs in the ordinary manner, leaving a sandwich filling of several inches of air trapped between the two plasterings. The dead air served as a kind of insulation.

Even though there is less space in the cavity of a back-plastered wall than in an ordinary one, you can certainly justify insulating it. Where our outside walls were back-plastered, we went ahead and blew in as much cellulose as we could in order to augment the seal provided by the back-plastering.

Incidentally, our modern thermal skylight made use of an insulating barrier of dead air (as did our storm windows and the double-layer thermopane glass in our new kitchen windows). The skylight had two transparent shells, one inside the other, with a layer of air in between that prevented condensation from forming on the inner surface, from which it would have drip-drip-dripped without a buffer zone between the cold outside and the warmth inside the kitchen.

Today all sorts of sealing products besides paint and caulk are on the market to help a homeowner close up the tiniest chinks in the building envelope of his house and so conserve heat. One of the simplest do-it-yourself projects is weatherstripping around doors and windows, especially doors. In an old house, most doors have gradually become poorly fitting, having over the years suffered from settlement, warping, or general sag. As doors began to stick, they would be planed down, often several times, thus growing ever smaller, ever draftier.

Modern weatherstripping comes in a number of forms and modes of operation, as you will see when you confront the constantly increasing display at your hardware store or lumberyard. Some are to be applied to the door itself, others to the threshold or to the casings. We won't even attempt a survey of the various products available to plug up doors and windows, but we will offer a few miscellaneous bits of advice. Don't shun the newer synthetic door gaskets. They're actually better than the old rubber ones, because they don't harden and crack. We don't recommend, however, the self-adhering tape with polyurethane foam on it, except for doors that will be retired from use for the winter, since with use the foam hardens and strips off, leaving behind the tape, seemingly stuck for life.

A quite different kind of urethane foam is available in spray cans, like shaving soap that hardens in the air. It is a convenient, though not cheap, way to fill in small voids, cracks, or unused keyholes and bellways. Every hole filled is a plus. But don't get carried away and risk short circuits by spraying the foam around receptacles behind switch or outlet plates on outside walls. Specially designed insulating gaskets are available for those locations.

Sealing up against infiltration is a commonsense procedure that doesn't involve complicated technology or a large investment. It pays dividends, and you can do it yourself. Replacing a furnace is another matter. It's a major investment and demands professional help. Before you commit yourself, be sure you have calculted the relative costs of starting anew and rescuing what you've got. Will you really save money by spending it? Our aged furnace was hopeless, but not every old one should be condemned out of hand until persuasive evidence is in.

The *forced hot water system* our furnace served is probably the most satisfactory kind of conventional system you will find in an old house. If you are lucky enough to have one, do what you can to restore it to a reasonable standard of operation. Unfortunately we had to do more than most. You need not expect to have to replace furnace, pipes, and radiators as we did.

You may find that your furnace produces hot air rather than hot water, and distributes it throughout the house via ducts and registers. A *hot air system* responds quickly but may deliver heat unevenly. A house heated by hot air can be rather drafty.

The least desirable alternative you may face is an elderly setup that provides *steam heat* to a squad of freestanding radiators stationed throughout the house. Steam heat is likely to introduce you to a host of problems caused by corrosion within the system. But you'd be wise to hang on until it's clear that you can't live with it any longer. Then switch over to a forced hot water system.

The ever-rising costs of electricity have given a bad name to *electric resistance heating units* installed as a series of baseboard units, which work on the same principle as a toaster. This system is what people usually mean when they refer to electric heat, and it does seem to be a very expensive way to heat a whole house these days.

You should be aware, however, of certain newer, more economical developments in electric heat. Some are simply auxiliary units, designed to supplement another kind of system. Others will do the whole job.

*An electric heat pump* is usually described as air conditioning in reverse. During the heating season, the pump (collaborating with a compressor) extracts warmth from the air outdoors and transfers it to air inside. This circulates through ducts, as in a conventional hot air system. The heat pump's efficiency descends as the outdoor temperature falls, but electric resistance heaters in the ductwork come on in stages to compensate. Below 30° they take over entirely. Estimated costs for this system are less than for electric baseboard heating and roughly comparable to gas heat. In summer the heat pump system can indeed be reversed, switched over to function as central air conditioning.

If you are determined to have air conditioning, and if you already have the ductwork of a hot air system (or because of the scale of your rehabbing are prepared to install new ducts), you may want to consider this option. Take into account that converted hot air ducts will not be as large as new air-conditioning ducts, and therefore won't be able to provide maximum cooling effectiveness. You will also have to add insulation to the converted ducts to prevent the condensation that air conditioning produces, and will also have to add the compensating electric heaters.

*Large-surface electric radiant heating* offers another alternative, when you are going to replace ceilings or walls anyway. A grid of wiring with insulation above or behind, sometimes enclosed in a kind of electric blanket, and designed to fit between ceiling joists, can be installed and then covered with a wallboard ceiling. Radiant heat will then be beamed down or out into the room. Wallboard panels are available with the wiring manufactured inside. They can't be cut into, but do come in both full and half sizes. An exact pattern of installation has to be precisely worked out in advance.

*Electric radiant heat units* also come in smaller sizes, as tiles or glass panels, and these are especially suitable for supplementary spot heating, as in a chilly bathroom, for example.

Another innovation is the *electric heat storage unit*. This is a cabinet, either free-standing or semirecessed in a wall, that is designed to heat an individual room and to take advantage of off-peak electrical rates, which are available in some but not all areas. The heat storage unit follows a cycle that goes like this: ceramic tiles or bricks with high heat-retention properties are charged up at night when power is cheap; then during the day these heat reservoirs give off the heat they have stored.

A fireplace may seem to be more of an asset in home heating than it usually is in reality. If yours lacks a damper, it is providing a constant escape route for the very warm air that you are trying to keep inside your house. Even if you already have or you install a damper, you have to open it when you light a fire. Ironically, the draft created by a burning fire siphons off more heat from a room than it adds to it.

One corrective approach would be to install a heat recirculating device inside the fireplace to catch the escaping heat that would otherwise be wasted, redirecting it into the room. A number of designs based on the same principle are available. Another tactic would employ tempered glass fire doors to prevent a net heat loss with every use of the fireplace by enclosing the blaze and preventing the siphoning effect. Fire doors also act as dampers when the fireplace is not in use. They are a particularly happy solution when, as sometimes happens, the construction of an old fireplace precludes the addition of a new damper.

The efficiency and safety of your fireplace and chimney will be increased by proper maintenance and repair. Check to see if any bricks need repointing, and arrange for regular visits from a chimney sweep. Our chimney was in surprisingly good shape and required only a cleaning, but we had a shallow hearth suitable only for burning cannel coal in a grate. Wood fires are the ones that cause large amounts of combustible residue to accumulate in chimneys.

You may decide to put a wood- or coal-burning stove in your fireplace or elsewhere. Be absolutely sure your plans conform to local regulations and specifications for stove location, heat shields, and stovepipes. The number of house fires caused by stoves is increasing in proportion to their new popularity, and improper installation is a major factor.

With every frown that crosses the faces of Middle Eastern oil potentates, new research and developments in both energy conservation and alternative sources are stimulated. Keep abreast of change by consulting your local state and federal energy offices, as well as utility companies, for details on the latest advances and techniques. Because the relative costs of electricity, gas, and oil are readjusting daily, and fuel availability varies, you can't rely on old accountings or prejudices from an energy-happy era. In this period of flux, heating design cannot afford to be as set in its ways as it once was. Keep an open mind, ask questions, and then make a reasoned decision that will suit your own situation.

### How to install fiberglass roll insulation in an unfinished wall

Be sure to wear a particle mask, work gloves, and long sleeves in order to protect your skin and your lungs from tiny fibers of insulation. These directions are for fiberglass rolls with a vapor barrier backing.

1. Measure the height of the studs in the wall.

2. Make a cutting pattern by transferring the dimension of the studs to the floor: make one mark for the bottom and a second mark, parallel to the first, for the top of the stud.

3. Place the roll of fiberglass on the floor with the cut edge aligned with the first mark. Unroll until slightly past the second mark.

4. Take a straightedge (a short piece of 2 x 4 is perfect), place it horizontally across the roll at the bottom mark, and step on it to hold it firm.

5. Using the straightedge as a guide, cut across the roll with a utility knife. The cut piece, or batt, will be exactly the right length and width to fit snugly in the space in the wall framing.

6. Put the batt in place between the studs with the vapor barrier backing facing into the room. Pull out the flanges of backing that run vertically on either side of the batt. Flatten them out on the inner edge of the studs and staple firmly in place. As you work along the wall, overlap the flanges of adjacent batts, to form a tight seal.

# 7
# Circulatory System

**Week 6**   When I checked in at this old house during the week, it still had a porch roof, but one that was pretty basic. All that was left were the horizontal joists. The pitched rafters were gone, and without them the structure looked like a shelf supported by some sticks (and our two indomitable old posts). ◄

A day or so later, the shelf had been further reduced, to a frame something like a grape arbor. Only one original post remained standing; the other was down for a close inspection.

We finally decided to allow ourselves a special kind of luxury. We arranged to have the two new porch posts we needed custom-milled out of single pieces of Philippine mahogany. A Williamsburg-type restoration could have done no more.

This decision involved some soul-searching on our part. We knew that the porch had been designed as the focal point of the house's exterior and deserved the best. But we boggled at the cost of excellence: an estimated several hundred dollars per finished post. The tooling up at the mill is what costs; the wood isn't as expensive as it sounds. No suitable domestic wood, like clear sugar pine, is any cheaper than imported mahogany. Besides, no sugar pine was available in the size we needed.

In other circumstances we might have been able to piece together respectable reproductions of the posts out of boards and molding. But, pressed for time, we had to bite the bullet. We gave the mill the go-ahead.

By yesterday morning the house stood bare, with practically no porch left at all. Board by board we'd gradually condemned and dismantled it. There just seemed to be no stopping point. As we looked closer and closer, we simply found too many trouble spots, too many problems, such as undersized or rotten timbers.

And so off to the dumpster the superstructure of the porch went, in installments.

The situation of the porch paralleled our problem with the kitchen wing, whose three exterior walls we ended up rebuilding. In both cases, time and economics dictated the same decision, to start all over and reconstruct rather than restore what little we had left. To have a carpenter, at his hourly wage, fool around with a prop-up-and-patch job is an expensive way to save some original but undistinguished construction.

Now all we had left of our porch was the floor, and that wasn't in the greatest shape. I was beginning to wonder if we wouldn't be wise to begin again with it too.

The morning was a beautiful one, clear and balmy, more like May than March. The boom truck from our major supplier arrived with a huge load of wallboard and two cast-iron bathtubs. We took advantage of it to deliver the pair of heavyweights as well as roughly half the wallboard directly to the second floor, right through the front window of the master bedroom. ▼

This spectacle attracted more than our usual quota of sidewalk superintendents, who followed every move the boom made, watching the slow transfer of the tubs with the total attention kids give to tightrope walkers. Would a tub actually fit through the opening, even with the window frame itself removed for the occasion? Or would it bash like a wrecker's ball into the wall on one side or the other? We were all relieved when everything slipped inside smoothly.

Russ Morash and I stood on the kitchen roof and consulted with Norm, who was finishing his labors on the east eaves. He already had put back up on the cornice the original brackets, slightly pared down to eliminate the rot-damaged bottoms, and he could give us updated predictions about how much longer the rest of the roof and eaves would take. The job had already taken almost twice as much time and effort as we'd estimated, partially because of the bad weather, partially because of the unexpected extent of the general rot. Around the corner Greg was finishing up the reshingling of the roof's north side.

Later in the day Norm installed our dramatic kitchen skylight. ◀ We had to go ahead and put it in place, even though we were taking a chance that the next week, when the men came to tar and gravel the roof of the wing, they would splat some of the tar on the Plexiglas dome. I was sure we could protect it with a plastic sheet. I was really impatient to see how the kitchen would look with all that light pouring into it from a completely new source. ▶

All things considered, we estimated we were at the halfway point with the exterior work on the house. And we were, of course, a little less than halfway through the time we had allotted for the whole project.

On the other hand, though we were roughly on schedule, we had to face one grim fact. We'd already used up our kitty of 20% over estimated costs that we were supposed to be holding in reserve for the unexpected. Certainly the snafus we'd already encountered were surprises. And there had been so many of them that we shouldn't have been taken aback by this accounting, but somehow we were.

Inside the house, both living and dining rooms looked abandoned, as if the major work on them had ground to a halt and the men had turned their attention elsewhere — which was, in fact, the case. The leveling of the living room ceiling had been finished, and the new coat closet that seemed to have backed into the room from the hall remained as it was last week, barely

framed. In both rooms gray drifts of cellulose insulation had blown up against the baseboards. Where was the action?

One scene of furious activity was in the master bedroom, where earlier in the morning Adam began remodeling the two side-by-side closets that dated from the 1939 remodeling. In a race against the clock, he had committed himself to finishing the basic reframing by the end of the day. ◀ I had faith that he'd make his deadline, but he looked mighty tense until the job was done.

This week's major accomplishments were not very showy. You might call them inside jobs. They were all work that would soon be covered up by wallboard or flooring. I'm talking about the basic wiring and plumbing that the electricians and plumbers had almost finished roughing in.

Wires and pipes when seen in the open are as easy to understand as blue veins and red arteries in an anatomical chart, or the highways on a road map. A layman is used to thinking of them as a mysterious network hidden under a skin of wallboard or plaster, paint, wallpaper, floorboards. He doesn't often get the chance to study a sight like our champion cluster, which included a large white polyvinylchloride (PVC) waste stack, eight electric cables, and five copper water and heating pipes. It was almost a shame to cover up such a collection.

But this was the time for the building inspector to check the roughed-in plumbing and wiring, all the work that would be sealed inside the walls once *the lathers,* the men who put up wallboard, came to do their stuff the following week. The inspector would check to see that our work conformed to all the requirements of the state building code, and we would pass. A final inspection would take place when the house was completely finished.

Today we talked with another visiting expert about one major aspect of the circulatory network in the house: the heating distribution system. Now that it was 95% installed, I had a few questions to review with the consultant from the gas company who had advised us when we planned it. I wanted to go over some of the technical innovations in the way our energy-saving furnace dispersed the heat it produced; to confirm the locations of our baseboard radiators, which were still to be installed; and to hear more about the whole concept of comfort zoning. So far, comfort had not been a conspicuous feature of our half-old, half-new house.

**J**oe Krol and I first consulted in the basement. He described to us how comfort zoning divides the heat circulation of a house into separate and independent facilities, each controlled by its own thermostat. In a house with zoned heating, the supply of heat in one group of rooms, or *zone,* can be altered without affecting the temperature in another group. Therefore you can lower the temperature in the specific areas of the house where there may temporarily be minimal demand. For example, our second- and third-floor bedrooms might be turned down to 60° during the school and work hours when they weren't in use, while the kitchen and family room, which were occupied then, might simultaneously remain at 68°.

In the bad old days, a single thermostat regulated the temperature for the whole house. About all you could say for that procedure was that it allowed no favoritism. If some cold-blooded person wanted a temperature of 72° in the living room, all of the remaining dozen rooms in the house had to be heated to 72°. The only alternative was to run around, upstairs and down, turning individual radiator valves on and off by hand.

Because of its flexibility, a zoned heating system doesn't waste expensive fuel. It promotes not only physical comfort but also financial ease.

That's the result of zoning, but how is it accomplished technically? What's the difference between it and our old one-hoss-shay system?

Before zoning, the hot water that heated the house was produced in the furnace boiler and pumped up through vertical *supply risers* into a horizontal *supply main* that ran around the perimeter of the house in a single circuit. The hot water detoured through *branches* to pass through and heat one antique radiator after another on the first floor, with more supply risers and branches on the second and third floors. When the single circuit up and around the whole house was completed, the water, no longer so hot, made its way back to the boiler in the basement via *return risers* and a *return main.*

In a new, zoned heating system like ours, the general principle is the same, except that the pipelines run in smaller, independent circuits. Each loop has its own route up from the basement, supplies a specific part of the house, and returns to the boiler on its own when the job is done. Each loop is controlled by its own thermostat.

When we studied the new furnace, we could see where a single large pipe left the boiler and then divided into four separate pipes with valves, one per zone, each with a bold yellow handle, that in response to four thermostats automatically controlled the flow into four separate supply risers heading upstairs. ◄

Our first comfort zone included both the living and dining rooms, and the foyer as well. In the completed system, the new baseboard radiators ran along the outside walls of the rooms. (They are almost never located on inside walls.) The controlling thermostat was installed in the living room on the partition between it and the dining room, to the right of the french doors in as draft-free a spot as possible. Thermostats should be placed where they won't overrespond to fluctuations of temperature.

That first loop up from the furnace rose in the southeast corner of the house, and went back down just west of the partition between the dining and the family rooms, at the exact spot where an old leaky radiator had once stood.

The second loop, which heated both family room and kitchen, turned no corners. It traveled only a short distance, straight along the north wall of the family room and the kitchen up to the closet beside the back door, where it descended. Because the east and south walls of the kitchen were fully occupied by base cabinets and appliances, leaving no room for radiators, it could go no farther. But the kitchen wouldn't be underheated because of this dead end, nor would anyone standing in

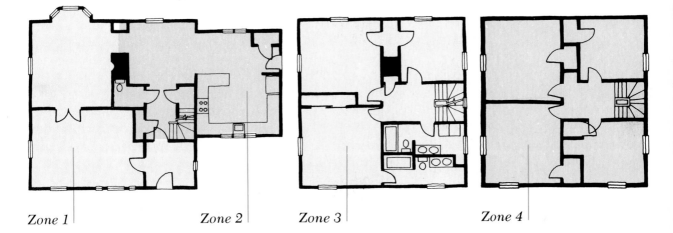

*first floor*     *second floor*     *third floor*

Zone 1      Zone 2      Zone 3      Zone 4

front of the sink ever get cold feet. The baseboard heating on the north end of the room was supplemented on the south by a single electric heating unit installed on the floor of the sink cabinet, with its register in the toe-space of the cabinet. The heart of our U-shaped work space would be warm.

Zones 3 and 4 were self-defining: the second and third floors respectively. Loop 3 circulated around the perimeter of the second floor, heating bathrooms and bedrooms alike, while Loop 4 repeated the pattern on the floor above.

Though we were advised on the new heating system by our friend from the gas company, its actual installation was done by the same men who had been working on the network of water and waste pipes usually referred to simply as "the plumbing." This was not unusual; many contractors double in heating and plumbing. Ours also installed the gas pipes that supplied our kitchen stove on the first floor, our clothes dryer on the second, and our hot water heater and auxiliary space heater in the basement.

A major plumbing job like ours is on such a large scale that, even if the building code permitted non-licensed workers to do it, no ordinary handyman in his right mind should plan to undertake it. Plumbing is not so simple to do as it seems when you're just gazing at pipes in a basement. Amateurs should maintain a healthy respect for the trade, which requires training, experience, and some specialized tools.

Downstairs, when we confronted our old plumbing, we could easily sort out the antique mixture of small metal pipes comprising the *supply system.* The supply system brings cold water directly and hot water indirectly (since it does have to detour through a hot water heater) to fixtures (sinks, bathtubs, toilets) and appliances (dishwasher, washing machine). We had no trouble distinguishing the massive cast-iron pipes of the *waste system,* into which all supply units drained. ▶

Fresh water is sent up through a supply system by pressure from the source, that is, the city main in the street. It is simple gravity, however, that brings the waste down through branches from each fixture and into the vertical *waste stack.* (Branches are never horizontal but tilt slightly downward.) The waste continues out of the house through the *main drain* and into the city *sewer* under the street.

Two parts of our inherited plumbing system that we couldn't see from where we stood in the basement were (1) the mineral-clogged old underground water

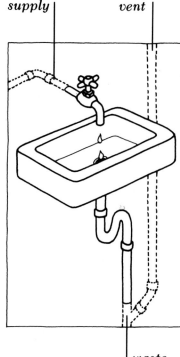

*supply*    *vent*

*waste*

main that came in from the street and by freezing up caused us to replace it, and (2) the pipes of the vent system, hidden in the walls upstairs, which go *up* toward an opening in the roof, rather than *down* into the basement.

The *vent system* is an unsung hero in the plumbing complex. Through it circulates not water but air, which is essential to the proper functioning of the waste system. Without the intake for fresh air and the exit for fumes that the vent system supplies, lethal methane gas would accumulate, and air pressure throughout the system would be unequal.

Though the main vent opens through the main roof of a house, there can be exceptions for branches. For example, the drain of our kitchen sink could be (and was) vented separately, right through the roof of the wing, because the exit could be located ten feet from the body of the house and so conform to code.

The main pipes of the three systems — supply, waste, and vent — together form a single *plumbing line*, which rises up through the house like a three-part tree

trunk. Branches go off it to serve various locations. The most economical arrangement is one that makes maximum use of a single existing line, minimum use of long, expensive branches.

For example, stacking bathrooms one above another, floor by floor, right on the line, is one approach. Another is to place them back-to-back, on either side of the line on a single floor, as we did our master bath and bath/laundry. There are limits to the feasible length of branches, and an expensive second plumbing line may have to be installed if a facility distant from the first line is to be added. Keep this fact of life in mind when planning.

We first discussed with Ron Trethewey, our plumbing contractor, the possibility of saving as many of our old plumbing pipes as we could, but he convinced us that would be a false economy. According to him, we had a real hodgepodge, with brass, copper, and galvanized-iron supply pipes, and cast-iron waste pipes, most of which bore some souvenir of past revampings of the system. The deciding factor was the cost of labor, for in order to save the old pipes, many hours would have had to be spent in breaking out and sealing them off, and in joining in new ones, as well as in repairing existing but weakened joints.

Finally we decided to go the whole way and put in all new pipes. ◀ We replaced the mixture of supply pipes exclusively with copper, with separate branches and separate shutoffs. In the waste system, we had the chance to switch over from cast-iron to PVC (polyvinylchloride) plastic, the economical, long-lasting modern alternative to metal. ▶ We also used it in all new work in totally new locations (like the first-floor lavatory). As long as we were revamping all the pipes in the basement we decided to spend just a little extra to install a new utility tub down there.

Upstairs, the new lavatory demanded some special consideration because it was an inside room. According to code, its windowless location had to be ventilated to the outside by an exhaust fan. Ours discharged through a long duct that led out through the north wall. It was concealed above the new dropped ceiling in the lavatory, and then snaked out through the old wall/ceiling construction between the dining and family rooms. Exhaust exits can be somewhat noisy, and some people prefer always to locate them in the roof rather than a wall, lest they build in an annoyance.

The kitchen and bathroom also presented a couple of special circulatory needs. The exhaust fan above the stove also had to have an exhaust duct to the outside. This led out through the south wall. Upstairs, we had yet another exhaust, the vent for the clothes dryer, in the east wall.

Ducts are large and unlikely to be overlooked, but the diameter of the copper tubing that was scheduled to lead from the water supply branch to the sink over to the automatic icemaker in our refrigerator was very small. Somehow it got mislaid in the shuffle until we remembered it, alas, *after* all the base cabinets were in place. The tubing had then to be threaded through the inside of the cabinets, a process no less demanding than sending a camel through the eye of a needle. There were a couple of polite but understandably irritated plumbers on the job that day.

Plumber John Hanson, when questioned, admitted that the hardest part of his job, even harder than compensating for oversights, was dealing with people who kept changing their minds. We were properly embarrassed when later we switched from a 36-inch to a 30-inch-wide vanity cabinet in one of the bathrooms. The supply and drain pipes were already perfectly in position for the larger model, and so was the toilet, farther into the corner than it needed to be for the smaller model. Plumbing fixtures can't be rearranged like furniture. There's no way you can try one of them "just a little bit more to the left."

Because our electrical system was antiquated and grossly inadequate, we had to settle for a complete job of rewiring, but we contented ourselves with the planning part, rather than actually trying to do the work. As with the plumbing, we left the performance to licensed electricians, while we worked in advance and behind the scenes.

The first inadequacy in the electrical system in our house was the amount of power the *service line* brought in. Electrical service is measured in amperes. Ours was a pitiful 30 amperes, while 100 amps is now common for new wiring in an ordinary house with ordinary demands for power. One that makes major demands because of simple size or energy-gobbling features like air conditioning may require 200 amps. We decided to increase our service all the way to 200 amps, but admittedly the extraordinary needs of our television lights and equipment were a consideration.

The electrical system in a house is controlled from a central *panel board.* ▶ (Ours was down in the basement.) There a *meter* monitors the amount of power actually consumed, and there the various circuits of

household wiring originate. There also are the *main circuit breaker,* which can turn off and on all the service into the house, and the *individual breakers* that control the separate circuits, automatically shutting off any one that is overloaded. In the old days, fuses would blow and shut down an overloaded circuit.

The second inadequacy in our wiring lay in the number of circuits we had. We simply had too few. Each circuit can serve only a limited number of outlets, switches, and fixtures without overloading. Most circuits carry ordinary 120-volt current and use wire of a size suited to that load. Major appliances like an electric stove or dryer require more powerful 220-volt current and heavier 220 wiring, and each appliance should be on a circuit of its own.

We increased the number of circuits and revised our central board accordingly. We also switched to modern circuit breakers from old-fashioned fuses.

We consulted with our electricians on the locations of new outlets and switches, as well as on the wiring for new appliances and light fixtures. These included such miscellaneous features as the light-fan unit in the lavatory, the chandelier in the dining room, the hanging lamp in the hall, the washing machine and wall lights over the basins in the second-floor bathrooms. The fact that the electrician asks you to spot all the outlets just when the building is only in skeletal shape makes for one of the hardest parts of planning. Decisions must be precise at a time when everything else is very rough. You need lots of imagination at this stage.

The wiring of an electrical circuit goes from one box mounted inside the wall to another. ▶ These boxes house switches, plug-in receptacles, mountings for fixtures, or the junctions of various wires, and all connections between wires are made inside them. Obviously it is easiest and best to map out and rough in all wiring, as well as install the boxes, while a wall is still open. But new wiring can be snaked in behind old finished walls and ceilings when necessary by maneuvering the wires through spaces between studs or joists and opening up small holes for the boxes. This is sometimes tricky, slow work, but it is done every day.

Our greatest challenge was the kitchen, always a planner's delight (or downfall). We were proud of the precision of our attention to detail, which meant that our electrical plan could be translated smoothly into a bright reality of ceiling-mounted light fixtures, under-cabinet fluorescent light strips, multiple switches controlling lights inside the kitchen itself and outside on the deck.

We also had to consider wiring from the refrigerator, trash-compactor, dishwasher, disposer, under-sink heater, stove, and hood, as well as the cavalcade of a half-dozen or so outlets for small appliances on the walls along the counters. Although we had lots of other demands on our time, we really worked over our electrical schemes, and as a result we got what we wanted.

**F**or homeowners who are untrained and unskilled in the technology of major wiring and plumbing jobs, the only feasible role in the installation of the circulatory system of the house is that of planner and tactful overseer. As always you should try to understand the general principles involved in a job so that you can keep watch to make sure details aren't overlooked. It doesn't take a mechanical genius to check to see that a copper tube has been installed from sink to icemaker, to cite an embarrassing example.

Electrical fixtures range in style from the ridiculous (the chandelier that dangles royal blue and red plastic prisms) to the sublime (the subtle translucent orb that can, nevertheless, light a whole kitchen). The selection is enormous, often overwhelming, and you can't expect your electrician to pick models that will please you. Nor can you rely on your plumber's taste in bathroom or kitchen fixtures, which also vary in material, color, quality, design, and price. You should take the responsibility for examining options, making informed choices among the alternatives available, and sticking to them without wobbling.

The simplest way to familiarize yourself with the market is to consult the catalogues, the displays, and the salesmen at your largest local supplier. There you can set up a general dialogue about the pros and cons of various types of equipment as well as examine specific models.

You can often get excellent free advice from electrical supply houses on indirect lighting and the functional, almost architectural uses of downcans or spot or track lighting, and other contemporary options that are, shall we say, light-years away from the brass wall sconces, the prim table lamp, and the traditional ceiling fixtures of the past. You can find out about indoor lighting regulated by timers or outdoor lighting on photoelectric cells, both useful for security and safety. You can investigate the possibility of having a central control panel in your bedroom that will enable you to turn on and off lights that are either outside or downstairs.

There is a point, however, at which any system can get too sophisticated. Zoned

heating is valuable, and no skimping should be encouraged if you are lucky enough to be able to install it. But too much reliance on automation in your controls can turn a simple repair or maintenance matter into a big deal. Hand-operated valves still have their place, in that they give you immediate control in an emergency or every day. In general, experience teaches that the more control the better in both heating and plumbing schemes. You might well discuss this issue with your contractor *before* you are launched with a system that proceeds as if on automatic pilot.

Incidentally, be especially careful to check exactly where your contractor plans to locate your thermostats. Decorating considerations are involved. For example, you don't want a thermostat plonked into the center of a wall where otherwise you might want to hang a picture or stand a bookcase. There are alternatives, and a thermostat doesn't have to be a decorating menace.

A related practical hint: don't use felt-tip pens to mark the location of anything — thermostats, electrical outlets, fixtures — on wallboard or woodwork that will be painted.

The ink will bleed through, unless you remember to shellac or seal it. The possibility is not worth worrying about. Use a pencil or chalk.

Ron was absolutely right when he said that patching together new and old pipes is economically self-defeating. ◀ You do often have to count on starting from scratch. Brass pipes are difficult to reuse. Sections of lead pipe can't be replaced. No one makes it anymore. And if you have to join a new PVC waste pipe into an existing cast-iron system like our original one, then you've got a labor expenditure so big that you can't really justify the scrimp on material.

By the way, old brass and copper have significant salvage value, so don't throw them away. Sell them to a junk man.

Circulating heat is an old story. The latest news, however, is recirculating it. The heat generated by certain appliances and vented straight to the outdoors has always been wasted, but now it can be saved. Check out possibilities for adapting your clothes dryer with a damperlike mechanism that can be switched on in the wintertime so that, while lint continues to be trapped or filtered out, heated moist air is returned into the house. This adds not only "free" heat but also humidity to the atmosphere inside. But remember not to exhaust the dryer into a closed area that could easily become over-moisturized. The idea is to dump it into a room or into the basement where it can circulate freely.

Central humidifiers can be added to hot air systems so that warmth and moisture are circulated simultaneously. They are not prohibitively expensive.

Another gimmick available today is designed to be installed in the exhaust vent of a hot water heater. The escaping heat, but not the escaping fumes, is transferred into a chamber inserted in the duct, from which it is forced out by a fan into the room, usually a basement. The idea is similar to the heating unit under our kitchen sink, but in this case the heat is "free."

Recirculation may be only a detour in the basic distribution routes within the house, but it is one more bright reflection of the new conservatism that is capturing the interest of energy-conscious rehabbers.

# 8
# Walled In, Walled Out

**Week 7**   Today, Dave Mullane, our roofer, arrived, and together we made a first ascent to the plateau on the top of our mansard roof to size up what had to be done. Silhouetted against the Boston skyline in the distance, I made the climb up the longest of our ladders. It was a little hairy for me, though Dave seemed matter-of-fact about it.

Though I had to report that it was cold and windy up there, my other news from the top was pretty good. The old roofing on the flat didn't have to be pulled up after all, and the dormer roofs, which were weathered and eroded along their ridges, could be patched. Our carpenters were already well along with the shingling of the sloped sides of the mansard. Happily, the new tar-and-gravel surface could be applied with no major fuss, after the old flashing around the chimney and vent stack was replaced. With its loose bricks that could be pulled out like drawers, that old chimney had given us some concern, but Dave assured me that he could rescue it simply by repointing. What a relief not to undertake a lot of rebuilding up there.

One level closer to earth, on top of the kitchen wing, tar-and-gravel reroofing was well under way. Here the old roofing had had to be stripped off, down to the bare wood sheathing below. Dave's brother, Mike, explained his work sequence: several new layers, alternating roofing paper and molten tar, would be applied, with a final surface of gravel spread over the whole that would, by the end of the day, finish the job. Several days before, Norm had installed gutters and edge flashing that, along with the newly milled small brackets, had completed all the prerequisite eave work on the wing.

During the week a regular caller, our friend the mounted policeman who patrolled the neighborhood, had dropped by to see how we were coming along with the front porch. By then we'd picked away at the structure until we were down to a couple of pretty basic timbers. My pessimism about salvaging the porch floor had been justified.

Anyway, we'd started rebuilding from the ground up, and I was able to bang in a few of the floorboards myself during the course of the day. We still hadn't decided how we would finish off the open space underneath the floor. One possibility we were mulling over was to make a stone foundation out of the rubble left over from the demolition of the doctor's extension. We'd have to see.

One of our two remaining original porch posts bit the dust during the week. Actually we had found that quite a few pests had been biting *it* over the years. Once we got it down, we discovered that it was alive with a population of infernal carpenter ants, who had chomped most of its insides out. We had to increase our order at the mill from two to three of those expensive items. ▼

Simultaneously we'd developed a small assembly line for brushing wood preservative onto floorboards

destined for our new porch, which were already cut to size. One of the guys would line them up across saw-horses and brush on the preservative to a bunch at a time. Working ahead, he'd already applied primer to clapboards in the same way and had put them up to dry on the garage roof. There they would rest until the carpenters got around to installing them.

Spirits were as high as the chimney I'd just inspected, and not simply because a purple crocus had popped up in the garden next door, though the signs of spring did help morale. This week had been one of those wonderful times when the whole project seemed to take a great leap forward.

For the past two or three weeks we had had a sense of suspended animation, in spite of the fact that the plumbers and electricians and carpenters were all on the job and working away at full speed. Their achievements, solid as they were, were comparatively unobtrusive and on a small scale. You can't compare the high drama and sense of accomplishment of bashing down a wall with the milder satisfactions of making a good tight joint in a copper pipe or of slowly assembling the elements of a heating system. We had been growing impatient for the next stage of the rehabbing process, one with some more grand gestures. Earlier this week, we got our wish.

Over the preceding weekend, the old house, deserted, quiet, and stripped bare, had had an eerie look to it. ◀ The rooms had somehow lost their identities, and were as anonymous as skeletons. Here and there stacks of wallboard stood patiently, waiting for something to happen.

The brand of wallboard we had laid in was *Blueboard,* which has a water-resistant surface and is used to finish walls that are to receive a skim coat of plaster.

Early Monday morning the lathers appeared on the scene. Working in pairs, they performed a kind of miracle in only two days. Speed is a lively concern of lathers, since they are often paid by the panel.

Using electric screwguns, our workmen installed the Blueboard with the long edge on the horizontal. ◀ The individual 4-foot-by-8-foot (or, in our case, sometimes larger, 4-foot-by-12-foot) panels are an awkward size and hard to handle, but one person working alone can manage a vertical installation. A horizontal job definitely requires two men, or one octopus.

Competent lathers avoid having seams align with one another or with the edges of door and window openings, and cut into the panels accordingly. Then they tape all seams; in our case, the tape was a self-adhering fiberglass gauze. ▶ The final step in preparing for the plasterers was to reinforce all outside corners with steel beading, so they would be strong enough to withstand the bangs and blows of daily life.

By the time the lathers' work was finished, our rooms looked like very neat packages, carefully boxed and taped as if for mailing. ▼ Suddenly the place was no longer a construction site, it was a house again, with real walls, recognizable rooms. It was alive, the skin back on its bones. We had passed an important turning point: there was nowhere to go but up from now on.

On Wednesday Sal Vassallo and his plasterers arrived in full force. They quickly set up shop in the first room to get the treatment, which happened to be the living room. They rigged up a kind of raised floor made of milk crates and planks in order to be able easily to reach the ceilings and upper walls, and at the same time to move freely back and forth. After mixing up a small white plaster mountain, they took as large a load of it as

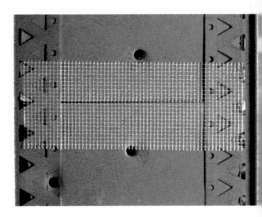

they could manage onto their carrying tools, known as *hawks.* Then using their *trowels,* they applied preliminary stripes of plaster, which they *scratched on* to taped joints and beaded corners, before proceeding to the double-layered skim coat.

The skim coat added a plaster buildup of only ⅛ inch, but that fraction made all the difference in the look of the finished walls. We'd decided that difference was worth the extra expense. (Our alternative would have been to settle for a so-called *dry wall* job, in which no finish coat of wet plaster goes on the wallboarded wall.) Our plastered surfaces were spectacularly smooth, with good sharp corners, even in a demanding area like the recess for our kitchen skylight. Also, the plaster surface would provide a much better base for wallpaper (and in years to come, for wallpaper removal).

Up on their raised platform of planks, the plasterers seemed almost to be dancing on the ceiling, ▼ or at least closer to it than most of us usually manage. Today, a Thursday, they'd been gliding over the wall and ceiling surfaces of the dining room and family room. The

speed and ease with which they worked made their trade seem like a cinch, and by the time they got to the kitchen, I couldn't resist asking Sal if I could try my hand at it. The fantastic glop of plaster was just too tempting. ▶

"Try to put it on the wall, not on the floor or on yourself," Sal advised, but too late. I had already splatted and smeared, and finally abandoned such an embarrassing public demonstration.

As Sal continued his work, he described to me how the veneer plaster he used, which is a combination of lime and plaster of paris, heats up through chemical

action, in effect baking itself to hardness within about an hour. For greater manageability, he added a retardant to the mixture to slow down the hardening time to about an hour and a half.

After the first real coat of plaster was applied to Blueboarded walls and ceilings, the second coat was put on almost immediately, before the first could harden. ▲ The heat generated in the drying of the double layer would firmly bond one coat to the other. But before that process got under way, the double coat was leveled with a piece of ordinary clapboard drawn across the surface, and then smoothed further with wide, damp brushes and more clapboarding. ◄ Any plaster that had gotten into electrical receptacle boxes would easily be cleared out later.

The temperature of 55° Sal encountered on our job was a good one for his work, but the wet, late March weather would slow down the total drying process a little. He estimated the average length of time after application that a homeowner has to wait before going on with work in a newly plastered room as from two to three days. The drying plaster does introduce a significant amount of moisture into the atmosphere of the house, and this can take much longer — sometimes weeks — to disappear entirely.

As, with a new respect, I watched Sal finish up with the kitchen, I was aware not only of the fine hand and wrist action of a virtuoso but also of how quiet a job plastering can be but usually isn't. Plasterers have a reputation as jokers and talkers comparable to that of barbers.

But, at least for the moment, all this cool whiteness and near-silence made a strange contrast with the molten black tar steaming outside, with the familiar bangs and squeals of carpentry. In the kitchen, though three men were working, all we could hear was a faint swishing and sliding like the sound of skates on ice.

**P**eople often think of windows as somehow separate entities, different from walls and not simply a variation in them. Windows are usually transparent and can be opened and shut, but the fact is that they are still engaged in walling out or walling in (depending on your point of view), just as is the solid surface that surrounds them. Some windows prove to be expendable, and make the transition back into solid wall with amazing speed and ease, as we demonstrated when we eliminated the old off-center bathroom window on the south side of the house.

Our windows were typical nineteenth-century double-hung models, and as is so often the case with the elderly, they needed a little rejuvenation. The double-hung window is raised and lowered by pairs of counterweights that hang from sashcords on pulleys, a mechanism in common use for centuries until after World War II. Many of our sashcords were broken and needed to be replaced and reattached to sashweights retrieved from where they had fallen inside the wall if the windows were ever to work properly again.

We made one pitiful experiment in substituting a modern plastic-and-metal spring-loaded sash balance. We rapidly changed plans after a morning in which we ducked as runaway springs ejected and shot across the room like rockets. We also found that in order to accommodate the new balances we'd have to trim down all the old sashes, an incredibly time-consuming job (and we had a couple of dozen old windows that would have to be altered). Philosophically, we decided that the old ways were the best ways and set about doggedly replacing sashcords. ▼

Among all our old windows, amazingly enough we had only two that were beyond repair, one in the

northeast bedroom, and the other in our laundry/bathroom. At considerable expense we had new ones milled — our windows were no longer stock sizes — and the cost of those two items made us sigh with relief that we'd succeeded so well in restoring all the others. We even reused one forty-year veteran, removing it from the south wall of the doctor's extension and transporting it backward to its new home in our rebuilt living room wall. Salvage pays off.

We weren't able entirely to dispel some lingering regrets that we hadn't decided to restore the two original floor-to-ceiling windows that had enhanced the south wall of the living room right through the 1930s. The style of the triple window that the 1939 remodeling had introduced was only slightly jarring, however, and we managed to justify its continuing presence by thinking of it as part of the record. It testified to the house as a structure that had developed and accumulated various features over the years since it had been constructed.

We knew what the old windows had looked like because we were lucky enough to have old photographs. If we hadn't had evidence, we would have been making a mistake to go back to a precedent we could only guess at. Conjectural restorations are usually a poor idea in principle.

The brand-new windows we installed in the kitchen were factory-assembled units with pre-cut trim parts. ◄ They were casement windows, rather than dou-

ble-hung, and had insulating double-glazing. Here we would not need storm windows, as we did in the main body of the house, where we chose the most unobtrusive white-enamel aluminum models we could find.

**T**he counterparts to our factory-assembled casement windows were our new pre-hung doors. These came already hinged to their *jambs*, which were ready to be set in place inside rough-framed openings. All that remained to be done was to level, fasten, and then trim them with their moldings, called *casings*. This is still rather precise work but much quicker and easier than starting from scratch.

We had a beautiful glass-paneled exterior door to install in the entrance to our kitchen from the deck. ▼ It also was pre-hung. All Norm had to do was shim it so that it was plumb, cut the shims off flush, fasten the side and top jambs to the rough frame, install the *brickmold* (trim) around the outside and the casings inside, and *voilà*, we were in business.

Luckily we didn't have to replace our old paneled front door. With some reputtying of the glass panes, some discreet sealing of joints that had opened up, thorough scraping and repainting, it was effectively restored.

The new doors that we added inside the house did not match all the others, which were the originals and paneled. We could have scouted around wreckers' outlets and secondhand lumberyards for duplicates, and might well have found close matches. But in both places where we planned to install new doors, we wanted to deemphasize the doors themselves and to cultivate instead the illusion of an unbroken wall.

The first area was the central stair hall on the first floor, where we had added two openings, one to the new lavatory and the other to the new coat closet. The hall walls already had several interruptions — a door to the basement, the stairwell itself — and we didn't want to add more distracting detail. So we chose to use contemporary flush doors for all the hall doorways, including the one to the basement. These we installed without casings, so that the eye would move smoothly along a surface that was as flat as possible, a simulated wall. We felt that in the family room and hall we were justified in resisting the pull to be "historically correct" and to go with the mood of our nearby and totally modern kitchen, where we also used a flush door for the closet by the back entrance. ◄

The second area where we used flush doors was upstairs in the master bedroom and master bath. The rationale in the bedroom was again that we wanted to give, with the sliding doors of the new closet, the look of an unbroken wall. We had to use a flush door for the new entrance to the new master bath. Inside the bathroom, like our kitchen a thoroughly streamlined modern installation, we used flush double doors for the closet there. Anything else would have drawn too much attention to itself.

In the bathrooms we had walls with special needs. No unprotected plaster surface can be expected to stand up to the moisture and torrents of shower water that assault the walls enclosing bathtubs. Both our bathtubs had walls on three sides.

Our first impulse was to choose a conventional solution, ceramic tiles. In the old days simply gluing tiles onto a wall surface — a *glue job* — was inadvisable, because the glue then available would deteriorate with moisture. The alternative then was a *mud job,* which involved setting the tiles in a thick bed of mortar, and it was universally recommended for anyone who could afford it. Today, however, with inorganic adhesives and thin-set cements that stand up to moisture, the modern equivalent of a glue job should provide a tight and durable tile surface for a tub surround.

Next we toyed with the idea of using fiberglass tub-and-wall combination units, which come all in one piece. These are getting better all the time, though perhaps the finish still does have a tendency to dull when scoured and can also be burned by a bathing smoker whose mind has wandered. Also, if a fiberglass tub is installed improperly, without its belly supported underneath by a mound of cement grout, a trampoline effect can occur, or, when the tub is filled with water and an occupant, the downward pull of the weight can drag the sides of the unit in from the wall.

We had gone so far as to order a pair of fiberglass units when we heard about an innovative kind of tub surround made of preformed plastic laminate. We decided to experiment, and changed our order from the fiberglass models to conventional porcelainized cast-iron tubs so that we could try the new surrounds.

Our installers, Paul and Tom Rae, described to us how, back in the shop, they had taken sheets of plastic laminate and bent them to our specs with a post-forming machine. Then they trucked the two three-sided constructions over to Percival Street. When installing them in the bathrooms, they would use a combination of mastic and a special heat-activated contact cement (to superseal the area abutting the seam between tub and surround where water leakage tends to occur). They would seal the seam itself with ordinary latex caulk. ▶

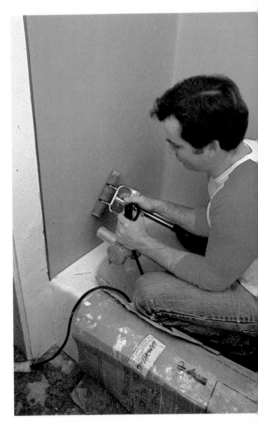

The cost of each installation was competitive with tiling. With no grout to maintain, these surrounds were much easier to take care of than tile, and they were permanently waterproof, since there were no corner joints. Each surround was a single seamless piece. In addition, plastic laminate comes in well over a hundred colors, many more than either tile or fiberglass.

When a rebuilt interior wall is finished — all smooth and white — it's easy to blot out the messy, intermediate stages that preceded such simple perfection. To review, in our kitchen wing alone we had at first struggled to save the old walls, had eventually demolished all of them and started over, had reframed, sheathed in the outside, installed insulation, put up Blueboard, and had finally applied a beautiful skim coat of plaster. Throughout the rest of the house we had stripped many walls down to the wood lath, and had proceeded from there. What a long sequence of steps

had gone into achieving finished surfaces that looked somehow so effortless, that were so easy to take for granted!

Finishing exterior walls required another long sequence of steps. But first we had a few preliminaries to take care of before we could get to the siding. The kitchen wing was a saga in itself.

1. After completing the framing of the walls, Norm and the other carpenters nailed on plywood *sheathing*. This was the first exterior layer to be attached to the framing, to wall *out* the elements, or wall *in* the house. ◀ Plywood really makes the modern housebuilder's job a lot easier. The old-fashioned method of sheathing used a series of individual boards. This surface was time-consuming to put up and also was far less tight when completed.

2. The carpenters' next step was to staple on a water-resistant layer of black 15-pound asphalt felt *building paper*, which protected the sheathing against

moisture and provided some draft resistance to joints around window and door frames. ◄

3. Finally, carefully measuring and leveling as they went, Norm and Greg worked around the three sides of the kitchen wing, nailing on preprimed new clapboards through the felt and the sheathing and into the studs. ▼ We used red cedar claps, ½ inch thick, 6 inches high, and anywhere from 2 feet to 22 feet long. For new work particularly, the longer the boards are the better, because then there will be fewer joints.

The men were careful to nail ½ to ¾ inches up from the bottom edge and about 2 inches from the end of each board, to avoid splitting. They used 4d galvanized box nails, which are just under 2 inches long. To finish off, they applied a bead of caulking along the joints where the clapboards met door and window casings. What a difference when the new siding was all up!

The same general sequence took place on the south side of the house, where we filled in the gap left by the doctor's extension, and also, above that, the one where the old bathroom window had been taken out and boarded in.

When our house was built in the 1860s, the conventional base for plaster was the spaced strips of *wood lath* we uncovered in room after room. ▼ The person who put them up was, logically, called a *lather*. His work must have been slow and tedious. In the search for improved ways to do the job, new products were eventually developed. An early successor was called *rocklath*, and though it performed the same function as the

old wood lath, it certainly didn't look the same. A precursor of wallboard, it came in strip panels 16 inches by 4 feet, and the lathers could put it up like crazy. It also came in a variation called *perforated rocklath*, which had a uniform grid of perforations that the plaster adhered to. Metal lath was available but more expensive and therefore less popular.

The various laths all required a full coat of plaster, which went on in several installments. With wood lath, a brown coat of rough plaster, which had sand in it, went on first, followed by a white finish coat that had almost no sand in it and dried to an extremely hard surface. The rocklaths normally had an initial scratch coat, followed by brown and white coats.

If you have this kind of double-layered surface on your old walls, you may find that the top, or white, coat will crack, buckle, and fall off in sections, particularly on an outside wall that is subject to variations in tempera-

ture. Happily, patching is simple. But when the whole multilayered coat of plaster bulges or sags away from the lath, you've got a difficult problem whose solution is likely to be more radical than patching.

In the housebuilding boom that followed World War II, developers latched onto a new building material. This was known generically as *wallboard* or *dry wall*, with varieties called plasterboard, gypsum board, or Sheetrock. All these came in the soon-to-be-familiar large 4-foot-by-8-foot panels that could be installed quickly and without an expensive full coat of plaster needed to finish their surface. Seams were simply taped over and masked with joint compound.

Nowhere along the way had the public stopped calling the installers of the various laths and wallboards by their original trade name. Lathers they had been, and lathers they still are.

Blueboarding with a skim coat of plaster bridges a gap between the old ways and the new. In our view it combines the best of both worlds: a base that can be quickly installed with the precision and smoothness of a full-coat plaster surface. It must be done professionally, however, and it is quite a bit more expensive than dry wall.

We were, we have to admit, perfectionists about our walls. When there was a problem with the old plaster, we didn't mess around, we just stripped the wall. For very practical economic reasons, you may not feel the same urge to get down to basics. There are alternatives.

Perhaps your wall doesn't have really major damage. It just has too many minor faults and blemishes to allow you to get away with only a paint job as a finish. If the texture is fairly bad, you might consider masking it by applying an *underlayment* of canvas backing, which will provide a smoother base for other, more decorative wall covering. The canvas will also serve as a great bandage strengthening a plaster wall that is not in peak condition. For less serious cases, a single decorative covering that can camouflage a lot would be grass cloth or any other heavily textured wallpaper.

Perhaps you have a serious bulge or hole in a wall, but the trouble spot is localized. Here is a case where patching may be in order. You will want to remove all of the afflicted section, ending up with the edges of the hole on or beside studs. You then cut a wallboard patch to size and nail it either to the studs or to extensions sistered onto them, so that the patch is as secure around its rim as can be. Perhaps you will have to shim your patch from behind to bring its surface up flush with the old wall around it. Using joint tape and joint compound and a lot of care you can then gradually blend in the border between new and old. Caution: this is not a job for the fast-and-sloppy worker.

*Joint compound* is an excellent material to work with, unlike old-fashioned spackling plaster, which sets up almost as fast as plaster of paris, and that's fast. It comes premixed in quart, one-gallon, and five-gallon cans. Though not as hard as plaster, it is more resilient and less likely to crack (though it does shrink), and it is homogenized so that it holds its shape and resists sagging on vertical surfaces. You can use it by itself to fill in fairly large holes in walls, places where wallboard patches are not justified. But because of joint compound's tendency to shrink when applied in a single thick layer, you will have to put it on in several thin applications, gradually filling up the hole.

After examining your walls and abandoning any illusion that bandaging, camouflaging, or patching can save your situation, you may be tempted to try your hand at installing dry walls yourself. Should you or shouldn't you — that is the question. One veteran we know states categorically that drywalling is one of the easiest things to learn how to do yourself; it goes quickly and gives a lot of satisfaction. Another counters, with equal conviction, that dry-walling is tough to do well and can't be done by an amateur without producing a horror show. (Unquestionably he is right when he says that a novice should never, ever attempt to install wallboard on a ceiling. Leave that to the pros.)

Certainly there are particular problems that occur when you are putting up dry wall in an old house that don't arise when you're doing the same job in a new one. In an old house the installer has to cut around existing door and window frames, and because old floors and ceilings tend not to be level, he has to trim the tops and bottoms of

his wallboard panels accordingly. All these cuts have to be very precise.

Also, if he is taking a shortcut and applying his new wall right onto an old surface, without stripping down to the lath or the framing, he may find that as he pounds his panel in place, pieces of old plaster may be dislodged behind and fall between the new and the old, making it impossible to lay the wallboard flat.

He also has to be sure that what he is nailing or screwing his wallboard to is firm and sound. Nothing is worse than having the member behind the wallboard bounce back and tear up the surface of the panel. Studs are the ideal target for nails; strapping, which tends to be bouncy, is not.

Yet another pitfall is the fact that, in an old house, studs are often not true in their dimensions, varying in depth, though the spacing between them may be fairly regular. Because of the variation in depth, an even plane is often difficult to achieve without some careful shimming or some other compensation.

Wallboard is not naturally flexible, though under certain circumstances it can be coaxed into a curve by scoring it on the back or by dampening it (only once). But in most tricky areas, like our vaulted stairwell, that are not based on the right angle, wallboard just can't be used. *Metal lath*, a flexible expanded steel mesh, can easily be bent into shape and attached. ▼ It will receive plaster and hold it tight to the curve, but a profes-

sional plasterer must be called in to do that job.

Read up in the detailed how-to literature of dry-wall installation, and make one of those grimly realistic appraisals we advocate, not only of yourself but also of any helpers you are likely to be able to conscript. Attempting to go it alone would seem to be a foolish decision for a beginner. The scope of your project is another consideration. A professional installer will certainly do a job better and faster than you can. Hiring him may be the wisest investment you can make.

In the course of renovating the original siding on the exterior of the house, we would patch wherever an old clapboard was badly cracked (a minor crack can be caulked) or showed other signs of deterioration. ▼ A demonstration of how to do that made it seem to be a feasible job for the inexperienced person to take on.

First the carpenter used a flat bar to pry the bad clapboard out from under the good one above it. Then he checked to see if the coast was entirely clear under the good clapboard by running his flat bar back and

forth behind it. Our original siding, it turned out, had been fastened down with old cut nails. If one of them had pulled through the good board and remained in place, or if part of the bad board had splintered off and was left behind, the carpenter carefully removed the survivor before proceeding.

Then he held up in place a length of new clapboard, butting one end against the adjacent board and marking the other end where the saw cut should be. He squared off his mark with a combination square. When he sawed through his line, he made a slight back cut, so that the slightly diagonal surface would be angled toward the outside of the joint, that is, the surface of the clapboard. A perfectly straight cut tends to open up where the boards meet.

Finally he slipped the new, cut-to-measure clapboard in under the old one above it, and nailed it in place.

Flush doors seem to arouse controversy. Some people just have a prejudice against them. The ordinary luan mahogany door does present some irritating problems, because its grain is so open that before it can be painted, a filler must be applied, and because it usually has a hollow core, it is fairly flimsy. A solid-core door is definitely preferable. A flush door that is of good, paint-grade, solid-core hardwood veneer, like birch, when either sealed with polyurethane for a natural finish or painted, can in the proper setting be just fine. We would never, on the other hand, have used flush doors in our living or dining rooms. There we tried to keep some sense of the historical period in which the house was built.

If you do decide to look around and find yourself some authentic old paneled doors, remember that old doors have often been planed down over the years so that they tend to be less than perfectly square. Realizing this, you'll be alert to the possibilities, and won't find, too late, that you've bought yourself a parallelogram that is impossible to hang so that it fits tight. If you encounter a door with a crack in a panel, don't give up on it. You can simply fill the crack with plastic wood, which is more gluelike than either caulk or spackle and won't pop out as easily.

Exterior doors really have to be quality goods. They take too much abuse from traffic

First you carefully remove the old glass, which you will probably have to shatter, and all the old putty. If you apply linseed oil to the putty and wait about thirty minutes, it will soften up and be easier to remove. Heat will do the same job. You could use a propane torch, but that can be dangerous; or you could use an electric heating tool specifically designed for removing putty.

Once the frame is completely clear of all old putty, you wipe boiled linseed oil (or kerosene) on the old wood. If you don't, the dry, thirsty wood will suck all the oil out of the glazing compound so that it won't adhere for long.

Next you lay a bead of glazing compound on the sash as a bed for the pane of glass you are installing. ◀ Then you set the pane on the bead and hold it in place on all sides with glazier's points inserted every four inches, which on an average pane amounts to two points on each side.

in and out, and from the weather. If flush, they must definitely be solid-core, paint-grade merchandise. Several manufacturers offer buyers a guarantee against warpage for five years or even longer. The "insurance premium" is figured into your purchase price.

### An Introduction to Glazing, or Repairing an Old Broken Window

Reglazing doesn't require enormous skill or experience, but because it is slow work, you'll save a lot in labor costs if you can afford to do it yourself. We had to reglaze a great many windows, not because the panes were broken but because the putty had deteriorated and had to be replaced.

You will have to lay in certain supplies:

1. Glass panes cut exactly ⅛ inch smaller than the dimensions of their destination in the sash
2. Linseed oil (or kerosene)
3. Glazier's points, to hold the panes in place
4. Glazing compound, a special type of putty.

Finally you press a second bead of glazing compound on top of and all around the edges of the pane. ▲ As a finishing touch you smooth and bevel it with a putty knife or special glazier's tool.

After a few days, when the glazing compound is thoroughly dry, you give it a coat of paint.

# 9 Grand Horizontals

Down on the neglected northeast slope of our property, down where empty bottles and beer cans had been heaved over the chain-link fence, and a crumpled snow shovel lay among snagged scraps of wet plastic wrap, the long-unpruned lilacs were trying to stage a comeback, their buds swelling in the cold drizzle of early April. Once, in the good old days, the corner had been filled with roses as well as lilacs.

The early morning seemed like a good time to go down and see about our north forty, in many ways the most public part of our lot, since it ran along the sidewalk of the main road. It didn't need to look like an annex to the city dump. Our next-door neighbor's tidy garden put us to shame.

 ◀ Looming over the site was our 1940 brick garage, a little worn around the edges, with some windows broken in spite of the protective wire mesh tacked across them, others boarded up, and a small side door as rickety as the sagging pairs in front that creaked as they swung. But the structure of the building was essentially as solid as the ledge it stood on, and we never considered for a minute taking it down.

We did at one point think we might paint the dark red brick to harmonize better with the house, but on second thought, we realized we'd just be creating a new maintenance problem for future owners. We decided to settle for a little face-lifting: eventual replacement of all the doors (making sure the side one was exterior grade, and switching to overhead models in front), and the installation of unbreakable plastic windowpanes, in order to foil passing target practicers.

The interior of the garage was a clear space twenty feet square, with no columns to break it up, that would nicely hold either two cars, or one car and a workshop. The building was free of cracks and leaks, and we'd been making good use of it as our warehouse. We appreciated its solid virtues.

Turning to the bombed-out area between the garage and the kitchen wing that had once been mud room and patio, I considered our latest plan for the deck we'd build there. Originally we had thought we would have a conventional single span the depth of the wing, the width of the patio. Then we realized that because of the way the land sloped away toward the south, the front corner of the deck nearest the garage would be about a yard off the ground, which would probably be as hazardous as it would look.

Going back to the drawing board, we came up with a revision: we would have a two-level span, something like two adjacent trays, the southernmost one set down a step from the other. This would reduce the height at the front, and perhaps the deck as a whole would even look more interesting than a single unbroken platform would have.

Glancing up from where I stood, I noticed that the sixteen new brackets we'd ordered from the mill a couple of weeks ago had already arrived and were in fact in place on the north eaves. We had restored as many of the old ones as we could, but we still came out a side short.

Around on the west side of the house, the carpenters had been busy filling in the last gap where the doctor's entrance had been with fiberglass insulation, sheathing, and new clapboards. Nearby, a hard-working apprentice was scraping and sanding away on the siding. Preparing the old clapboards for eventual repainting was a giant task that would take weeks. ▶

On the interior of that same west wall, inside the dining room, all of us — camera crew included — watched with interest as Judy Selwyn, our visiting consultant in historical preservation, gave us a mini-seminar on the results of her research during the week. She had come up with the answers to our questions about the colors the house had originally been painted, and even had samples of the three shades. Now we would have to decide whether we wanted to turn back the clock.

Sal Vassallo and his plasterers were finishing up the stair hall, which would complete their work on the house. I told them I thought they'd done the best job in town.

Once they had completed their work in the kitchen, Norm had been free to go ahead with his finish carpentry there. The preassembled casement window that had come from the factory ready to go into the

rough-framed opening over the sink had long been in place and waiting for the final touches of woodwork. All Norm had left to do was to install in the proper sequence the various pre-cut pieces of interior trim: first the *sill,* the surrounding *jambs* and *casings,* and finally the *apron,* the horizontal piece under the sill. Happily the modern casings were as simple and unpretentious as the old moldings elsewhere in the house; new and old went together well.

With plastering out of the way, the plumbing-and-heating men were also able to move ahead with their installation of the last baseboard units. ◄ They'd already finished with the first floor, and were almost through on the second. The radiators didn't have long to wait in line.

Dave Nobis had returned with his insulation installers. He discussed with us the insulation in the kitchen wing crawl space and showed us how cellulose is blown into an exterior wall. I knew I couldn't get through a whole day without climbing onto at least one roof, so it was with a certain resignation that I climbed up on top of the porch with him to look while his men prepared the exterior of the bathroom wall by removing clapboards and drilling holes.

But at least we did have a porch roof once again. During the week we had gone from nothing at all to a full frame, whose rafters clearly showed the pitch of the roof, and on to the next stage, the slippery, rain-soaked sheathing on which Dave and I were trying our best to stand firm.

Once again down on the level, on the flat new floor of the porch, I could see above me that the furring strips were nailed horizontally in place across the joists, ready to anchor a parallel plane. ► Our new porch ceiling would be made of Texture One-11 plywood, which is scored to look like the traditional tongue-and-groove boarding used in Victorian porch ceilings. We hadn't resorted to many such money-saving shortcuts so far in our rehabbing. We felt, at this stage of what we laughingly called our budget, that it would be wise to slip at least one in.

So far in this weekly record of current events in our old house, we have paid a good deal of attention to its verticals: the studs, the many pipes ascending from basement to rooftop, walls (inside and out). But along the way, we have of course been concerned as well with various surfaces on the other plane, the horizontal. After

all, what is a house without floors to walk on, ceilings to stare up at?

When completed, the floor of our front porch looked at first glance just like the ceiling above it. The ceiling, as we've confessed, was to be sheets of plywood masquerading as something else, while the floor was the genuine article, a carefully laid pinstripe pattern of individual 1 x 4 fir boards. These we had pre-cut to size and treated with clear wood preservative, as effective as and easier to maintain than paint. Fir is an especially good wood for an exterior surface; treated respectfully, it should last a good long time.

We had wanted to make sure that we laid the flooring properly, leaving enough space between the individual boards so that water could run off and dust and leaves wouldn't collect. And so we employed a little trick. In order to keep the gaps between the boards even, we used a 16d common nail, ordinarily referred to as a *spike,* as a spacer. ▼

First we'd nail down a floorboard, right into the joists, using an 8d galvanized finish nail. (I recommend

the so-called *hot dip* nail, which has a rough texture and grips into the wood better than a smooth, electroplated version of the same nail.) Then we would place the spike between the board just nailed down and the one to be nailed next, pushing the second one as close to the first as the spike would allow before we nailed it. These steps, repeated, guaranteed a floor with uniform spacing between the boards.

One thing we had to remember, however, was always to make the last few hits of the hammer light ones (and then to set the nails below the floor surface with a nail set). Otherwise the surface would have suffered the hammer marks known as rosebuds, and these are blossoms that really mar the finish of a new floor.

Inside the house, we'd been committed from the first appraisal to replacing the really sagging old lath-and-plaster ceilings with Blueboard. ▶ Once plaster has separated from lath in a ceiling to produce a sag, the stopgap measures of repair sometimes suggested are a waste of time. It's better to get a messy task over with at the beginning, when it's not inconvenient, than to face it as an emergency later, probably at the most disruptive and inconvenient time possible.

The first step in replacing the old ceilings had been demolition. We had had to strip off both plaster and lath, going right down to the *furring strips*, narrow pieces of wood attached in rows across the joists to provide a supportive framework, from which, in our house, the lath originally hung. A pattern of narrow white strips of plaster alternating with wider bands of bare wood where the lath had been remained on our furring to testify to former dimensions.

We had counted on using the old furring to hang our Blueboard on, and so we were concerned when we discovered that the joists underneath varied considerably in size. In the dining room ceiling, for example, about half the joists were 2 x 10s, the remainder 2 x 12s. The furring wasn't attached to every one of them. If it had been, it would have rolled across the room in 2-inch ripples, as wavy as the ocean. If we had ignored the smaller joists and left the furring attached only to the larger ones, we'd have had insufficient support for our final surface of Blueboard, which would have ended up as springy as a canvas tent. (These randomly sized old joists were a far cry from our new ones in the kitchen. Those were uniform and as truly horizontal as they could be, with their ends securely fixed in place by the sturdy metal supports called *joist hangers*.)

When I set to work in the dining room to demonstrate how to establish a firm and level base for the old furring, and therefore, indirectly, for our new ceiling, the procedure I followed was this. At every intersection where a furring strip crossed a joist, I nailed on a horizontal piece of scrap wood, so that it extended the joist (and readjusted the furring) down to a set level. The reference point for this level was a string guide ◄ set at an arbitrary point slightly below the lowest joist edge.

Then, with two *ring nails*, which have sharp-edged ridges that lock into wood fibers like barbs and greatly increase holding power, we secured each furring strip to each extension. ▼

There were a lot of intersections to doctor up in this way. The job of ceiling straightening is, let's face it, a little tedious — but easy enough for a beginner to consider doing.

Nearby, in the area composed of the family room, the entranceway from it into the kitchen (where the old arch had once been), and the stair hall, we indulged in

some out-of-sequence floor straightening, a project very similar to straightening the dining room ceiling.

There were some differences, however. First, the floor wasn't wavy; it simply sloped downhill. Second, the scrapwood extensions we added brought the nailing

surface of the joists up, not down, to a more level plane, not perfect but near enough. ▲ Third, we didn't have to install a framework comparable to the furring strips in the ceiling. The plywood subfloor was strong and rigid enough to bridge the gaps between the joists it rested on without bounciness, and the pull of gravity wasn't the disadvantage it is when dealing with a ceiling. Anyway, when the plywood subfloor was all laid, we sanded its seams smooth to form an even base for the oak flooring that would go on top.

Ordinarily we would have straightened this swatch of floor *before* the walls were plastered. That would have been the proper and sensible order, but because the space functioned as a center or key hall, through which pretty much all the traffic in the house had to pass, we were forced to deal with it when we could, not when we wanted to. We just couldn't afford to have everything grind to a halt when logically it should have. The timing was not ideal.

The flooring we chose for the kitchen was unorthodox, but much more practical than it seemed at first glance. It had proved its durability in such hard-wear districts as a busy restaurant in Nantucket and other large family kitchens we knew. The material was natural-finish oak, cut into ⅞-inch-square blocks that looked like blank Scrabble tiles and when laid formed a kind of mini-parquet.

**151**

These little blocks are not put down individually, one by one, but are laid in groups fixed on an 18-inch-square paper sheet, larger by half than a conventional vinyl floor tile. The paper is attached to the top surfaces of the blocks with a water-soluble glue.

Norm demonstrated for us how easy this kind of flooring is to install. First he drew a line on the subfloor, to indicate the path of the first row. That line was squared off with the room. He'd made it at a 90-degree angle to one of the walls, usually from the center of the main doorway to the room. Sometimes it's also useful to nail another guide, one made of a thin strip of wood, or *batten*, at a right angle to the line, to ensure square corners.

▲ Next Norm applied just the right amount of a thin mastic, using a toothed or notched trowel, onto a small section of floor along his line. He didn't want to put so much down that it would squeeze up through the joints and smear all over the surface of the blocks, but he didn't want to skimp and risk a poor bond. In order to avoid having the mastic dry up, he spread only enough to set a couple of sheets of blocks at a time.

After he'd laid several sheets, making sure they butted up tightly against one another, he took a sponge and wet the paper surface. Then he used a hammer to tamp all the blocks down as evenly as possible. When the water-soluble glue had softened, he was able to peel off the paper layer, leaving behind the many little tiles, all neatly in place.

Later, when the mastic was completely set, the surface of the parquet would be sanded to a uniformly smooth finish, and several protective coats of moisture-cured polyurethane would be applied to give the floor a waterproof, hard-wearing surface. The completed floor, resembling textured butcher-block, managed to be both elegant and informal. We liked the look.

Upstairs, somewhat the same procedure was carried out in both bathrooms, where the floor material we had selected was brown matte-finish ceramic tile, which came in the Scrabble-tile size officially known as *mosaic tile*. Domestic tile is made of clay with minerals introduced to give it its color. It is fired to a temperature of 1,200°. No wonder tile floors endure. Because our choice was not highly glazed, it had a natural rather than an industrial look to it.

These mosaic tiles also came in sheets, but they were larger in size, strips about 1 foot wide and 2 feet long. The tiles were linked together by dabs of glue rather than by a backing. Our tiler also used a notched trowel to spread waterproof mastic right onto the plywood subfloor, which had been screwed down to avoid any chance of springiness. ▶ An alternative method of installation would have been the so-called *mud job*. This would have required first laying down builder's paper on the plywood, then attaching wire mesh, and finally spreading a very thick layer of mud (cement mortar), into which the tile would be embedded. A mud job would have cost 50% more than ours, and its additional weight would have put an extra strain on the framing supporting the floor.

After our bathroom tiles were laid, there was a waiting period of a couple of days before the tilers returned to fill in the joints between the individual tiles with the thin mortar called *grout*. ▶ The pause allowed any gases rising from the mastic to escape, and also made sure that the tile had bonded completely.

Our grout was tinted slightly so that it would be more compatible with the color of the tiles themselves. Often a bright white grout will contrast too dramatically with dark tiles and will produce a busy effect. The tiler spread our brownish grout all over the floor with a trowel, forcing as much as he could into the joints. Then he used a burlap rag to scour in more grout, as well as to wipe off the excess. The grout contained a retarder so it wouldn't harden and adhere to the surface before the cleanup could be completed. (A safeguard: any grout that can't be wiped off can later be removed with a light acid wash.)

The final touch was the installation of immaculate white marble thresholds. Let the bathwater splash and the steam settle. Our new bathroom floors were as tight

against water problems as we knew how to make them.

The original fir floors on the second floor were essentially sound, but dull and worn. They needed only a cosmetic treatment, not total replacement, and George Hannon was the man to spruce them up, with his electric sanders and his know-how.

The larger of the two machines he used was an upright *drum sander*, ◄ which had a cylindrical roller to which sheets of various grades of sandpaper could be attached. The big machine couldn't sand right up to the walls, and so for finishing close to baseboards, his assistant used a smaller, hand-held edger, a *disc sander*. ▼

Before he started sanding the guest room, George went over the whole floor and carefully set any nails that seemed to have worked their way up above the surface. One protruding nail can destroy a sheet of sandpaper in an instant and waste both time and materials.

He made his first series of passes over the floor with the drum sander loaded with coarse sandpaper to take off whatever remained of the old finish, and he always worked with the grain of the wood. That first sanding made the most dramatic difference in the look of the floor, which was stripped bare in no time at all.

Reloading with a medium-grade paper, George then made another attack, this time cutting down any high boards and producing a smooth finish.

The edges of the floor, inaccessible to the drum, required some close attention. George finished them up with the disc sander where he could. In awkward or confined areas (as under radiators, around pipes, and in corners), he had to resort to handwork with a scraper and sanding block.

After one more overall sanding with very fine pa-

**155**

per, he vacuumed up any leftover sawdust that his two machines had failed to suck into their attached bags. Once the whole surface of the floor was absolutely dust-free, he applied the priming coat of polyurethane. This both penetrated and sealed the bare wood and produced the natural finish we were after. To ensure proper adhering of the second and last coat, he sanded lightly once again before he applied it.

After an interval of about three days, the newly finished floor could be waxed with a high-quality paste wax and polished with an electric buffer. From there on in, twice-a-year waxings, with occasional buffings in between, would be sufficient to keep the floor in good shape.

Tongue-and-groove oak strips have a reputation as the most popular hardwood flooring for new home construction in America. Certainly the narrow oak strips got our vote as the choice for the new floors in the main body of our old house: in the living room and the family room/hall area. Besides, we wanted to match the single surviving old floor in the dining room that we'd decided to try to refinish.

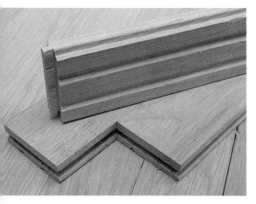 ◀ Each of our tongue-and-groove floorboards was 2 inches wide and ¾ inch thick, but they were of random lengths, and none had more than one simple flat surface. Of the six sides of each board, only the top was flat. Both ends and both sides had been milled with either tongue or groove, so that the individual boards would interlock in all directions, and the bottom was grooved.

A board is fastened down through its longitudinal tongue, which disappears into the groove of the next board, so that the nails driven through the tongue are invisible. The first few rows of boards, which are awkwardly close to the wall, must be nailed through their faces and by hand, as in the old days, but thereafter professional installers now use a *power nailer*, a machine that is activated by a swift blow with a five-pound mallet. The mallet head is rubber on one side and metal on the other. The metal side drives the nailer, but the rubber is used to position the wood strips close to one another without damaging them.

George's brother-in-law and partner, Jim Bannon, was already at work in the family room when we turned up to watch. We were hypnotized by his performance, a cross between dancing a jig and playing in a one-man band. Before beginning he had arranged a field of strips, placed loosely in order, with end-to-end joints staggered as in bricklaying. Once he was in full swing, he would use one foot to hold the strip he was about to nail both

down on the subfloor and up against its neighbor, one hand to hold the power nailer in place, and the other to wield the mallet. He had to have perfect balance and aim, as he moved along the row with a steady rhythm of push, swing, bang. With one bang a board would be butted closely to another, and with the next, a nail would shoot diagonally through the tongue of a strip and into the subfloor. ▲

Once Jim had completed laying all the new floors downstairs, George took over again with his sanders. The only really tricky part of the assignment was refinishing the old oak veneer in the dining room. It could have been too thin to have taken another sanding, as our appraiser had feared. George began, and we crossed our fingers. Luckily, nowhere did the machine sand down so far as to expose the tongue-and-groove joint, or did it even cut through the veneer anywhere. When finished, the old surface was as smooth and gleaming as the new ones on either side of it, and mirrorlike reflected the silhouettes of the old four-paned windows.

**157**

**I**f you feel comfortable with machines and tend to keep a cool head, you may be a candidate for refinishing your own hardwood floors. (Softwood ones are fairly tricky.) The equipment — the sanding machines and the floor polisher — can easily be rented. That's not the problem. The difficulty with on-the-job training is that the job can be over before you have mastered the skill, and you are left to live with results that are less than professional.

A drum sander can seem to have a mind of its own, and if you panic and fail to keep it moving smoothly ahead or forget to raise the revolving drum from the surface of the floor, you will dig those telltale trenches known as *drummers*. Working on the edges takes time and, in the case of the hand scraping, a lot of elbow grease. You should be aware that you may invest valuable time and energy only to be disappointed when you've failed to measure up to your own high standards.

But remember that if you do give refinishing a try and things don't go well, you can simply stop where you are and call in a professional. There's nothing dishonorable in facing up to limitations. So many do-it-yourselfers commit themselves irrevocably to do or die once they have undertaken a project. In floor sanding, as in other brave endeavors, a wise and strategic retreat is always an option.

The light natural finish, which we liked, that results from simply polyurethaning sanded oak or fir is not universally popular. Some people want a deeper color. If you're one, before you get involved in staining your floor, consider some problems you are likely to come up against.

Oak is a porous or open-grained wood, which means that a filler has to be applied in order to get a smooth finish and an even color. But polyurethane varnishes are not always compatible with the filler, nor is polyurethane with an oil stain.

Because there is always a chance you will stain too dark or unevenly, you should always make samples on scrap flooring, starting with the lightest stain option and moving toward the more intense. Remember that floors darken more with time, and you have to take that into account.

All in all, staining a floor is a sophisticated business, and you should plan to have an extensive seminar with your supplier about the materials you'll be using. Remember that a darker floor presents continuing maintenance problems. It shows the dust, and it will wear in high traffic areas. And then ask yourself once more, is staining worth the trouble?

If you have an impossible floor, perhaps softwood, that doesn't seem worth refinishing, and you don't want to lay a new one, then wall-to-wall carpet may be your shortcut solution. Heavy hair-and-jute padding underneath carpeting can mask a multitude of irregularities. Though wall-to-wall may not be absolutely true to the period of your house, this may be one situation where you may want to compromise. We did, on the stairs and in the second-floor hall.

Ceramic tile floors like those in our new bathrooms are durable and easy to care for, but their installation may intimidate an amateur. We recommend them, but if you are determined to choose an alternative that you feel confident you can do yourself, do avoid sheet vinyl, which is hard to handle in itself and involves making a precise cutting pattern. Try instead vinyl tiles, which are much easier to work with, and offer less chance of a minor miscalculation's causing a major disaster. Carpet tiles, either shag or with a flat indoor-outdoor surface, are another alternative. With both vinyl and carpet tiles, however, watch out for corny patterns — multicolor imitation mosaic, or lurid synthetic shades of yarn — that will be hard to live with and obtrusive in your old house.

Taste enters as well into decisions about ways to deal with ceilings that are sound enough structurally but inadequate visually. Beware of the temptation to take the easy way out and put up a dropped ceiling, the kind that hangs panels in a metal grid suspended from the offending surface. The panels absorb dirt and cooking odors and are hard to keep clean. Most important, the dropped ceiling not only is out of character in an old house, but also simply doesn't look residential, no matter what the period of the residence.

A related alternative in this situation would be to have a wooden grid constructed on the ceiling and wallboard hung from it, taping seams carefully and painting, perhaps with a textured paint, to try to create the look of a plastered ceiling. The look probably won't fool anyone who knows about plastered ceilings, but it will certainly be an improvement over suspended panels or the stark commercial ceiling tiles that don't belong in a mellow room. Never rule out the miracles that can result from conscientious plastering of cracks, scraping, sanding, and fresh paint. The simplest solution for a problem ceiling may sometimes be the best.

When dealing with ceilings you must always be sure not to cover up any electrical fixtures or outlets. Building codes are very stern about this and demand that access to them must remain. You can provide that by installing the removable caps available for this purpose.

Ceilings and floors, floors and ceilings — it's hard to remember that these horizontal surfaces are mirror images, identical twins. But they are, and this fact suggests a useful architectural trick. When you are planning, considering alternatives for a room that's so cluttered with furniture or debris that your thoughts about it are confused, stop a minute and gaze up. Looking at the ceiling of the room is like looking at a bare, abstract floor plan. You can get a fresh sense of the dimensions of the space, and clear your buzzing head.

# 10 On Top of Things

Speckled and piebald, our old house looked a little mangy this morning. From the outside it was hard for anyone but us to tell how really sound it had become after many weeks of solid work.

The men were scraping and sanding away on the mottled siding, as the mammoth drudgery of paint preparation continued. But it wasn't all primitive handwork, as I demonstrated on the front porch wall when I tried a power sander equipped with a special guide that made stripping the clapboards a less nerve-racking proposition.

Inside, we had gotten to work on the same kind of picky, seemingly endless, and certainly undramatic job of removing old paint from the woodwork. Patience, fortitude, and some precautions were essential, because old paint is usually lead paint and is dangerously toxic. We had let ourselves partially off the hook by sending the original paneled doors of the second floor off to a professional paint stripper. For about twenty dollars a door, we'd eliminated some labor and risk, and perhaps more to the point, we'd saved valuable time.

But we knew of no rejuvenator where we could send our windows for treatment, and so, in odd moments, work doggedly continued on the great double-hung window renovation project.

We had some fun ahead, however. The base and wall cabinets for the kitchen had arrived; still in their cartons, they were stacked like so many large toy blocks.  ◀ Before long, those of us who couldn't restrain ourselves until time for the actual installation took the cabinets out of the boxes and pushed them more or less into place. It's tough not to jump the gun and try to accelerate the steady sequence of events. We'd gone through a lot of slow, hard work to get this far with the kitchen. A

**160**

little impatience was as natural as the urge to sneak a look at the end of a thriller to see whodunit.

Upstairs, one mid-tan plastic laminate tub surround was already in place in the master bath, and during the day I tried to lend a hand with the installation of the second one, a bright daffodil-yellow number, but Paul and Tom Rae had the situation well under control without me. The surround had been waiting for them in the guest room, and they managed to maneuver it out, through the hall, and into the bathroom/laundry, and then demonstrate their expertise in getting the bulky thing over protruding plumbing pipes and stuck in place straight. It was clearly a two-man job for pros.

Back outside, Norm took time off from building new steps for the porch to discuss work in progress on the deck. During the week he and Greg had accomplished miracles with the kitchen wing. They had finished clapboarding the walls, had installed the back door, and had gotten the small brackets back up on the cornice. Now they were ready to roll with the deck. They'd found time to pour the concrete foundation and, as Norm explained early in the morning, were about to assemble the frame for the deck floor itself.

During the day they kept up the pace, ▶ and before we left for home, the late afternoon shadows were falling on a beautiful expanse of deck, newly framed. The stepped effect would prove to be a great success, we all thought, but we'd have to wait until the flooring was on to be sure.

Last week we'd had to be careful in walking on the slippery plywood sheathing of the front porch roof. This week, that same roof was completed, with a tough new surface made of roll roofing. Traction was no problem up there now.

**B**efore we got to work on any of our roofing surfaces, we had to take care of our major difficulties with the rotted edges of our main roof, the problematical eaves. During the course of our work on the old house, the carpenters probably spent as much time on the eaves and the mansards as on any single aspect of the rehabilitation. But we slid into the commitment gradually.

Our first estimate of the effort we would have to put into eave restoration had been based on a distant and outside view. We had seen from where we stood on the ground that there was trouble — leaks, rot, seepage, the works — but we didn't guess what we knew for sure once we got up there and inside. We thought originally we would have to count on two carpenters spending three days per side, or a total of six man-days per side, or about two and a half weeks in all.

Our experience should be a cautionary tale for anyone who might otherwise underestimate any work old-fashioned boxed eaves might require. Natural optimism should be left behind, and binoculars focused sharp.

Once we had opened up the patient, and found that the rot extended into the sheathing and well up into the framing, we began recalculating. By the third week of the rehabbing, Norm's projection was sobering, to say the least. He estimated then that it would take two carpenters five or six days per side, for a total of ten to twelve man-days per side, or about four weeks altogether.

Actually, as it turned out, the south side, which was the first one we did and the source of Norm's pessimism, was the worst side of all, while the one on the north needed comparatively minor work. If this seems strange, remember that what wreaks damage on the edges of a roof in a cold climate is the destructive action of melting and refreezing snow and ice, which may back up under the surface of the roof — in our case, the shingles — or leak into the structure through open cracks. In the winter, the cold north side tends to freeze and stay so, while the alternation of liquid and solid that causes the trouble occurs almost daily on the warm south side. There the sun may beat down at noon, but the cold grips at night.

From the first we wanted to retain the period look of the eaves. Although the brackets had departed from our twin house across the way, we wanted to save ours. The first thing we had done was carefully to take the old brackets down from their places on the cornice boards and set them aside for safekeeping until we had time to work on their restoration. Next we had removed the *fascia*, the cornice boards that formed the vertical surface or face of the boxed eaves, and then the horizontal *soffits*, or the bottom of the box.

Even with the eaves opened up this way, we couldn't grasp the full extent of the damage until we removed the shingles on the lower edge of the mansard roof. Then we could see how many of the old sheathing boards had to be replaced. All rotten ones had to go, and so did the damaged sections on the end of the supporting framing members.

The next step was to start replacing those damaged members or at least parts of them. Norm was able to *sister on* — that is, attach a double to — the old *look-outs* that had been trimmed of their rot. A look-out is the short horizontal timber that supports the boxed eave construction. ▼

The major defect in the original construction of the eaves had been this: instead of mounting the gutter on the outside of a single fascia board, the builders of the house had attached the gutter directly to the ends of the look-outs, and had completed the fascia enclosure by adding one narrow board above the gutter and another below. This plan provided the maximum number of seams that would pull apart and admit water right into the roof's interior. No wonder we had problems.

Rather than restore that ill-conceived design, Norm substituted a single wide board for his fascia and did what should have been done in the first place — attached his 5-inch wooden gutter to its surface. The gutter itself was a single span as long as the house was wide, which meant that there was no joint, no potential leak, except at the corners. Before that, however, Norm and Greg had to install a new soffit and reattach the old brackets, trimmed of their bottom inch or so.

That cosmetic surgery took place inside the house in our impromptu bracket workshop. In almost all cases the rot was confined to the bottom section of a bracket. Since the section was marked by a natural break in the design, the affected part could simply be sawed off uniformly, and the remainder sanded and primed before it was returned to service up on the roofline. ◄

We had had several alternatives: (1) to mill all new brackets at $58 a throw; (2) to can the brackets altogether; (3) to replace the amputated sections with blocks cut to fit exactly and reattached with a good waterproof glue; and (4) to do what we did, which was to save the brackets we could, and replace when we had to. In fact, we found that once the old brackets were back in place and painted to match the woodwork, it was almost impossible, even for us, to detect the little shortcut. Until then, however, there were a few telltale signs, as when new-and-revised met old at a corner.

The most demanding detail of the renovation was tailoring all the new molding, with its many mitered corners, around each and every one of about sixty brackets. That kind of small-scale, precision carpentry is almost cabinetwork, which is hard enough to do on ground level, let alone up in the air.

It is very important that tightly boxed-in eaves have sufficient ventilation, as Dave Nobis (our consultant on insulation) pointed out to us. Otherwise, moisture builds up inside the boxes, and dry rot can be the result. Insulation should not be installed in such cavities, but small metal vents should be added in order to allow air to circulate.

**W**hen the men had finished with the eaves on the south side, they tackled the next stage, the long overdue shingling of the curved sides of the mansard roof. (The flat top would get its own treatment, but not with shingles.) In dealing with the mansards, standard operating procedure was to finish up all the stages on two sides before moving on with the scaffolding to the other pair. ▶

The first step in applying our new shingles was to get rid of the two layers of brittle old ones. The first layer dated from 1921, when the original slate roof had been removed, with the first layer of asphalt shingles as their replacement. An asphalt shingle surface can usually be counted on to last from twenty to twenty-five years, so the second layer was probably added early in the doctor's ownership, or in the 1940s. The roof was

due for reshingling just about the time he moved away in 1965, but after his departure, maintenance lapsed.

It is sometimes possible to reshingle right over one earlier layer but not over two. We had to strip and start over. Using a claw hammer, Greg pried up the long-suffering old shingles, some of which had served for fifty-eight years. ◄ There was the original board sheathing underneath. Once all the old shingles were off, Norm rolled out the roofing paper, the *underlayment* for the new shingles, and stapled it into place. Then the insulation went into the mansard, before the shingle covering.

Shingling gets off to a comparatively slow start and then goes amazingly fast. First the roof edges had to be prepared carefully, for as we knew all too well, that's where trouble can start.

As Norm summarized his preparation, the initial step was to nail on an 8-inch-wide *drip edge*, a strip of aluminum that comes with a molded edge designed to divert the rainwater that rolls down a roof so that it falls slightly out and away from the vulnerable surface of the fascia and into the gutter.

Then he applied a single run of roofing paper, a yard wide and in one seamless piece the length of the side of the roof.

We had chosen a style of shingle that had an irregular rustic look to it; it had the standard three tabs per strip plus an extra overlapper on every third tab that gave a certain texture to the finished expanse. But for his first four rows, or *starter courses*, Norm installed absolutely plain self-sealing shingle strips that had no tabs at all. In this way the susceptible edge was sealed in as tightly as possible. ◄

Before too many courses he could no longer reach his work from the scaffolding, and from that point on had to work from a kind of ledge or shelf, a single scaffolding board securely braced against the roof, about halfway up it.

Though our shingles were all self-sealers (dabs of adhesive having been applied at the factory) we took the precaution of adding an extra dab of roofing cement to those decorative single tabs that might tend to catch the wind and lift. ▶

A hip roof and a mansard have four things in common, the four corners where their shingled surfaces meet. The problem of protection is the same as in the ridge of a gabled roof. The angled intersection must be fitted out, as Greg demonstrated, with an extra cover of a single row of shingles molded over the corner.

Up on top of the roof, we had found far fewer problems than we might have. When we learned that we wouldn't have to remove the old surface from the flat, or peel off and start from scratch on the dormer roofs, which were worn away on their ridges, or rebuild the chimney, we gave a great sigh of relief.

Picking up on various clues, Dave Mullane, our roofing contractor, had been able to estimate off the cuff that the surface had originally been installed fifty or sixty years before, with one resurfacing about twenty years later. A telltale sign, he said, was our *flashing*. Flashing is a metal sheet or membrane; it is installed at roof protrusions, eaves, valleys and ridges, and so on, which are problem areas in roofing and require continuous coverage against leaks rather than individual shingles. The flashing around our chimney and vent pipes,

as well as that which formed the finishing edge around the rim of the flat roof, was original, and it was made of zinc. In the period during and after World War I, copper, the preferred metal for flashing, was scarce, having gone to the war effort, and builders had to settle for the less desirable zinc. Incidentally, copper remains the first choice — flashing made of it is virtually indestructible — though the cheaper aluminum is popular.

Dave's educated guess about the age of the roof had been confirmed by our research into building department records, where we'd found a 1921 building permit for removal of slates and application of new asphalt shingles. No doubt the tar-and-gravel top surface had been installed at the same time, and had been refinished whenever the second layer of shingles had gone onto the mansards.

Now, up there on top of things, we had to remedy several decades of erosion. First we had to repair the dormer roofs. ▼ Where the weather had worn through three plies, or layers, of roofing, Dave's men scratched back eighteen inches on either side of the ridges, then patched with three new layers of roofing and tar, and followed that up with a thick top coat of gravel, which gives both thermal and physical protection. In miniature this was essentially the same process they used on the larger area of the flat. When the whole job was done,

Dave ventured one more educated guess, that our new roof would last another fifty or sixty years.

As for the chimney with its many loose bricks — so astoundingly loose that it's hard to imagine how they managed to stay in place at all — we simply mortared the bricks firmly back where they belonged, and re-pointed other joints and the corners. ▼

Chimney flashing is installed in two interlocking layers: *base flashing,* mounted flat on the roof, essentially; and *counterflashing,* which wraps around the sides of the chimney. The more vulnerable counterflashing had long since blown off our chimney, and we had to replace it. The final touch would be the cleaning of the flue by a top-hatted chimney sweep.

**T**he renovation of the flat top of the mansard roof was a matter of resurfacing, while the roofing of our kitchen wing was a case history — from beginning to end — of installing a *built-up,* or tar-and-gravel, surface. There's a lot more to building a road than simply run-

ning a steamroller over some tar and gravel, and the same is true of a roof. We had to spend a lot of time on preparation.

The original roof on the wing had seen better days. Much of the gravel had washed off, and the general look of the surface was as mangy as our siding. We swept what was left away from the place where we planned to cut the opening for our skylight. Though the roof looked flat, it actually had a very slight pitch. There are few absolutely flat roofs; the dangers of standing water and leaks, as well as the question of structural strength under a heavy load of snow, have given flat roofs a bad name.

Before we started work on the exterior of the roof, we had had to perform some preliminary structural reinforcement inside. The carpenters had installed a 6 x 10 beam across the ceiling of the kitchen, a sturdy number we found at a secondhand lumberyard and bought at a very good price. Then they had built the interior rough framing for the new skylight. As Norm explained, "We had to strengthen things and head off the weight of the skylight."

Outside, when Greg built the exterior frame for the skylight, he designed it to provide a level base in the slightly pitched surface but with sides canted so that water would run away from the skylight. Then the men had lined the new unit up with guidemarks on the frame. After Norm had squirted a bead of butyl or rubber-based caulking compound all around the four sides where it would rest, they ceremoniously lowered the skylight itself into place and nailed it down. The skylight unit came with its own self-flashing. The layers of roofing paper and tar would come up right over the canted wooden frame. (For pictures, see pages 110–111.)

Still more preliminary work had to be done before the actual roofing could begin. ◄ The eaves of the kitchen wing were renovated in a sequence smaller in scale but similar to that for our work on top: (1) new look-outs were sistered onto the rafters; (2) then new soffits and fascia went on, as well as some new roof sheathing around the edges that completed the boxed enclosure; (3) finally, on went the new gutter and brackets. We had had to invest in twenty-five newly milled brackets for the kitchen wing. Smaller than those on the main house, they cost "only" $26 apiece.

When the roofers arrived it took them only about half an hour to rip off the old roofing. Its condition was much too bad to justify adding a new layer of tar and gravel on top of what was there. We'd managed to get away with that successfully on the main roof, but if we'd tried it on the kitchen wing, we'd have ended up with a really bumpy, unsatisfactory roof.

Once the old surface was gone, the men nailed on two plies (one lapped layer) of roofing paper (felt). It comes in yard-wide rolls. The rolls come with white guidelines that ensure that 18-inch overlaps can be kept even easily.

Then a roofer went to work to install our beautiful top-quality copper flashing all around the perimeter of the roof. ▼ The copper strip was angled so that part of it went from the edge of the roof up onto it for a depth of 3 inches, and the other reached down from the edge into the gutter itself. At the intersection of side and top, on the edge, a kind of lip called a *gravel stop* rose up like a small wall, designed to prevent the erosion of gravel right off the roof and into the gutter.

At last we were ready for the most dramatic part of the tar-and-gravel resurfacing: the mopping-on of the molten asphalt. Steaming buckets of it were hauled up from the boiler that was bubbling away by the garage, and it was poured into a rolling cart-container. While one fearless roofer mopped on the liquid, the other unrolled the roofing felt. ◄ The two components fused together as the asphalt cooled.

In all, three layers of roofing paper and asphalt went on, giving us a built-up surface that was five plies thick (including the two plies first nailed on). Finally, the roofers raked on a coat of gravel. Another major job was completed. ▼

**M**ost rehabbers don't have to get involved in actually reconstructing or even repairing the framing of a roof. If you're lucky, all you'll have to do is replace a few shingles and seal a few leaks. What's more likely is that you will have to replace a worn-out surface with a complete new layer of shingles, or some other covering. You may be able to *over-roof*, that is, put a second layer right on top of the existing one. But two layers is the maximum. If you already have two, you will have to strip both off and start anew, as we did.

Nevertheless, in the interests of general education, you should understand something about the way an ordinary pitched roof is built. The one on our front porch is a clear and simple illustration of framing basics, and its construction is worth a brief review.

Some of the basic members in that roof are familiar: the horizontal joists and header. The *joist plate* and the *rafter plate* are also clearly horizontal. It is when you come to the *rafters* that you encounter a new consideration. Left behind is the simple certainty of the 90-degree angle; the diagonal underpinnings of a pitched roof bring up oblique matters. ▼

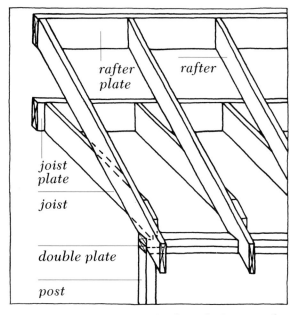

In framing a pitched roof, three tricky angles have to be dealt with: (1) the cut of the rafter end at the point where it is attached to the house, or, in a gabled roof, to the *ridge;* (2) the cut at the opposite end of the rafter, or at the edge of the roof's overhang; and (3) the notch that must be cut in the lower edge of the rafter in order for it to fit over the header and allow the slope to proceed downward at the proper pitch.

After the framing is completed, *sheathing* goes on top. The plywood panels we nailed onto the rafters provided a solid base for roll roofing. ▲

The *roll roofing* we used on our porch roof can be thought of as a bolt of the basic material from which asphalt shingles are cut. Though much lighter in weight, it is also asphalt-soaked felt that has a gravel surface. The long sheet itself comes in a roll 1 yard wide and 36 feet long, enough to run the length of an ordinary-sized roof without a seam. ▶

Though less pleasing to the eye, and only half as long-lasting as asphalt shingles, roll roofing compensates by being inexpensive and both easy and quick to install, even for a beginner. On a slightly pitched roof like the one on our porch, it is the material of choice, because its comparatively seamless surface is more waterproof than shingles would be on such a gentle slope. Shingles, like slates, will actively shed water but only when they are installed on a suitably steep roof.

*Asphalt shingles*, like those we used on the sides of our mansard roof, are the most popular roofing material, by far, in the country today. Cut from compressed fiber or felt (wood-and-rag composition or, in the most modern type, fiberglass), the basic shingle is saturated with asphalt and finished on one side with a light coating of gravel that is ground almost as fine as coarse sand. Shingles are fire-rated — A, B, and C — with C being the grade most people choose. Some brands feature wind-seal ratings as well.

Asphalt shingles don't come singly like the more expensive wood shingles or slates. They are manufactured in strips 1 foot wide and 3 feet long, divided by cuts halfway into the width usually into three tabs per strip. ▶ The single rows of shingles you think you see on a finished roof are not what they seem. Each successive course of strips is laid,

starting at roof edge, so that the halves with tabs overlay and conceal the uncut halves of the preceding row. Make sure you choose shingles that are self-sealing; that is, those that come with spots of adhesive which is activated by the heat of the sun and anchors down the tabs. Even so, you may want to add extra adhesive, as we did, to be on the safe side.

Once upon a time asphalt shingles came only in a conservative spectrum. Classic black, gray, tan, dark red, and green were the standards. Now the range of colors has really taken off, and some subtle new shades are available, though you do have to pay a premium for the latest thing. One look to avoid, at all costs, is ersatz "wood grain."

The kind of *built-up roof* we had our contractor install on the kitchen wing can almost be thought of as a custom-made version of the other felt-asphalt-gravel roofing materials. Because it is the most waterproof of all, it is used on flat or near-flat roofs, which have the greatest potential for leaks.

Theoretically, the application of roll roofing and shingles is within the capacities of the ordinary, inexperienced home handy- **175**

man. The height and pitch of the roof, to be sure, may be the crucial factors for a do-it-yourselfer. But a built-up roof should always be installed and repaired by professionals, who have the know-how, the equipment, and the crew for the job. Amateurs shouldn't mess around on high places with asphalt that can be as hot as 500°F.

Slate and tile roofs also require professional attention. They are expensive to put on and to maintain properly, but they are extremely durable. As we have said before, if you have a slate (or tile) roof, treat it as a major asset, and take good care of it. You won't get a better roof, no matter what anyone tells you.

◄We chose to install wooden gutters. Aluminum is another option for both gutters and downspouts, but the metal will corrode, especially in salt air, and is also susceptible to denting and loss of shape. A newer alternative is PVC, which is a very easy material to work with. The main disadvantage of the PVC gutters and downspouts now on the market is that so far they come only in white, a fact that limits freedom of choice in color schemes for the house. White gutters against the dark brown trim of our house would have called too much attention to themselves.

Another lofty question concerns skylights. The amount of work that Norm had to do to prepare the framing of our kitchen roof for the skylight we installed might make it seem that the job is beyond the average rehabber. This is not the case. Our roof had special problems of structure and pitch that made a little more work for us. Because skylights come preframed, with their flashing in place, the trickiest part of the installation is the cutting of a hole in the roof.

Thermal or double-dome skylights come with both the inner and outer shells made of clear plastic. They also come with the outer shell clear and the inner one frosted or tinted. This reduces glare without diminishing light particularly, and also mutes the messy look of debris that falls on the outside surface. Some people can't bear to have the same old leaves and twigs staring in at them week after week, but don't relish climbing up to sweep them off.

**A** healthy sense of self-preservation usually keeps someone who has to go up high or on top of a house from taking too many foolish chances. If you are considering mounting ladders or scaffolding, you should be aware of a few safety rules that are not as obvious as making sure that a ladder rests on level ground.

Don't tilt your ladder too steeply. Imagine a right triangle formed by wall, ground, and ladder as hypotenuse. The leg on the ground should be at least a quarter as long as the leg on the wall. Then the ladder will lean at an angle that is safe.

Remember also that an aluminum extension ladder is designed to be used vertically. It is less strong horizontally, so don't use one as a substitute for a solid scaffolding plank. If you stand on the ladder, it may bend. A plank won't.

The rented scaffolding we used had heavy wooden posts as the uprights, which were fastened in place by metal braces bolted right through the walls of the house. The horizontal work platform was a series of 2 x 10 planks 12 feet long. These rested on adjustable brackets called *pump jacks,* which travel on the uprights and move the platform down or up (safely, to a height of 30 feet). This arrangement is far less cumbersome than metal pipe scaffolding, really necessary only for large commercial jobs.

A less complicated setup will do for less demanding jobs. A pair of extension ladders can be used as the uprights for a platform no longer than 9 feet, no higher than 20 feet. Metal *ladder jacks,* hung from the ladder itself, support the platform and brace the ladder against the wall of the house.

Scaffolding whose verticals rest on frozen ground can be a problem when a thaw occurs and the supports settle into mud. The whole business can suddenly pull away from the house and cause serious injuries unless you have made sure it is securely anchored to something stable.

# 11
# Fresh As
# Paint

**Week 10**  Suddenly, with just three weeks left to go, we found our interests switching from the way things were built to the way they looked. Cleanup and decoration were our new focus, inside and out.

The bare earth of the front yard, the stone rubble left over from the demolition of the former entrance, the scraggly bushes, the spotty look of the siding, all of this seemed to get to us. Because we could already see in our mind's eye exactly how the finished house should look, the mess of the intermediate stages was a reality that was just plain irritating. When the wind blew, the dust swirled up from the desert that was our front lawn and into our eyes. We were impatient and frustrated and a little worried. How could we possibly get everything squared away in time to meet our deadline?

During the week we made a mild beginning down in the basement, where we scurried around and cleaned the place up. It's a plain and honest old unfinished basement, but a neat one now. There's nothing like starting from the bottom.

The vanguard of our team of landscaping consultants arrived today to talk to us, just at the right psychological moment. Phyllis Andersen and I strolled rather briskly around the grounds, for though the sky was clear, the mid-April breeze was cold. She summarized her ideas about ways we could transform the place into a proper setting for the house. Experienced in a city-sponsored neighborhood improvement program called The Greening of Boston, she had special expertise in planting in an urban environment.

Clearly we had a massive cleanup ahead. Phyllis pointed out example after example of overgrown shrubbery (much of which was hopelessly clogged with dead wood) ▶ and unhealthily sited trees that would have to be moved if they were to survive, or else cut down. She suggested regrading, fertilizing, pruning, all sorts of basic manual labor.

On the more positive side, she had a whole sheaf of ideas for such improvements as new planting and other landscaping. She painted an inspiring picture of the future: flowering trees and shrubs, a low picket fence, paths, a new front walk. The land would bloom again as it had in past springtimes.

Norm and Greg had finished flooring and applying preservative to the deck. They had also installed its new steps, just in time for a special guest, the mayor of Boston. Kevin White came by to see what we were doing and to talk about some concerns common to rehabbers planning to settle in marginal but reviving sections of a city: possible reassessment and higher real estate taxes, once the rejuvenation of a house had increased its market value; the quality of neighborhood schools; and local police protection.

As we inaugurated the deck as a place to sit and talk, the mayor assured me that we would have a three-year freeze on our original assessment (which at $7,500

was ridiculously low), and that any change thereafter in our tax of $1,500 annually would have to be part of a city-wide, across-the-board increase. We wouldn't be penalized for having rescued a dying house. Mr. White predicted a boom in neighborhood real estate comparable to that of the downtown waterfront, where "seven years ago I had to *give* away buildings." At $17,000, our house hadn't been a giveaway, but perhaps our investment was like buying low at the beginning of a bull market.

Today Norm and I had the long-awaited pleasure of putting up some of the kitchen wall cabinets. ▲ This was for real — no more playing house as we had last week. In the days since, the walls and ceiling of the room had been painted, and Norm had attached temporary supports of 2x4s to the east wall. The tops of these *deadmen* reached exactly to a leveled line on the wall marking where the bottom of the cabinets should come. We would brace the cabinets on the deadmen while Norm screwed them into the wall studs, all at one time.

Previously Norm had lined up outside all the cabinets for the east wall and had fixed them together by attaching another temporary brace, a horizontal piece of wood across their tops, that joined them into one manageable unit. We were then able to carry the assembly into the kitchen and install it in a single operation. We avoided a lot of individual leveling and fussing by using this shortcut.

Elsewhere in the house, paint preparation continued steadily, as it also did outside. We had to be getting close to the end. The carpenters had been replacing the last of the deteriorated clapboards on the west wall, ▼ while up on the porch roof Norm took time out from his work to talk to me about what he was doing. He and Greg were installing new clapboards, as neat a job as they had done on the kitchen wing, and the last traces of the old bathroom window had already disappeared. Pretty soon all our scraping and sanding and repairing would be completed, and the first coat of paint, a primer, could go on. One of our new garage doors was already up and primed. We'd get to the other one soon.

s John Hewitt had pointed out when he appraised the house, the exterior paint buildup was almost a quarter of an inch in some places. When multiple paint layers have over the decades accumulated to that thickness, it's no surprise to find the phenomenon known as *checking*, or *alligatoring* ◄ (a more extreme form of the same disease). The surface has crazed, with chipping or peeling the result — a pretty depressing mural. Other problems arise where there are a lot of joints in woodwork, as on window frames and eaves, where water steals behind the paint through cracks and lifts it, while soaking into the bare wood itself.

When at last we finished preparing all the exterior surfaces that would be painted, from a distance the house didn't look much better than it had when we first saw it months ago. But from a closer vantage point, anyone could see that the siding was clean and solid and dry, all ready to be primed. ▼ We'd spent a lot of

time on details, such as preparing the engaged front porch post. The drudgery hadn't been half as satisfying as stroking on the final coats of paint would be, but it was one job that, like it or not, simply had to be done.

In most ordinary jobs, where there is less scraping down to the wood than there was in our orgy of preparation, painters would simply *spot prime*. In our case, there were so many spots that we in effect applied a single coat of primer all over most of the walls. The thirsty wood drank it up.

The primer was a light neutral shade, an off-white. ► What color would we finally have? From the first we had toyed with the idea of turning from the

white that was on the house when we bought it to one of the dusky tones characteristic of 1860s taste. In order to find out, if we could, exactly what color our house had been originally, we had called in preservation expert Judy Selwyn to investigate. The former tenants, Georgia Packard and her sisters, recalled that the house had been white in the 1920s and 1930s, and they also remembered that our twin house across the drive had then been a muted color, either gray or buff. But our consultant would delve deeper in the past than that.

When Judy arrived on the job, she had an odd assortment of professional equipment: a microscope, a hand lens, and a sharp cutting and scraping tool something like a surgeon's scalpel or an X-Acto knife. Her mission was to establish a *paint chronology*, to discover the colors that had been painted on the house, and in what sequence.

She prowled around until she found protected areas where all the layers of paint would be intact, sheltered from the elements. One of these was on the southwest corner of the house, which the 1939 addition had covered. Another telling item was a bracket that had been taken down from underneath the sheltering eaves.

To make a boring into the layers of paint she took her scalpel, stuck it into the sample she wanted to study, moved it around slowly and at an angle until gradually she had exposed a kind of cone, in which under the microscope the successive layers of paint lay revealed, like the rings in a crosscut section of a tree.

Judy found ten layers of paint, plus a primer that was very thin, most of it having been absorbed into the original new wood. The original finish coat turned out to have been a medium brown, almost a cocoa. ▶ The porch, the detail on the eaves (including the cornice board and brackets), and other decorative trim had been a very dark chocolate brown, while the shutters and the front door were in yet another related but contrasting shade, a light coffee tan.

The second layer indicated that when first repainted, the body of the house was changed to an ochre, with the trim remaining brown. On top of that were more dark colors, alternating back and forth with the strong shades then so popular.

Sometime after the turn of the century and before 1922, when the continuing effect of the Colonial Revival that began in the 1880s still converted Americans to white as the preferred choice for even the most flagrantly non-Colonial home, our old house got the treatment and turned pale. After 1939, when the doctor's addition went up, there were four more coats of white altogether, but none, it is safe to say, since 1965.

In summary, half of the coats of paint were dusky and Victorian, and the other half white and Colonially inspired. Our best estimate, and our painters' guess as well, was that the house hadn't been painted for about twenty years when we took it on. That's a long drought for parched clapboards. The usual interval between paintings for a city house, which is subject to more pollutants and grime than a country or suburban place, is approximately six years. (Rural siding can probably go for about eight years and still look good.) In the clean air of nineteenth-century Dorchester, the interval must have been somewhat longer, if from the original coat in the 1860s to about 1920 there were only four other paintings, or one every dozen years or so.

We were fascinated to get the straight facts on the old house's paint chronology, but we were left in a minor quandary. We'd sort of planned on painting the place an ochre with brown trim. Now we were torn between our own taste and absolute authenticity. Judy assured us

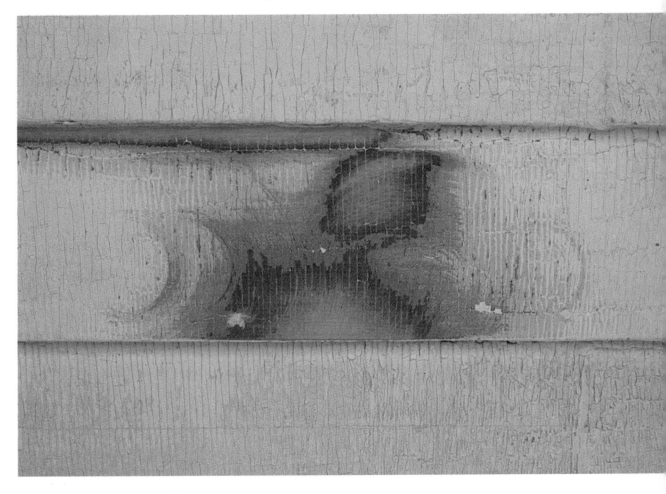

that ochre was a "period typical" color and would be perfectly appropriate. Besides, she continued, the original choices are not graven in stone like some arbitrary commandments. Personal taste is always a factor to balance with authenticity. She herself, however, was actually in favor of returning to the original combination of browns. She thought the effect would be extremely handsome.

Right down to the wire we alternated between ochre and brown, brown and ochre. Finally we bowed to history, and decided to opt for the original scheme of three shades of brown.

Our painters, John Buckley and Sam Zarzour, reviewed for us the work sequence followed in preparing and painting the exterior of the house.

Step 1: Scraping ▼ and sanding, including the feathering of the edges between old paint and the bare spots.

Step 2: Spot priming new wood and old.

Step 3: Caulking joints where surfaces meet; filling nail holes with putty.

Step 4: Applying *first primer* (off-white), almost everywhere.

Step 5: Applying *finish prime coat* (battleship gray), everywhere. ▶

Step 6: Applying *finish coat* (cocoa brown) to body of house; then painting contrasting trim (dark brown and tan).

The interval between applying the two finish coats should be minimal. We used oil-based paint, whose drying period is typically from 12 to 48 hours, and the second coat went on as soon as the first was dry

in order to ensure that the chemical bond between the two would be firm, that they would *key* into each other. As John explained, "You don't want the coats to separate. That would be the worst thing that could happen," and Sam added, "A lot of people get uptight and think that the second coat shouldn't go on too quickly, but it's actually better that way."

When John demonstrated the proper way to paint clapboards, he used a 4-inch Chinese bristle brush, which was an investment, but a good one. Properly cared for, a good brush will last for some time and be a joy to use. First he ran his well-loaded brush along the underside, or the *butts*, of two or three clapboards, and then he went back, with plenty of paint, and coated their vertical surfaces. And so he proceeded, repeating the two successive steps.

If a primer is too close in color to the finish coat, it's hard for the painter not to miss spots. Sam said he always tints his primer as close to the finish as he can without causing confusion between the two colors. In this way he manages to strike a delicate balance between having a primer that is hard to cover because it's such a contrast, and one that's hard to distinguish from the final color.

Sam took on the job of applying the final finish to our deck flooring. Norm had already given it a preliminary treatment with one of the many colorless ◄ modern wood preservatives available. Smelly creosote is now a thing of the past. It's cheap but it stains wood a dark walnut shade. Don't think of using it. We wanted to keep our deck floor a natural tone, and certainly had never considered getting into the perpetual maintenance problems of floor and deck paint.

Anyway, Sam's final touch was an application of *boiled* linseed oil, which he mixed with turpentine and brushed on in sufficient quantities to really soak and penetrate the grain of the wood. Raw linseed oil takes forever to dry; you usually end up with a surface that is sticky and very attractive — to flies only.

Inside the house, preparation for painting was somewhat easier, but equally slow and even less mechanized. For example, sanding and scraping baluster after baluster on the staircase by hand was no quickie job. ► We had to make sure, too, that any previous finish, including the children's poster-paint graffiti in the guest room, that might bleed through the new paint had been removed or sealed.

We made a deliberate decision about the painting of the inside of the house. We would sidestep the question of "interior decoration" with all the overtones of the term, if we possibly could. Because of our special situation and the way we were to sell the house, a couple of decorative commitments were made for us that we might otherwise have postponed, such as the wallpaper in the kitchen and bathrooms.

On our own, we preferred to restore the house only to the point at which everything structural had been done and it was pure, almost abstract, as if waiting for the future owner to add his own colors, his own individuality. We painted all walls and woodwork white, and left both our stripped old doors and our new flush ones in their natural tones, echoing the oak and fir floors.

The Victorians went in for what they thought of as the subdued colors of nature: shades like olive, ochre, rust, and dark gray. And they particularly liked them in intense combinations that highlighted architectural detail.

Andrew Jackson Downing, the most influential of early proponents of this spectrum, writing in 1850, objected to the bright white of the widely popular Greek Revival style as so "gleaming and conspicuous" as to be absolutely painful to the eye. He compared the look of white houses, dazzling in the landscape, to the "silly expression" that very white teeth give to a face.

Advising that man in his houses should avoid all those bright and artificial colors that nature avoids, except as accents of yellow, red, and blue, Downing went on to recommend adopting the colors of the materials used in construction, all the browns, fawns, drabs, and other wood and earth tones that soon became fashionable in exterior decoration.

For the early part of its life, our house must have been in the height of style, especially since, as Downing also advised, its body and its trim were painted in contrasting shades, in order to accent "the features that confer expression on a house," as eyes and eyebrows do in a human face.

But for more than half a century, until we returned it to its original trio of browns, it was blanked out, all in white. However unsuitable that was historically, a widespread feeling prevailed around the 1920s that old houses were most respectable when they were white.

In general, white and lighter shades like pale yellow, soft beige, buff, and pale gray, with trim in even lighter shades, were characteristic not only of Greek Revival but also of the earlier Federal houses at the beginning of the nineteenth century. Even the still earlier Georgian houses of the eighteenth century, while they did tend toward more intense shades like yellow ochre or deep buff or dark blue and brown, made less of a point of contrasting base color and trim. Today homeowners are more sophisticated in their understanding of period colors and pay more attention to researching appropriate choices for their particular house.

No matter what color you choose, if you paint an insufficiently or improperly prepared surface, you'll be wasting your efforts. The job will look okay for a limited time only, and then you'll be back approximately where you started.

In order for paint to adhere, or to form a strong bond with a wooden siding like that on our old house, it has to be applied to a surface that is (1) dry, (2) solid, and (3) as clean as possible.

**Dry.** If an area to be painted will continue to be exposed to the same source of water that originally afflicted it, the new paint will blister and peel just as the old did, no matter how good the quality of the material or of the application. For example, we had to fix our leaky eaves in order to prevent the waterfalls that had done so much damage whenever it rained.

But water doesn't always attack in such obvious ways. There is sometimes sneaky subversion from within. When insulating we dealt with the problems of water vapor leaking from the interior of the house and damaging its structure within the wall cavity. The moisture doesn't stop there, however, and in continuing on its way out can undermine the exterior paint.

**Solid.** No one can depend on paint alone to glue together crumbling wood or fill in large cracks, though it may disguise them for a short while. That's why we were so scrupulous about repairing and replacing clapboards and woodwork, and caulking around window and door frames.

**Clean.** This means that not only ordinary dirt but also other debris must be removed from the surface to be painted. Because it had been so many years since our old house had had a face-lifting, we had an unusually extensive assignment in the scraping and sanding department. The old paint exhibited almost every stage of deterioration, everything except mildew. Our hillside site had exposed the house to conditions where maximum weathering occurred.

Preparing a surface for paint is like dieting. There's just no easy way to do it, no miracle in a bottle. Chemical strippers are fine for taking the finish off a chair in the basement, or even under certain circumstances for dealing with interior woodwork. But chemicals would be both impractical and too expensive for a massive outside job like our clapboards and trim. In a case like ours, you've got to make sure someone does the job right, or you can summon up your will-power and get to work yourself.

Besides great amounts of elbow grease, you will need some equipment: ▼

1. *Work gloves* are essential.

2. *Plexiglas goggles* will keep paint chips from flying into your eyes.

3. Hooked *pull scrapers* with replaceable blades are your primary hand tool. Have a file handy, so that you can sharpen your blade every so often.

4. A *face mask,* or respirator, will protect your lungs.

5. See if you can rent a *rotary* or *disc power sander* with two grips and a trigger,

set up with guides designed to help you in running evenly along clapboards. The one we used saved us a lot of time and mental anguish. Ours didn't use sandpaper, but featured instead a metal disc studded with Carborundum chips, an infinitely long-lasting abrasive surface. When the Carborundum disc gunked up, all we had to do was clean it off with a wire brush or soak it overnight in solvent.

6. *Wire brushes* are extremely useful for scouring off loose paint, especially from irregular surfaces like moldings. As with the pull scraper, work with a firm but light hand, or you may gouge or otherwise damage the wood underneath.

7. *Electric paint removers* that soften the old paint so that it can more easily be scraped off are on the market. They work on the principle of an iron, are useful for small areas and details, and are certainly safer to use than a propane blowtorch. A torch should never be used on the body of an old house, which tends to be tinder-dry. It may be used to soften paint on detached ornament, but only if you are *sure* that you're not dealing with lead paint.

**A**t several points we ran into a hazard peculiar to old houses, one we heard about in no uncertain terms from our more safety-conscious fans, and that was the very real danger incurred when removing lead paint. When we checked into the matter with Boston's Lead Paint Poisoning Prevention Project, we discovered that burning off lead paint, as we had been doing on the porch posts, is actually against the law in the city. We changed our ways immediately and investigated the proper procedures to use.

If you have an old house, the chances are overwhelming that you do have layers of lead paint. In fact the more expensively built the house was originally, the higher the lead level in your paint will be. In the mid-nineteenth century, all house paint was mixed from scratch by the painter, and one period recipe for it began, "Take 50 lbs. best white lead. . . ." The higher the proportion of lead in the mix, the higher the quality of the paint and the more long-lasting.

Health and safety experts advise that you treat lead paint as the deadly poison it is — that is, with great respect. Young, rapidly growing children are physiologically about five times as susceptible to lead absorption as adults, with those between ages one and three the most vulnerable. The result is, for them, irreversible brain damage. In view of the consequences, no precautions are too excessive.

Fumes are just one way lead paint can contaminate. It does its damage in other forms. Chips may fall from the siding of a house and into the soil. There the lead may then be absorbed into any root or leafy vegetables that may be planted (though fruited vegetables like tomatoes are not affected). Or children playing in the yard may ingest particles, as the dirt on their hands contaminates their food or toys.

Other dangers present themselves when sanding and scraping are going on. One is known as the *ambient lead hazard*, which is a technical way of saying that airborne lead paint dust can drift over a large area, particularly outside, when the wind blows. The dust can be inhaled or can settle on skin or clothes or can be widely distributed.

At first it seems you are faced with an impossible choice if you have a lead paint problem: it's dangerous to take it off, and it's dangerous to leave it on. The federal government has spent many millions of dollars since 1970 on trying to figure out some way to solve the dilemma, but so far none of their experimental schemes has proved feasible or effective. Lead paint removal remains a hazardous and labor-intensive job, but for safety's sake it has to be done. ▶

Removing the paint is something you can save money on by doing yourself, but there are certain basic precautions that you must follow scrupulously.

**First,** always wear a mask, goggles, gloves, and clothes that protect your skin, like long-sleeved shirts and long pants.

**Second,** on outside jobs, lay tarpaulins or drop cloths on the ground and bushes beneath where you are scraping or sanding. Use a shop vac regularly to suck up accumulations of chips and dust. Do not work on a windy day. Don't smoke or eat in the work area.

That goes for interior work as well. Inside, you are of course in an enclosed area, so you have to be especially careful. The best precaution, especially if you're preparing a number of rooms and therefore will be exposed to the lead paint for a long period, is to wear a double-cartridge filter mask (the cartridge should be changed once a month, the filter daily), but any kind of mask is better than none. Keep the room where you are working closed off from the rest of the house, so that the lead dust doesn't spread, but maintain sufficient ventilation within the room. Cover up any hot air registers. Evacuate any children for the duration.

After you have finished a room, do not use it for a specific amount of time, because lead dust is very fine and continues to sift down for many hours. The rule of thumb is that eight times the height of the room equals the number of hours you must wait before using the space again. If your room is eight feet high, then to be completely safe you should wait for sixty-four hours before reoccupying it.

To be as careful as possible, according to official safety standards, you should also segregate the work clothes you have worn from other laundry. Wash them separately, so that the contamination doesn't spread onto other garments.

These safeguards may seem fussy and a pain in the neck, but ignore them and you take a chance. Lead paint removal is a job you'll do just once. Do it right, and you'll never be sorry.

Painting the outside of a house can seem to be an overwhelming task, one you would never undertake yourself, even though you might well plan to do what might actually be a comparable job inside. Still, doing exterior painting yourself is well worth considering, as long as you take several factors into account in making your decision.

1. You will save an appreciable sum of money, since a large proportion of the cost of a professional paint job goes for labor, both for preparation and for the actual application.

2. The job is most efficiently done over a short, concentrated period of time, rather than dragged out weekend after weekend. How long it will take obviously depends on the size of the house, the number of coats of paint necessary, the crew of dedicated helpers you can conscript. It's a pretty long and lonely job for a solitary worker.

3. You have to figure in your chances with the weather. Three consecutive days of rain can set you back four work days, because you will have to wait twenty-four hours before you can resume painting. Certain seasons are better than others. Winter is obviously out of the question, and summer's extreme heat can present special problems. Paint will not adhere properly when it's too hot, nor will it spread easily, and the painter will swelter. Given seasonal limitations, can your own personal timetable be adjusted accordingly?

4. The job can be a physical endurance contest. Are you in training?

There is one shortcut in a project that otherwise doesn't seem to lend itself to mechanization. You can rent a sprayer. You probably won't want to use it on siding, because large-scale spraying is tricky, there are sometimes local regulations against doing it outdoors, and it uses twice as much paint as hand application. But spray painting of detailed areas and specific items like shutters can save you as much time and aggravation as it saved us. Be sure you get an *airless sprayer* and follow the directions carefully.

One technique that doesn't get sufficient publicity is *back-priming*, which provides extra protection to surfaces that aren't directly exposed to the weather and are therefore often shortchanged. These include the backs of clapboards, trim, and other boards. We back-primed the new brackets we installed on our cornice board, for example.

Back-priming stabilizes the material and minimizes warping and curling. New clapboards that are back-primed will absorb what moisture they do at an even rate, because both sides have been treated the same way and are equally stable. All trim should be back-primed before it is attached, and the bottoms of all doors should be painted so that they, too, don't suck up moisture and swell.

One note: any priming is a great job to assign to kids who want to help out.

The controversy about oil-based paint vs. latex is one that arouses strong partisan feelings. Latex advocates claim that it's faster drying, easier to clean up after, "breathes" so that moisture is not trapped between it and the wood underneath. Advocates of oil-based or alkyd paint (the two terms are for practical purposes synonyms), who form the conservative wing (which includes many professional painters), admit all that. But they insist that their choice covers better and lasts longer, advantages that make slower drying and the slight inconvenience of having to use turpentine or mineral spirits as a solvent seem to be really minor matters.

But one thing everyone seems to agree upon — and this may determine your choice for you. That fact is that latex may not adhere properly to an existing finish of oil-based paint. To be on the safe side, you should stick with the kind of paint you already have. We stuck with oil-based, outside and in for use on wood. Latex flat for interior walls and ceilings is, however, deservedly popular, and a different matter.

Preparation for interior painting is generally less arduous than that for exterior work. Sometimes you can get away with simply washing down woodwork to remove dirt and grease and provide the necessary clean surface, finishing up with a little light sanding. You may, however, have to work harder: stripping and sanding deteriorated window-frames, ◄ filling holes and cracks in walls and ceilings and doors, removing clogging layers of paint from paneling or other architectural details, or from hardwood that deserves to be returned to its natural finish, like our stair rails. But interior painting does lend itself to a room-by-room, piecemeal approach that seems to make it more appropriate for part-time work.

In addition to lead paint, there is one finish found in old houses to look out for. That is *calcimine*. Once widely used on ceilings, it is water-soluble and will wipe off on a wet sponge, which is how you test for it. If you paint over it, your new coat will simply peel off. Scrape and wash off as much of the calcimine as you can, and then apply the special anticalcimine primer that is available before you paint.

## Painting equipment
### Exterior preparation: (wood siding)
1. Pull scraper, with removable blades
2. File
3. Wire brush
4. Cold chisel and mallet, for removing old caulking
5. Safety goggles
6. Face mask
7. Putty knife and putty
8. Caulking gun and caulk
9. Electric paint remover, optional
10. Disc power sander with clapboard guides, Carborundum-surface disc

### Exterior application:
1. Flat paintbrush, 4-inch
2. Sash brush
3. Extension ladder
4. S-hook, to hang paint can or bucket from ladder
5. Rags

### Interior preparation and cleanup:
1. Detergent and sponges
2. Sandpaper (medium and fine) and sanding block
3. Putty knife
4. Joint compound
5. Window scraper (razor-blade type)
6. Masking tape
7. Drop cloths
8. Gloves (vinyl throwaways are practical)

### Interior application:
1. Brushes:
     3-inch flat
     2-inch chisel-edge
     angular sash
     oval sash
2. Roller, 9-inch with extension handle
3. Roller cover, plastic-core, with nap suited to both surface to be painted and kind of paint
4. Mixing paddle

# 12 House and Garden

**Week 11**  The daffodils next door were out in clumps, our inherited forsythias had astounded us by blooming in spite of their ragged winter look, and I was in shirt-sleeves. Our landscape consultants were busy supervising various rites of spring here and there on the property. Raking, clipping, pruning, and digging were all in full swing.

We were shifting into high gear now, as we moved into the final phases of so much of our work on the house itself, and began in earnest our labors on the great outdoors.

Norm, in an even better humor than usual on this balmy day, didn't seem to mind my interrupting his work on the new steps he was building. He joined me in taking stock of — gloating over is another way to put it — the week's progress on the front porch. A few days before, Greg had put the finishing touches on his restoration of the original engaged post taken down from the wall to the right of the front door. Then, replacing the temporary 2x4 supports, the single old veteran and the three newly milled freestanding posts went up. ▶ So did the scored plywood ceiling.

The new look was terrific. It's amazing how restoring an authentic detail like four ornamental posts can anchor a house in time, and give it a real personality. Suddenly our rebuilt porch wasn't just raw and new, something separate that we'd tacked back onto the front of the house. It was once again part of the house, an extension *of* it, not an addition *to* it.

We've all seen uneasily remodeled old porches, with substituted posts, like stark 4x4s or spindly wrought-iron jobs, that just don't carry their weight visually, though they may be adequate structurally. They look makeshift and out of period. I was glad we'd been able to manage the expense of having posts that were

exact replicas of the originals. In place they were a satisfying sight, and the house did look right.

Meanwhile the mighty backhoe had arrived to undertake a variety of heavy chores that needed its brute strength. One of the first jobs was to scoop out the pitiful privet hedge bordering the driveway. ▲ Unlike the blooming forsythias that had managed to justify their existence in the nick of time, the privet was too woody and unhealthy to bother with. After making quick work of the hedge, the backhoe moved on to tackle the debris from the demolition of the 1939 addition.

We would also use the backhoe to transfer large stones salvaged from the rubble over to the street side of the front yard where the gap in the retaining wall would be rebuilt. It also served to help with and clean up after the excavation for the new water main in from the street.

Ever since the near-zero days of February when the main froze, depriving us of water and leading to the total collapse of the old furnace, we'd been waiting for the ground to thaw so that we could take care of that subterranean problem. This week the big dig finally took place, ▶ the pipe installation was completed, and we were back in the mainstream.

Later in the morning the backhoe worked on a rescue mission, when we moved a picturesque if stunted birch from one side of the north yard to the other. But before we got to that, we had to attend to important matters inside the house.

In the dining room we dealt with some stone that was certainly more elegant than the rubble lying around what we laughingly called the front lawn. Larry Albre had come to show us how our Carrara marble fireplace could be cleaned up and returned to its original status as the most distinctive decorative detail of an interior that was essentially pretty straightforward and simple.

Years of smoky service had badly discolored the marble, ▼ and somewhere along the line the mantel shelf had split. Also, in the course of our own work, someone reaching from a ladder had absentmindedly braced his foot on the right side of the mantel itself. The whole piece had fallen right off the wall — a discouraging moment.

We had scouted up a replacement for the shelf, but as sometimes happens (unless you're of the play-it-safe-and-measure-a-dozen-times school) we'd miscalculated and bought ourselves a secondhand slab that was beautiful but about an inch and a half too short. We had to trade it in for one that fit.

Larry had some practical and professional suggestions for the restoration, and he pointed out exactly how worthwhile it was. His estimate of the cost of reproducing the installation today — including imported marble, piecing, carving, and the cast-iron work — was $2,000.

The detached side had already been anchored back in place and a new slate hearth installed when Larry and Co. turned up to demonstrate how to clean the stained marble. Simply scrubbing marble accomplishes nothing, because the discoloration is not on the surface. The soft stone, which is 99% calcium carbonate, has actually absorbed the stains right into its pores. The only way to remove soluble ones is to apply a chemical poultice that draws out the embedded stains.

The poultice slathered onto our mantelpiece was a commercial product, a drawing agent that was basically paint whiting and hydrogen peroxide, which reacted chemically with the calcium carbonate. ▼ Because such a poultice requires moisture in order to work, it had to be covered with a polyethylene sheet, which was taped down securely around the edges to seal it. The poultice takes about forty to seventy-two hours to complete its drawing effect. When the time was up, we washed down the surface so that we could inspect it. Sometimes a second application is necessary before the final buffing and sealing complete the job.

Before we could check off the fireplace project, we'd have to set the new mantel shelf when we managed to get one that was the right size. Larry showed us how to do that by cutting brass wire into little pigtails that would anchor the shelf in place. One end of a pigtail would be fastened into the plaster wall and the other end would be hooked into a hole bored into the marble itself with a $^3/_{16}$-inch carbide-tip drill. In this way the shelf would be reinforced to resist most normal downward pressure.

Today was certainly floor-laying day in the old house. Other men in Larry's crew were upstairs working on the tile in the bathrooms, while in the kitchen Norm was finishing up the oak block parquet. He just had his project under control when someone outside shouted in to him, "Here come the counters!"

They were accompanied by our second Larry of the day, Larry Lauria, with his sons Bobby and Kevin. They were carrying large spans of plastic laminate in the burnt orange color we'd chosen. ▲ These counters would complete the base cabinet installation in the

kitchen. Custom-made back in Larry's shop in several large sections, all the pieces were seamless except for the longest counter, which would go on the south wall. This had to have a seam by the sink, since the section itself was 15 feet, and plastic laminate comes no wider than 12 feet. The opening for the sink was pre-cut.

All the countertops had been made with a small backsplash attached and were self-edged. The piece that topped the base cabinets of our peninsula had been designed to extend beyond the cabinets so that stools could be drawn up under it. Its two outer corners were not sharp and hazardous to hips but were finished with curves. (Eventually we would apply the same orange laminate to the *soffits*, the panels enclosing the space ◄ between the wall cabinets and the ceiling.)

All this was the most demanding precision work, with no margin for error. Larry had made careful measurements, but after our own mantel shelf fiasco we were a bit nervous. There were a few hairy moments with the largest section of countertop, but we finally did maneuver it into place. The fit was absolutely perfect.

Another visitor joined us in the kitchen today. Rick Salon dropped by during the afternoon to discuss the burglar alarm and fire detection service his firm would be installing soon. The glass-paneled back door was an especially vulnerable point of entry. It would be fitted out with a timed exit-entry delay system activated when the door was opened and the magnetic contact between metal inserts recessed in both door and frame was broken. By punching in a code on a discreet push-button board located on the wall next to the door as soon as he'd entered, the homeowner would routinely deactivate the alarm before it sounded. An intruder, having no way to stop it from going off after the short period of grace, would be out of luck.

Photoelectric units and ultrasonic motion detectors, as well as smoke and heat detection devices elsewhere in the house, would provide further protection against crime and combustion. Another master control panel mounted on the wall in the master bedroom would make possible the arming and disarming of the whole system from upstairs. The homeowner would simply have to punch in the same numerical combination used on the board downstairs.

We all climbed upstairs to look over the location of the master control and to test the two distinctive beeper tones that would alert the homeowner at the same time that the system reported to the monitoring service that would summon police or fire departments.

Rick told us about another feature of his system, the "wireless panic," the term in the trade not for an unstrung state of mind but for a wireless remote control. Easily portable, it would enable one to activate the alarm from out in the yard or on the deck — anywhere within a range of a hundred and fifty feet of the house.

When the complete system was installed and at work, the hypothetical family who would be living here would have reason to feel they were as safe as modern technology could make them. Not everyone might want to spend $2,500, the cost of our exemplary system, in order to acquire our degree of coverage. But not to install at least some means of protection would probably be a dangerous gamble to make.

Outside, our backhoe was raring to go. The small birch was all ready to be moved. Years before, it had seeded itself there on the high northwest corner of the property in one of the most exposed spots we had, and ever since had been struggling to survive. We felt it deserved a second chance. ▼

During the day the landscape gardeners from the nursery that would be providing the plant materials for our spectacular reforestation had dug a slit trench right around the birch, isolating its roots. As we watched, the mighty paw of the backhoe lifted the tree up, while the men wrapped burlap around the root ball, ◄ and then hoisted it onto a waiting dolly.

Over at the new site, in what we thought of as our woodland area, a large excavation was ready. Once the tree was out of the ground, we saw how much of its growth had been underground. Wayne Smith, our good friend who owned the nursery, estimated that, root ball and all, it weighed about five or six hundred pounds. It really needed a sizable hole to accommodate it.

Four men and a lot of push finally got the dolly rolling, ► and then momentum carried the tree along past the blooming forsythia and toward its new home at such a clip that it almost overtook Wayne and me as we sauntered ahead.

**T**he dictionary says that the word "landscape" comes from a Middle Dutch word composed of two other words meaning "land" and "condition." Well, the condition of our land when we acquired it was pretty dismal. Even in 1818, when its very first owner, one John Parks, took possession, it probably didn't look quite as unkempt. There's something especially ramshackle about land that has been cultivated and then allowed to go to seed.

Because we took over the place in midwinter, our reclaiming process got off to a slow start, but by our eleventh week of work things were moving along. We'd already carted off three truckloads of leaves, branches, trimmings, and general dreck and debris.

When the first of our team of landscape designers, Phyllis Andersen, arrived to go over the property with me, we didn't know exactly what direction we'd be taking, or how extensive our work could be. Nothing had been done at that point, and all our construction trash and general wear and tear had made the front yard look even more depressed than ever. Phyllis was undeterred and began right away to suggest alternative plans.

The concrete walk leading from the driveway to the front steps might possibly be salvaged, she suggested, but if it couldn't be, we had two general options. We could replace the concrete with a *soft* material, like gravel or stone dust, with a containing edge to help keep it in place, though some problem with dispersal and tracking would still remain. Our other alternative would be a *hard* surface, either flagstone or brick. We finally went with flagstone.

The slope of the front yard would have to be regraded for better drainage and topsoil added, she said. The stumps of bushes and trees that we were getting rid of would have to be dug up. These included the privet hedge, a few hopeless lilacs, and an unwelcome black cherry in the southwest corner. Phyllis's general plan was to replace the overgrown and scraggly bushes with a healthy border of flowering shrubs along the driveway.

She also suggested that the most appropriate way to contain and define the new front garden would be to install a rather long span of picket fence along the driveway. It might run from the front walk west to the streetside corner and right around toward the chain-link fence that already enclosed the rest of the property. Though the old fence wasn't the most beautiful thing in the world, it was in good shape and we couldn't justify getting rid of it. We decided to leave a short space between the end of the picket fence and the beginning of the chain-link, and then to fill in the interval with planting, blurring the transition between one and the other.

Stock-sized 4-foot pickets would be a bit too high, Phyllis thought, and she recommended that they be cut down to 3½ feet so that they would be on a scale more compatible with the house. She suggested that the fence be painted to pick up the lightest trim color, the tan we'd chosen for the shutters and the front door.

In the very spot where the old maple that had fallen in the 1938 hurricane had once stood, a flowering tree, like a hawthorn or a crab apple, would make a decorative replacement whose scale would not be overpowering. At this early stage of planning, Phyllis was also considering restoring a trellis and wisteria to the west end of the front porch, for privacy and also as a nostalgic gesture to the past, to the porch as it once had been.

When we walked around to the back of the house, Phyllis commented on the irregular shape of the lot. It certainly was far from four-square, but she found the oblique angles interesting. It was then that she pointed to the little birch fighting for life in the northwest corner and suggested that we transplant it to a more congenial spot.

She did condemn as hopeless our landmark from the early weeks when we were tearing down and reconstructing the kitchen wing: a gnarled black cherry on the north side of the house. About forty years before, it had had the bad luck to seed itself right on ledge, where it proved that trees with tenacity can adapt to the most unlikely situations. Now it was infested with insects and wouldn't last too much longer. Phyllis recommended that we take it out while we had heavy machinery around to do the job.

The large and unusual old oak tree to the west of it and the sycamore maple to the east were both in good shape and could remain. The oak would need only to have the soil around it loosened, to have mulch added, and to be fertilized in order to continue in good health. It was a great asset.

Many of the existing spirea, forsythia, and lilac bushes in back of the house could also be saved by some judicious cleaning up and pruning to induce new growth from the bottom that would fill out their rather leggy silhouettes.

Victorians didn't use foundation planting. Though we did want to restore the mood of days gone by, we weren't going to be that purist. For example, when we followed the final planting plan, we didn't hide the foundation of the west wall, we just softened it slightly with a combination of low evergreens and deciduous shrubs, most of them flowering.

Diane Ridley, Phyllis's partner, commented to us on their choices when she presented the new plants along the west wall. The dominant axis of their scheme was horizontal, with the exception of one azalea that provided a vertical accent.

The team had made a point of selecting species of plants whose blooms were white or creamy, as some of their names suggested: Glacier, Boule de Neige, Delaware Valley White. These light and neutral shades would contrast effectively with the dark browns of our siding and trim.

Occasionally, elsewhere on the property, the light shades of the freestanding flowering trees and shrubs would blush a little. The colors of our new lilacs, crab apple, viburnum, and roses ranged from delicate yellows and pinks to a shade that was well on the way to purple. But none of our foundation planting was in that spectrum. Nowhere did we have a bright red variety of azalea, for example, that when set against the cocoa and dark brown of the house might well have looked like a maraschino cherry on a chocolate fudge sundae.

All of Diane's and Phyllis's recommendations appeared graphically, and to scale, on the final planting

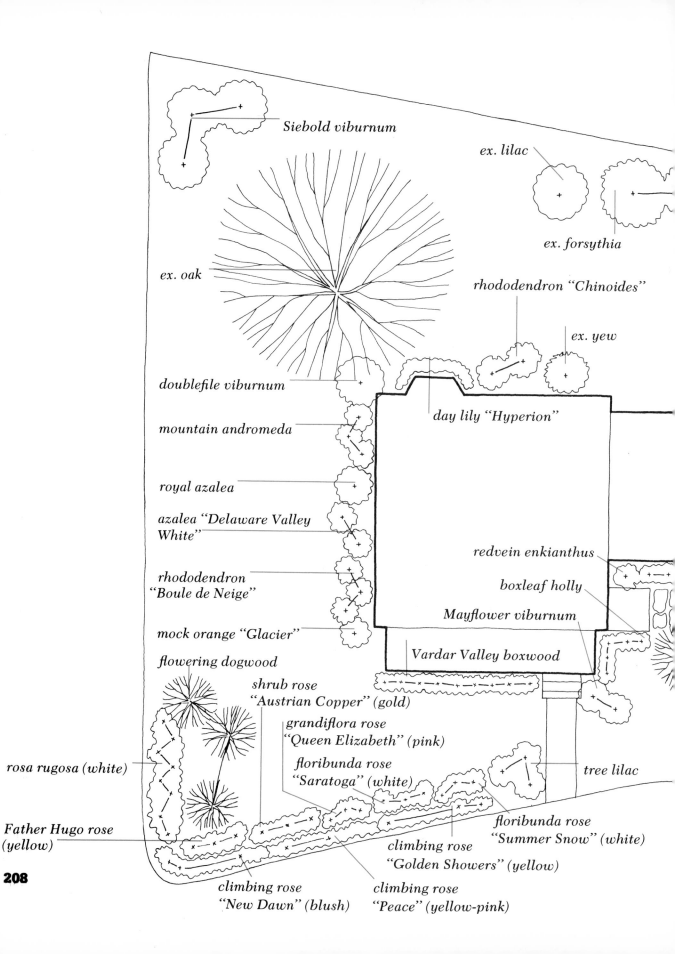

Siebold viburnum

ex. lilac

ex. forsythia

rhododendron "Chinoides"

ex. oak

ex. yew

doublefile viburnum

day lily "Hyperion"

mountain andromeda

royal azalea

azalea "Delaware Valley White"

rhododendron "Boule de Neige"

redvein enkianthus

boxleaf holly

Mayflower viburnum

mock orange "Glacier"

Vardar Valley boxwood

flowering dogwood

shrub rose "Austrian Copper" (gold)

grandiflora rose "Queen Elizabeth" (pink)

floribunda rose "Saratoga" (white)

rosa rugosa (white)

tree lilac

floribunda rose "Summer Snow" (white)

Father Hugo rose (yellow)

climbing rose "Golden Showers" (yellow)

climbing rose "New Dawn" (blush)

climbing rose "Peace" (yellow-pink)

plan they drew up. On it the massing of the various shrubs and trees is indicated schematically, and their botanical names are given. Items marked *ex.* (ex. lilac, ex. spirea, and so on) were already *existing.* ▼

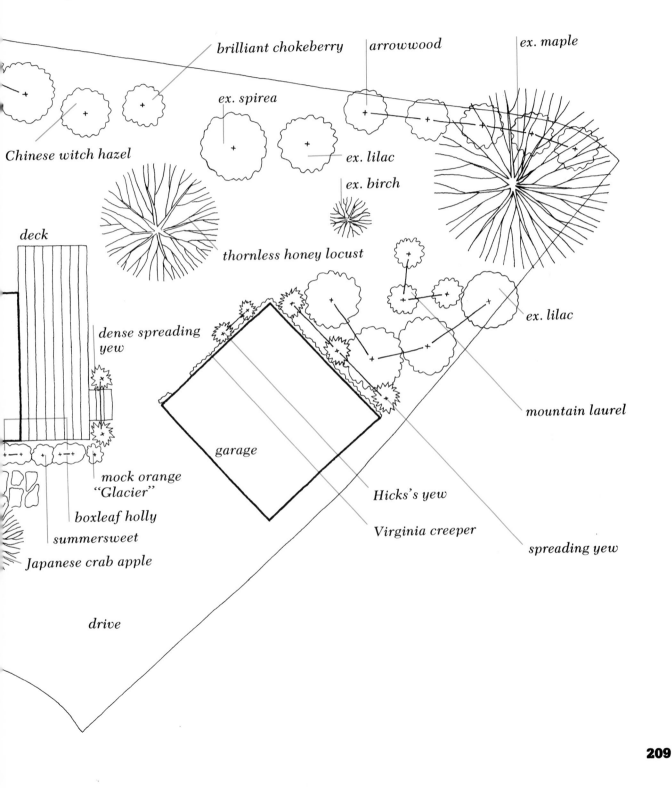

brilliant chokeberry

arrowwood

ex. maple

ex. spirea

Chinese witch hazel

ex. lilac

ex. birch

deck

thornless honey locust

ex. lilac

dense spreading yew

mountain laurel

garage

mock orange "Glacier"

Hicks's yew

boxleaf holly

Virginia creeper

summersweet

spreading yew

Japanese crab apple

drive

Once we'd worked out the details of our planting plan, we moved right along to the mighty job of what can only be described as The Greening of 6 Percival Street. Manpower and horsepower collaborated. The gnarled black cherry went down with a crash and was hauled off. Beside the deck, near the newly planted birch, the backhoe dug another, even bigger, hole for our largest import, a 25-foot-tall honey locust that Wayne Smith selected for us. It arrived in state on the back of a large truck, ▼ and together men and machines gingerly jockeyed it toward its destination, being careful not to skin its bark. This load weighed in at over a ton.

Wayne explained why he had suggested a honey locust for the site. The species is very hardy, both wind- and drought-resistant, and would thrive in the exposed location north of the deck. In the summer, the tree's fernlike foliage would provide some shade but would not be so dense that it would cut off the view of the park, as an evergreen would, for example.

A honey locust is a fast-growing tree. Ours, Wayne estimated, was over twenty years old. Its interesting asymmetrical shape would show to good advantage in such a prominent place. ▶

I collaborated with Wayne in planting a much smaller tree by the south wall of the kitchen. This one we coped with ourselves, without the help of the back-hoe. It was a flowering crab apple eight feet tall that would eventually grow to a full height of about fifteen feet. ◀ The hole we set it in was, as prescribed, about twice the volume of the root ball.

More heavy industry in the landscaping line took place in the front yard. Out of a chaos of rocks and slag, Paul Panetta, our stonemason, chose stones to recycle as

he filled in the gap in the retaining wall where the brick steps up from the sidewalk had been. ▶ At first we hadn't thought we'd be able to reconstruct the missing section, but when we found we could, we were delighted. Now that both the doctor's entrance and the walk up to it were gone, having a stairway that led nowhere was senseless.

The scrap salvaged from our own demolition work was the same random rubble that the existing retaining wall was made of, but even if we hadn't had leftovers on hand, we could have duplicated the material at a masonry yard.

The mortar Paul made for his work was in the proportion of one shovelful of Portland cement to two shovelsful of sand, mixed together dry, with water gradually added. The ideal consistency is neither crumbly nor so mushy that mortar seeps out of the joints and stains the surface of the stones.

He proceeded to set one stone next to another on the bed of mortar he'd troweled on. Then he filled in the joints, ▼ first using the *trowel* for the rough work, later a *tuck-pointer*, or joiner, for smoothing and finish-

ing. After the mortar had dried a bit, he cleaned off the surfaces of adjacent stones. As he worked, the pattern of neatly fitted stonework emerged. ▼

All this looked like a specialized skill that would be beyond the grasp of a beginner, but Paul assured me that a novice could manage it, *if* he were patient and took his time with the job.

Victorian Dorchester is a museum of beautiful masonry retaining walls. Architectural historian Douglass Shand Tucci described to us how in the late nineteenth century wealthy Bostonians moved to Dorchester from the city center and built homes more like town houses than suburban villas. Residential blocks of these detached but closely spaced houses were unified by the characteristic retaining walls that linked the separate properties into a single parklike streetscape.

Years ago our own wall was known as McGinty's Wall. Traditionally a neighborhood Memorial Day service has taken place on top of it, at approximately the spot where we'd found the little birch. A solitary trumpeter plays "Taps" and the notes float out over our lawn and the park below.

We installed a ready-made lawn of sod. It arrived in rolls, like so much carpet. But sodding a lawn is not as simple as rolling out a rug. As we discovered, the area must be prepared as carefully as for seeding, with the topsoil raked into a properly receptive surface.

With the warmer weather, we found that instead of huddling by the space heater in the basement for our breaks as we had in February, we gravitated to the new deck, where we could sit in the sun and enjoy springtime in our developing city garden.

Unself-consciously we were falling in with another old tradition of the place. Former occupant Georgia Packard had described to us how her family had used the east side of the yard as a kind of terrace, complete with outdoor furniture. The space where the garage was later built was then part of the garden. A heavy-laden grape arbor nearby screened in the area from the common driveway.

A modern deck can be a pleasant and useful addition to many an old home, as long as it is sited carefully so that it doesn't dominate or distract from the house itself.

Norm and Greg, who are skilled professionals, built ours with great speed. A step-by-step replay is perhaps in order, mainly to illustrate some general principles of planning and building any such construction.

One obvious difference between our deck and our front porch, which in some ways resembled each other, was that the deck had no roof or supporting posts. Another was that the deck needed more extensive work on its foundation.

### Deck: foundation

At its north end, we already had a start in the concrete slab left over from the old patio. What we had to do was to complete the base for the south end of the new deck by providing four new corner supports. Our overall plan called for the two halves of the deck to be on slightly different levels, the one to the north higher than the one to the south. We had to work out some exact heights for the pair, using the givens of back door sill, patio foundation, and the ground level.

The four new corner supports were concrete and were constructed in two parts: (1) the *footings*, and (2) the *piers*. To make the forms for the footings, Norm and Greg dug four holes about 10 inches deep and 2 feet square, though slightly wider toward their bases. The holes would mold solid supports for the weight of the deck.

At first Norm mixed by hand in a wheelbarrow the concrete he would pour into the molds. Later on, someone lent us an antique electric mixer; it wasn't the latest thing, but a cement mixer isn't a tool that requires space-age technology. A mixer can also be rented by the day for about $20. ▶

In all, we used about six bags of premixed concrete, which comes with all the dry ingredients in the proper proportions. Norm added water sparingly to the sand, gravel, and cement because he didn't want to end up with a soupy mixture.

**215**

After pouring the concrete into the holes for the footings, ▲ Norm and Greg smoothed the surface of what looked like puddles. As the concrete began to harden, they inserted upright steel anchor bolts that would rise up through the piers and protrude enough for the deck frame to be attached securely to them.

To mold the piers, the men used prefabricated cylindrical cardboard forms. Though fairly expensive, these are time-savers and probably end up costing less than the labor and materials necessary to make plywood forms. They come waxed inside, so they can easily be slipped off the hardened concrete. ◄

### Deck: framing and floor

Previously we had had to determine the difference in height between our two decks, as well as the

level of the lower one. Otherwise we wouldn't have known how high to make the piers.

The ideal height for any step or rise is about 7 inches. We had to have one step down from the back door to the upper deck, and a second step down from the upper to the lower deck. Two steps would measure about 15 inches down from the back door sill, so we had established a level line at that point as the height of the floor of the lower deck.

After boring holes in the floor joists, the men slipped the timbers over the anchor bolts in the piers and proceeded to level them with bits of shingle before finally securing them.

Constructing the upper deck on the old patio foundation demanded some more precise leveling ▼ and some heavy joining, but with joist hangers in the act, the framing went quickly.

Before long the entire deck was floored, ▲ with the same spaced, square-edged fir decking we used for the front porch. Norm sanded out any unevenness and applied preservative. The final touch was a simple linseed oil finish.

### Deck: steps

We still needed a set of steps down from the lower deck to the ground. These required a concrete footing of their own.

Then Norm showed us how to measure and cut stair *stringers*, which are the diagonal supports for the horizontal *treads* and the vertical *risers*.

First he had to figure out how many steps he needed. The distance from grade, or ground level, to the top of the rough framing of the upper deck was 26 inches, or, at approximately 7 inches per riser, 4 steps. But the lower deck was already one step down from the upper, which meant that the stairs from the lower deck to grade need only be about 19 inches high, or 3 steps. Therefore we needed stringers with three risers, each a little less than 7 inches high.

The ideal relationship between the depth of a tread and the height of a riser is indicated by a total, when both measurements are added together, of approximately 17 inches. Norm settled on a riser height of 6½ inches and a tread depth of 10½ inches.

Then he clamped his square to a piece of wood ▶ that had a straightedge so that the legs of the square measured 6½ and 10½ inches. Sliding the straightedge and the clamped square down the 2x12 from which he'd cut the stringer, he easily drew his pattern. From the last riser he subtracted the thickness of a tread (in our case, ¾ inch), because that one would rest directly on the ground. He wanted to have the exposed part of every riser the same height. ▶

The last addition to the deck was the vertical boarding Greg installed to enclose and mask the piers and the black void under the deck. ▼ The men would add an old-fashioned crisscross lattice to the front porch for similar reasons but a slightly different effect.

When completed, both extensions of the house into the garden were firmly anchored to the ground, visually and structurally. Before long, their straight, hard edges would be softened by shrubs, and the ground on which they stood would be bright with new grass. All that would be left for us to do would be to draw up a deck chair, lie back, and enjoy the sun and the fragrance of lilacs. Easy living lay just a few weeks ahead.

**219**

**W**hen you first confront a major landscaping project, you should be on guard against making two common mistakes in your approach.

The first mistake is to think immediately in terms of specific planting, imagining a rose bush here, a crab apple there, day lilies everywhere.

The second error is to consider the project as simply the sum of its parts, not as a whole with subdivisions. The front yard may seem to be one separate unit, the back yard another, and the vegetable garden a third, but they are all parts of the landscaping, as rooms are of a house.

Planning that tries to move from the specific to the general, rather than the reverse, can get bogged down in details along the way. Remember that landscaping includes not only planting but also grading, fences and walls, decks and terraces. All these subsidiary projects will make competing claims on your attention, but you should try not to let them distract you from your overall goal.

Unless you have a total plan clearly in mind, you will find that you won't be able to divide the project into its logical stages. You will be tempted to strike out impulsively in several directions at once, and your random choices may produce results unrelated to the realities of your land, or to your own real needs. You may be disappointed by the discrepancy between effort and outcome.

Before you can plan intelligently for future landscaping, you must determine what you have in the present, the *existing conditions* of your property. This stage parallels the initial appraisal of the structure and condition of the house itself.

Ask yourself these questions:

1. Do you have any major *site problems*? Perhaps, like us, you have underlying ledge that will limit the planting you can undertake. Are there sharp differences in grade that you should consider changing or that you will have to plan around? What are your screening needs? Is there an unattractive view that you will want to block out with planting, or will you want only to screen for privacy, as we did in the northwest corner and beside the deck?

2. What *exposures* do you have to work with? Where do the sun and the shade fall in your yard? How many hours of full sun do you have in various areas? Remember that the house itself casts a shadow on potential garden space. Trees shade, of course, and they also have large root systems that monopolize moisture and nutrients in the soil around them. Their demands must be taken into account.

3. What about existing *plant materials*? What do you have? What condition is it in? Which existing plants are worth trying to save, and which should be taken out right away? How much dead wood do you have in your trees?

4. What is the *soil condition* you have to deal with? Test your soil for acidity and to find out what minerals are lacking and that you will have to supply. Will you need to bring in new topsoil?

What you have is one thing; what you want is another. When you have completed your appraisal of existing conditions and considered the implications of them in your planning, you should then move on to think about human needs, not just the needs of the site. How do you and your family want to use the land? Are there special features that you want to plan for? What are the practical limitations on your needs that you must account for?

One way to organize your thinking is around these defining categories.

### Circulation

How will guests approach the house? How will the family? Where will you want paths? To the front and back entrances? To the basement? From garage to house? From one part of the property to another? Where will trash cans be in relation to the house?

### Specific needs

Are there going to be special features you should plan for because of the demands of children, pets, outdoor seating, eating areas, hobbies or sports, other miscellaneous considerations? For example, we wanted to have planting appropriate to a certain histor-

ical period, since we were basically doing an exterior restoration.

### Maintenance

How much time are you willing to spend on taking care of your property? Your self-appraisal will help you decide the relative proportions for you of *soft surface*, like lawn and garden, and *hard surface*, like terrace or deck. Do you want perennial borders, which require more maintenance than evergreen shrub borders? Do you want a living hedge, or a fence that needs minimal care?

### Budget

Don't put this category first in your basic planning. A budget doesn't determine what you need or want — it determines what you can have. If you can't afford at the start all that you need or want in your landscaping, then you either have to approach the project in easy stages, or you have to give up some of the features that are less important than others. Then, even if you never get beyond the first stages, you at least will have proceeded logically.

Only when you have answered these questions in your own mind are you ready to settle down with graph paper and pencil to make a precise *planting plan.*

If you find that this prospect overwhelms you, you may want to get help. Like an architect, a *landscape designer* can work with you in a small way or a large one. You may feel that you simply want to have a professional opinion in general terms, that you want an overview, especially when you are appraising existing conditions. A landscape designer, for a flat fee on the order of $50 for the first hour, will walk around with you, as Phyllis did with us, and give on-the-spot opinions and suggestions (with a written follow-up).

Stepping up services a degree, the designer could make a *concept plan* for you. This would not be dimensioned but would indicate schematically what should be done where. You would then implement the scheme yourself at your own rate of speed.

Finally, in a full-scale service, the designer would draw up an exact planting plan like ours, and would contract out and supervise the actual work, for which he would receive as fee a percentage of the cost of the total job.

You can't depend on getting significant design help from the average nursery, but you can expect to get good advice on choosing plant materials, on various species and their care, as well as their appropriateness for your site. The nurseryman can tell you such things as which trees thrive in city or exposed locations and which shrubs and perennials need sun or can take shade, and they are experienced in the peculiarities of your immediate locality.

Pay careful attention to instructions for the actual planting of trees and shrubs. The most common amateur mistake is to plant in holes that are too small. The old adage goes, "Don't put a five-dollar plant in a fifty-cent hole." Also, be sure you are scrupulous in following all directions for adding nutrients to the soil. You don't want to take chances on wasting all your hard work because you were stingy or lazy at the end.

Our landscaping was a major project, and we implemented our plan all at once. We didn't have to wait for anything. We used sod for an instant lawn, rather than waiting for seed to sprout. We brought in a large tree that would screen our deck immediately, rather than a less expensive sapling that would have to grow into the job. All shrubs went into the ground in a couple of weeks. We were fortunate to be able to make such an exciting transformation, one that showed what *can* be done when all systems are go. But most homeowners aren't so lucky, and would probably need to tackle a comparable landscaping less dramatically, following a long-range plan whose stages might stretch over several years.

No one should be under the illusion that the procedure we followed is typical or necessary. As a matter of fact, there are certain advantages in going more slowly, in living through the cycle of all four seasons before making major commitments. You can learn firsthand about the seasonal patterns of sun and shade, and will also have a sense of how your family actually uses the property. You may even find you will want to revise your initial thinking.

To illustrate how any overall plan can be broken down into its components, here in order of priority is how we would have done our job in stages.

First, we would have cleaned up the whole site, concentrating on the north side of the property, ▲ particularly the slope between the garage and the street. We would have taken out dead wood, removed the dangerous black cherry, carted off prunings, leaves, and debris. Then we would have embarked on a general revitalization and maintenance program.

Next, we would have moved on to the front of the house and worked on the way the house related to the garage, the driveway, and the street. The important southwest corner required early attention because we had to revise where we'd removed the walk and

excavated for the water main. We would have implemented as much of the plan for fencing and planting as we could have afforded, postponing what we had to.

The third priority would have centered on planting around the deck.

Fourth, we would have attended to planting that would screen out any part of our view that we wanted to deemphasize.

Finally, we would have done the foundation planting. This comes at the bottom of the list because it was purely decorative. Nothing had to be screened or masked. The fact that foundation planting wasn't a Victorian usage also made it a less urgent priority.

**223**

# 13 Of Time and Money

**Week 12**

Now we were really entering the countdown stage: one week to go, and a million minor jobs, it seemed, to get finished. We faced reality and took stock.

### Exterior work left to do:

1. Install second garage door, side door, and window replacements. Clean garage. ◀
2. Prime, paint, and put up shutters. Scrape and prime dormers. Complete all exterior painting, prime and finish coats.
3. Install storm windows.
4. Finish landscaping.
5. Complete vertical boarding along sides of deck.

### Interior work left to do:

6. Install sinks in lavatory and laundry/bath.
7. Finish all moldings, door and window casings, baseboards.
8. Prime interior woodwork.
9. Hang all doors.
10. Carpet stairs and hall of second floor.
11. Complete floor work.
12. Remove temporary partition from third-floor hall.
13. Install kitchen appliances. ▶

Impossible? Well, maybe, but we were determined to give it our best try. I remembered a conversation with Judy Selwyn, our preservation consultant, about a month ago. She said then that it seemed to her that the last 5% of the work on a house always *seems* to take as long as the first 50%, and that all the little hitches that happen during that last bit are particularly aggravating, because by that time everyone concerned has had it.

Certainly the place was buzzing with activity today, and morale still seemed okay. On hand we had all sorts of people working their heads off to help us meet the deadline looming over us: 4 landscape gardeners with 1 supervisor, 2 landscape designers, 2 floor men, 2 plumbers, 2 carpenters, 3 apprentices, 2 painters, and 1 stonemason. Plus me, the television crew, and a slightly larger than ordinary complement of sidewalk superintendents and fans.

The commotion didn't seem to bother Paul Panetta, who was intent on finishing up his job on the retaining wall. I began by strolling down to the sidewalk to talk with him about his work. By the end of the day, he'd be all through.

John Buckley climbed down from the high place where I found him to describe to us the painting procedures he recommended. The dark gray prime coat he and Sam Zarzour were applying looked odd, but he assured me that the final coat of cocoa brown would cover it completely. The two were quick workers, and by 1 P.M. they had painted down to ground level and were finished with the next to last coat on the south

side. Then they went right back up on their ladders and
started on the eaves of the west side. ▲

Yesterday the backhoe regraded the front lawn
and spread new topsoil around. All traces of the water
main project were gone. Later today the truck delivered
our new honey locust, among other major plant materials, and we embarked on what was our own local Arbor
Day. We planted the locust by the deck and the little
crab apple in front of the kitchen wing.

Norm had completed all the clapboard patching
during the week and his work on the front steps early
this morning. Next he and Greg tackled the installation
of traditional crisscross lattice, a decorative and authentic way to finish off the crawl space under our beautiful
Victorian piazza. It's not hard to do, at least as Norm
described it.

First he made a frame out of 2x4s and fastened it
to the porch.

Because the lattice strips are small — 1⅜ inches
wide by ⅜ inch thick — they form a fairly dense open-
work pattern when they are installed that is hard to

paint. So Norm had the strips primed before cutting them. All the pieces were laid out, and a roller used to apply the primer to many of them at the same time, just as we had previously primed clapboards. This left the painters only the finish coat to do once the lattice had been nailed in place.

Each strip had to be cut to certain lengths and at a 45-degree angle. To save measuring and therefore to save time, Norm set a *jig* on his miter box. A jig is a guide used when you're cutting a series of identical pieces. It enables you to work with the efficiency of an assembly line.

Norm and Greg worked together to attach the strips. Greg got a head start with the first layer. ▼ Using one strip as a spacer, he set the pieces of lattice that slanted in one direction. He nailed the strips only at top and bottom, and not in the middle, using 4d box nails. Norm followed up, repeating the process in reverse as he nailed on the second layer, all those strips that

slanted in the opposite direction. The top pieces held the lower ones in place.

Finally, Norm finished off the lattice screen with 1x4 pine boards that completed it like a picture frame. ▶

Inside the house we were making progress on our list of things to do. In the family room and hall, Jim Bannon was busily nailing down the new oak strip floor, while upstairs George Hannon gave a lesson in how to sand a floor, and I countered with a demonstration of how not to. I underestimated the forward drive and brute power of the big drum sander, and it very nearly ran away with me. I felt as if I were being pulled along by a team of wild horses. Luckily I remembered to tilt the machine up so that the cylinder of the drum wouldn't

**227**

be in contact with the floor, and we stopped. It was a narrow escape, but I did manage to avoid digging a trench in the floor, or plowing into the wall, or mowing down either of the intrepid cameramen recording the great moment.

Comparatively restful was my discussion with John Hanson, who showed me the completed installation of all the plumbing fixtures in the master bathroom. One interesting feature he pointed out was the single-handle faucet in the bathtub/shower. The building code now requires that the hot water in a shower be no hotter than 110° as a safety measure. Our controls were designed with a stop that would temper the mix of hot and cold to the required limit.

We still had a little way to go in the bathroom/laundry, where the sink was not yet hooked up, though the gas clothes dryer was already in place.

In the kitchen we were all prepared for the appliances that soon would be delivered. Everything was in order, the floor, lights, cabinets, and counters all ready and waiting.

We'd come a long way in three months. I found it hard to recall with any vividness the sad sight that had been the old abandoned kitchen of our first week of work. How many hours of labor, and how much money had we invested in it since, I wondered.

I was just musing, my question basically a rhetorical one, but perhaps this is the stage of our story in which we should pause for some accounting.

First of all a disclaimer. As we've said before, our house was a special case, not a representative one. Our purpose wasn't to show how economically a house can be rehabbed or to chronicle a typical renovation. Far from it. Our purpose was to show how we did everything we thought had to be done. We aimed to illustrate many more options than, realistically, most people would undertake.

The issue is further clouded by the fact that we received many contributions of goods and services. The donors' generosity often stimulated us to do things we might not have undertaken otherwise.

Finally, the pressure of our tight schedule sometimes meant that we had to choose the expensive but quick route, or that we didn't comparison shop, or get as many estimates as we knew we should have.

Given our special circumstances, we have devised a special sort of accounting that may satisfy the merely curious, and yet be of some practical use to the homeowner contemplating a rehabbing of his own. It is in general terms and deals in relative costs, not in dollars. Unfortunately it looks as though inflation will continue and will soon date exact figures, but the proportions of parts to whole should remain comparatively stable. We have worked out percentages of the total cost of the project spent in various subcategories, such as carpentry, plumbing, and insulation. Within each category, we give the relative proportions of the cost of labor and the cost of material. These seem, if not absolute prescriptions, at least representative and should give prospective rehabbers some idea of what to expect.

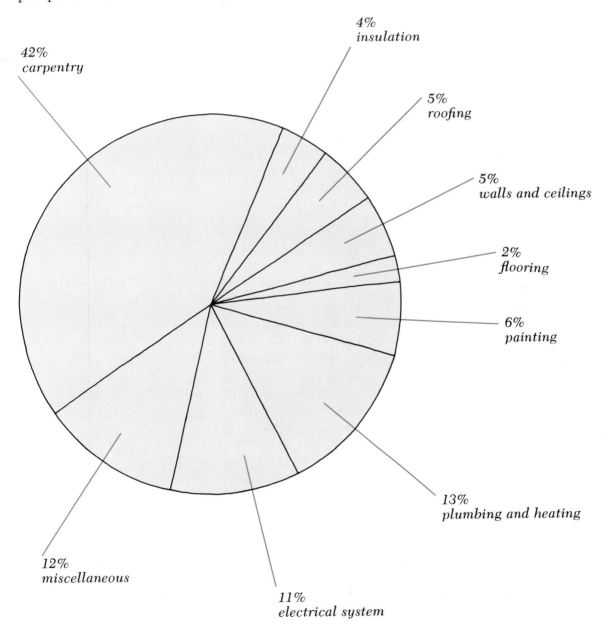

4% insulation

42% carpentry

5% roofing

5% walls and ceilings

2% flooring

6% painting

13% plumbing and heating

12% miscellaneous

11% electrical system

The grand total on which we base our percentages includes only the costs of labor and material incurred in renovating the body of the house itself. It does not include the purchase price, or the fees for the various consultants, the landscaping, and the security system.

Our original estimate of what the grand total might be was optimistic. We thought we would spend $30,000. John Hewitt — and at the time he said he was teasing — suggested we might spend twice that amount. We ended up spending a third again as much, or about $80,000. This figure does include the value of donations as expenses.

## Carpentry
### 42% of grand total

Our major expenditure was for carpentry. This is hardly surprising, given the extent of the work we did.

To summarize the main achievements on the exterior alone, our carpenters demolished the doctor's addition, walled in where it had been, rebuilt the front porch, repaired and reshingled the mansard roof, restored the eaves and brackets, rebuilt the walls of the

kitchen wing, renovated the garage, and repaired the siding.

Inside the house, they demolished various old walls and reframed new ones, stripped and leveled ceilings and floors, renovated old windows and installed new ones, hung doors, applied casings and other woodwork, hung cabinets, and laid the kitchen and lavatory floors.

Materials accounted for 58% of the cost of the carpentry work, while 42% went for labor.

Materials included (1) all lumber used for framing, siding, and general construction; (2) millwork, including all the new brackets and porch posts; (3) all doors and windows, including the skylight, storm windows, garage doors, and the bulkhead into the basement; (4) miscellaneous building products and hardware.

### Insulation
### 4% of grand total

We spent the lion's share here on the cellulose insulation. Our installer said that the ordinary job of cellulose insulation should pay for itself in money saved on heat in three to four years, the so-called payback period for this product.

A couple of hundred dollars in this category went for materials, primarily fiberglass batting, that the carpenters put in themselves. We can't, however, separate out from the total of all carpentry labor the cost of their work specifically on insulating.

### Roofing
### 5% of grand total

Here the major expenditure was for resurfacing the main and the dormer roofs as well as for a new built-up roof on the kitchen wing. This work was done by a roofing contractor whose bill accounts for 84% of our roofing expenses.

This category also includes the cost of other materials, which the carpenters installed themselves: shingles for the mansard sides of the roof, and roll roofing for the front porch. These materials represent the remaining 16% of the total roofing costs. Again, we can't separate out the carpenters' labor from the carpentry category.

### Walls and ceilings
### 5% of grand total

This category includes (1) all lathing, (2) plastering, and (3) the tub surrounds in the bathrooms.

The total cost of the lathers' work represents 43% of the money spent in this category. Within it, materials (Blueboard, specifically) represent 42% of the cost, while labor was responsible for the other 58%.

Plastering represents 44% of the cost of all wall and ceiling work, and the amount we spent was almost entirely for labor.

The total cost of the two tub surrounds represents the remaining 13%.

## Floors
### 2% of grand total

This category includes (1) the refinishing of the old fir floors on the second story and the old oak veneer floor in the dining room, as well as the laying of all new oak floors downstairs (except the parquet in the kitchen and lavatory, which was carpentry work) and (2) the ceramic tile floors in the bathrooms.

Our installer told us that a little over half the cost of an oak strip floor like ours represents the cost of materials. The combination of laying and refinishing our wood floors accounts for 69% of the expenditures in this category.

The remaining 31% was spent on tiling the bathroom floors.

## Painting
### 6% of grand total

This category includes interior and exterior painting, plus the extensive preparation for it (scraping, sanding, and so on), and miscellaneous items like wallpapering, door stripping, and equipment rental (wallpaper steamer and paint sprayer).

We had to do more exterior preparation than is typical, because of the extraordinarily poor condition of the siding. The cost of labor on preparation alone, inside and out, was about 30% of the total expenditure in this category.

Materials represent 45% of the total spent; labor accounts for 55%, of which a little less than half was spent on the actual application of exterior paint.

## Plumbing and heating
### 13% of grand total

This category includes all of the contractor's rough and finish work for both the new heating system and the revised plumbing system. We contracted for a first-class job, we got it, and we paid for it. Included

here are the cost of the replacement of the water main, the furnace, and the expense of various emergency calls and start-up work incurred before our contractor came onto the job.

Labor represents 69% of the costs in this category. The contractor's men put in 247 hours on rough work and 55 on finish work, 302 hours in all.

The cost of the new water main represents 7% of the total in this category.

### Electrical system
### 11% of grand total

We spent a lot, but we did do a complete rewiring and increased the service all the way to the maximum of 200 amps. The electrical work compared in scope to the plumbing and heating job.

Materials represent 28% of the total we spent on electrical work. The cost of light fixtures mounts up more than one might expect. They alone accounted for 13% of all we spent on materials in this category.

Labor amounted to about 240 hours of work, at a cost of 72% of the total here.

Anyone of a mathematical bent will now ask: what about the remaining 12% of the grand total? Actually this percentage has no real identity as a category but simply represents the total of miscellaneous expenses, some of them rather large. These range from the cost of all appliances, kitchen cabinets, and counters to the rental fees for scaffolding and dumpsters. To account for them all, one by one, would not be generally enlightening.

**N**ot surprisingly, the most expensive rooms in the house to redo were the kitchen and bathrooms. Both required extensive plumbing and wiring, new appliances and fixtures, special new floor and wall surfaces, lighting, and cabinetry. The work was slow and demanding, and therefore expensive.

In our kitchen the retail value of the appliances alone came to about $3,000. Our new cabinets and counters weren't cheap either, and we didn't even have top-of-the-line custom cabinets. The cost of the cabinets and counters almost equaled the cost of the appliances.

In comparison, plumbing fixtures for bathrooms seem to be surprisingly inexpensive. For example, our cast-iron tubs were only a couple of hundred dollars each. Fiberglass tubs would have been 25% less. But the rough plumbing work that must precede the installation is another matter. Remember that our contractor estimated the cost of labor alone on the two new bathrooms as $3,500.

One builder we talked to estimated that the cost per square foot for kitchens and bathrooms is easily double that of the other rooms in a house. These rooms are obvious money-grabbers, a fact you can count on and plan for. Their demands on time and money come as no surprise, unlike the spiraling involvements represented by our experience with the eaves. Norm's original estimate of the amount of time the job would take (and consequently of what the labor would cost) *doubled* once he got into the work and saw how much had to be done. The front porch also turned out to be an unexpectedly larger, more expensive project.

Eaves and porch had one thing in common besides the extent of the work they required. Both were restorations, in which we had to duplicate original architectural details, the brackets ▶ and the turned posts. Restoration is always expensive. It is labor-intensive, requiring as it does hand and custom work. The high price of such fidelity may seem worthwhile to those of us who are committed. But before going blindly into a restoration, the homeowner should be aware of what he's getting into. To us, the cost of milling forty-five new brackets and three new porch posts was justifiable, even though it amounted to 15% of the total expenditure on carpentry materials.

A little jolt of pessimism, just enough to alert the rehabber to reality without breaking his spirit, is probably a good idea. Of the discrepancy between an initial projection and what actually happens, Charles Wing in *From the Walls In* says, "My personal fantasy factory is 2x — everything costs twice as much, takes twice as long, is twice as hard — as I have learned from hard experience."

**S**uppose you were committed to rehabbing a house that was roughly in the same shape that ours was. The chances are that, unlike us, you couldn't afford to do it all at once. The question is: where would you, where should you start?

In the broadest terms, the directions in which you should move are these. You go (1) *from the roughest work to the most finished,* for example, from demolition to painting, (2) *from the concealed to the exposed,* for example, from wiring and plumbing to plastering; (3) *from life support to decoration,* for example, from heating system to wallpapering.

With this general progression in mind, you might well consider your priorities in this order.

Start with the necessities, with obvious hazards and code violations in heating and electrical systems. If you are going to be living in the house as work proceeds, you may want to include plumbing among the necessities.

Next, take care of weatherproofing the exterior of the house. You don't want leaks and water damage to subvert your interior work. Weatherproofing includes sealing up roof, walls, and windows, and taking care of gutters and downspouts and other drains. Any major structural problems, such as foundation work, should also be attacked early. If you are not living in the house, you may decide to put this stage first.

Once the bare necessities are taken care of you can proceed with work that is less urgent. This includes remodeling of the floor plan, insulating, modernizing kitchens and baths, restoring architectural detail, and finally redecorating.

The economic advantages of doing a major rehabbing stage by stage are obvious. You can pay as you go, and you can also live in the house while the work goes on around you, as you probably couldn't in a blitzkrieg like ours.

There are psychological advantages as well, particularly for the indecisive who would rather spread minor choices over a longer span of time, sometimes really designing as they go. There is, however, no escaping the need to make certain major decisions at the start, if a coherent master plan is to organize the whole process for you. You should keep your long-term goals in mind, even if your progress toward them is stately.

One disadvantage in not mounting a campaign on the grand scale is that you lose a certain momentum and may sacrifice efficiency. You may have to get the same workmen back again and again as you inch forward, stage by stage. Start-and-stop work wastes more time than going full speed ahead to the final destination.

Another disadvantage is primarily psychological. The job can begin to strike you as a life work that you will never complete, especially if you are doing a lot of the work yourself. You take on too many chores at once, and all around you are half-finished projects. Demoralization sets in.

Before undertaking do-it-yourself projects you should be clear in your own head about whether you are doing so because you *want* to or because you *have* to. Assigning yourself too many uncongenial or overly difficult tasks is unrealistic.

Most people don't spend enough time assessing a project before they get into it, but simply go off half-cocked without thinking through all its implications. If you start by doing this, will you then be committed to doing that? Try to predict what lies around that next corner before you turn it and come face to face with something lying in wait.

Ask yourself some hard questions. Is the project you are planning to do yourself highly technical, requiring special equipment, special knowledge or experience that would be difficult to acquire rapidly enough to do acceptable work on the job at hand? Is time an issue, with a deadline pressing you? Is your own time worth more than the money you're likely to save? If the answers are yes, perhaps you'd better reconsider.

But if the job is one that will really give you a sense of satisfaction to do, if you have enough time and energy to do it properly, and if you already have some of the prerequisite skills or natural aptitude, and either want to buy, have, or can rent the necessary equipment — then the light is green for you. If it is a labor-intensive job that requires dedication but not expertise, the large amount of money you will save by contributing your own labor will be persuasive.

One way to calculate is to get an estimate on having the whole job done professionally. Then figure out the cost of materials and subtract it from the estimate. This lump sum of potential savings may tell you all you need to know, but you can continue and divide the difference by the number of hours you think the job will take you to do. The answer will give you the hourly wage you will then be paying yourself. Ask yourself if it still makes sense for you to do the job on your own.

Certain categories of work save more money than others. One working rule is that labor costs are on the average 60 to 75% of the total spent on a project. Our labor costs actually ranged from 41% of the total for carpentry to 81% of the total for walls and ceilings. No rough rule is perfect, but 60 to 75% is a reasonable approximation.

*Money* magazine made a comparison of what the savings would be on a number of possible do-it-yourself projects. The percentages ranged between two extremes, from 80% saved if you were to install a 400-square-foot flagstone patio or to dry-wall a small room, down to only 16% saved if you replaced a wooden screen door with a pre-hung metal screen-and-storm door. On the exterior and interior painting projects cited you could save 77% and 54% respectively. By laying your own asphalt shingles over existing roofing you could save a tidy 48%. If you insulated an 800-square-foot attic using 6-inch fiberglass batting, you'd save 32%.

The catch is that various projects range in degree of difficulty as well as in their rewards. Almost anyone can paint, but not everyone is up to shingling. Looking back over the work we did on the house itself, these are the projects we did that we can recommend to beginning do-it-yourselfers:

1. Demolishing
2. Straightening ceilings
3. Insulating with fiberglass batting
4. Restoring windows (repairing sash cords and reglazing)
5. Painting (including preparation)

The experienced home handyman could well take on the following additional projects:

1. Laying wood parquet and vinyl tile floors (ceramic tile would be more of a challenge but possible); laying outdoor decking; refinishing wooden floors
2. Putting up dry wall (except on ceilings)
3. Installing a skylight or bulkhead; installing and trimming pre-hung doors and preassembled windows
4. Shingling; roll roofing
5. Clapboarding
6. Building a deck
7. Installing lattice
8. Hanging cabinets
9. Wallpapering

**A**s a consumer group, do-it-yourselfers who are primarily concerned with saving money are susceptible to various false economies. Competitive manufacturers and aggressive merchandisers have put on the market a lot of junk that looks quick and easy. This stuff is a constant temptation to inexperienced buyers for whom price is the main consideration. A lot of it is not worth your time or money.

Here is a cluster of things to look out for. Examine the kitchen cabinets that seem to be such a bargain to see how they are put together and what materials have gone into them. For example, do the drawers travel steadily on side guides, or do they wiggle back and forth on a single center track? Are the components simply stapled together? Don't economize on cheap hardware. Beware of bargain lumber. It can be twisted or full of knotholes, and you'll waste a lot of time compensating for its defects. Beware also of imitation or simulated anything. It may look terrific to you who have never encountered it before, but not to anyone who's been around. There are very few all-plastic items that you will find in a quality job anywhere. Avoid the latest fashion in items that you'll have to live with for a long time. Fads date quickly.

A related false economy is to buy cheap material and then either pay the going rate for labor or else try to save even more by installing it yourself. One example is bargain carpet, which will have to be replaced sooner than quality goods. Having to repeat the installation will consume the initial savings on material. You can, however, save wisely by buying from odd lots or discontinued lines.

A different breed of consumer may go overboard in the opposite direction and feel compelled to invest in the best of everything in order to justify the time he's going to spend installing it himself. Unnecessary extravagances are his temptation. Instead of wasting his labor, he may waste materials if his skills are not up to the job.

The price differential between the top and the middle of the line can be considerable. It's clear that you shouldn't buy the cheapest embossed vinyl tiles whose printed pattern will in effect wash off, but on the other hand, you really don't need to make a major investment in the opposite extreme, solid-core vinyl tiles. There is an acceptable happy medium.

In appliances the price range is often staggering. The monolithic refrigerator/freezer may have every feature known to man, but it may also cost twice as much as one slightly less elaborate but certainly adequate.

Another unnecessary extravagance is to overequip yourself with more tools than you need to own and that are more powerful or elaborate than you need for the kind of job you are likely ever to do. Don't get an 8-inch circular saw, for example, when a 6-inch model will suit you fine. Buy yourself a basic complement of good quality tools, and rent the special items on the rare occasions when you need them.

Right now insulation is on everyone's mind, and the maxim that more is always better seems sometimes to be unchallenged. You can, however, overinsulate so that you can never earn back your investment in money saved on fuel. The advantage of having a professional energy audit is that you get help in determining the practical limits of an insulation program for your house, one that realistically establishes priorities and considers the payback.

The beginning rehabber who wants to work with contractors rather than do the job himself has other temptations to resist. One is to neglect the process of getting competitive bids, often for no other reason than it seems vaguely impolite to pit bidders against one another, or underhanded to go behind the first bidder's back to get second and third opinions. Nonsense. Getting competitive bids is reasonable and is expected. It can make a big difference. For example, the lowest bid we got for exterior painting was 35% of the amount of the highest bid.

When you are evaluating your bids, be sure you actually call the references the bidders supply. Strange to say, many inexperienced employers assume that the mere fact a reference is given means that when it's checked out, it will of course prove satisfactory. They don't bother to check, sometimes to their sorrow.

If you plan to save a little money by working along with your contractor, remem-ber that you are making a commitment to finish your share of work when you say you will. You must be as professional in living up to your deadlines as you expect him to be. Budget your time wisely, realistically.

You can help your contractor to avoid expensive delays by getting busy early on the kinds of choices you are qualified to make — in fact, really should make. These are matters of style, color, alternative models. Ask to see samples and to be directed to the distributors he recommends so that you can settle on alternatives in tile, flooring, hardware, colors of plastic laminate, appliances, and plumbing fixtures. With kitchen cabinets, it is especially important to see the actual cabinets, not just photographs in a catalogue. If you make up your mind early, orders can be placed early. You will minimize the chances that your project will grind to a halt when the supplier informs you that the item you have chosen "is no longer available" or "won't be available until . . ."

One final word on time and money. Construction companies submit bills promptly and expect you to pay up equally promptly. When you are dealing with a credit card enterprise that is in effect lending you money at interest, you can put off payment in good conscience. When you are billed by a construction company, you are not dealing with an anonymous bureaucracy. The men who have been working for you are waiting for your payment to come through the company directly to them. You should have a healthy sense of urgency. To get the best work from your contractor, try to pay your bills on time.

# 14
# This New House

**Week 13**  This was it, the big day we'd been working toward all these weeks. Our new house was about to make its debut, but as usual in such great ceremonial occasions — graduations, wedding, premieres, and ship launchings — there had been a lot of frantic last-minute preparation.

With remarkable good humor, everyone had pitched in. A small boy from the neighborhood, who had long been an extremely serious but faithful sidewalk superintendent, finally smiled when he was conscripted to help us wash windows. Long after hours yesterday, the most unlikely candidates wheeled barrows of bark mulch, scrubbed the tubs, and primed woodwork. Our elderly paint-and-plaster-splatted vacuum cleaner gave its last full measure of devotion, until at last it could hardly suck up one more ounce of sawdust.

This morning the sun rose with fierce tropical splendor, as if nature had decided to end our project as dramatically as she had begun it. I remember all too well seeing my frozen breath before me as I introduced the old house in the midst of that deepest of deep freezes. Now I would show it off in a sizzling heat wave that was the opposite extreme. With the temperature unseasonably in the nineties, the "sweat of our brow" was no figure of speech.

Instant summer was a little hard on our instant landscaping, particularly the new sod. We kept the hoses going, watered like mad, and hoped for the best.

During the week a crowd of shrubs was delivered to the front yard, where they waited patiently in line while Wayne Smith consulted the planting plan. A ◄ charming low border of miniature box bushes went in along the front porch, against a background of lattice. Also planted were those old-fashioned favorites, mock orange and viburnum and lilac, a selection whose com-

240

bined fragrances were almost guaranteed to arouse free-floating nostalgia.

The pattern in which the sod was laid, with staggered seams, echoed the way Jim Bannon had laid the oak strip flooring inside the house. With no need for nailing, the lawn laying went incredibly fast. ▲ It was the careful preparation of the surface that had taken time.

What a startling difference the new grass made! This morning when I came down Percival Street and turned into the driveway, the sudden sight of it really took my breath away. Rolling out the green carpet, rather than seeding and waiting patiently, may constitute an extravagance at a cost of from 13¢ to 20¢ a square foot (depending on how much you buy), but for instant gratification, sod can't be beat.

We watched as the two new flagstone walks in front were laid, one double row up to the front steps and a single row leading from the driveway to the bulkhead. Their installation involved a simple little trick worth passing on.

**241**

First the gardener put the flagstone down on the sod exactly where he wanted it. Then, using a linoleum cutting knife, he cut into the sod, carefully following the contour of the stone as if it were a pattern. Then he put it aside, lifted out its green shadow, like a cookie he'd cut, and replaced the stone in its custom-made bed. The flagstone looked exactly as if the grass had grown up around it. ▼

The sodding stopped short of the new picket fence that the men finished installing today. As planned, the fence began about a yard from the front walk, ran west along the lawn and around the corner, and stopped about ten feet before it would have met the existing chain-link fence. We set up a kind of demilitarized zone between the two kinds of fence and planted it with new shrubs, craftily sited so that when they grew to full size they'd be a diplomatically leafy screen across the gap.

I talked with Sam DeForest, who represented the company that manufactured and installed our fence, and asked him about materials and methods. Our fence, he said, was completely cedar, both posts and pickets, and every nail used in its construction was galvanized. Using

a manual *post-hole digger,* which is essentially two shovels hinged together, his men dug holes 36 inches deep and 6½ inches in diameter into which they set the posts. (Suppliers usually provide their own specs; the rule of thumb is that the depth of the hole should be one third the length of the post, but no more than 3½ feet.) The pickets went in next, section by prefab section. ▶

The men ran into a few tough installations when they hit ledge. In these cases, they bored the holes right into the rock and then, using steel-pin anchors, set the posts in them in hydraulic cement. This is the strongest way to set a post, but it's not the ordinary method.

Our solid new fence will be around for a while now. Sam estimated its life expectancy as from twenty to thirty years. ▶

An average home handyman could install a fence like ours himself if he followed the supplier's instructions faithfully. He could rent a post-hole digger. He would also need to supply himself with gravel backfill and plenty of wood preservative. An easy way to treat posts is to stand them up overnight in a bucket of preservative.

Work space was at a premium, and earlier Greg had taken advantage of the clearing on the porch by the front door to cut some glass for a few last-minute replacements. His successor there today was engrossed in cutting tackboards for the stair carpet installation when we edged by him to go inside.

The rug we'd chosen was a neutral wheat-color Acrilan. We needed eleven yards of it for the stairs and the second-floor hall. When I asked whether carpeting stairs with turns like ours might be a do-it-yourself project, the answer was emphatically no, this was not something the average homeowner should attempt. Working with bulk and acute angles requires experience: the potential for expensive errors is just too great.

Inside the house, we'd completed a lot of finishing touches in all directions during the week. Paper went on the bathroom walls. A brass chandelier in the dining room and a hanging brass lantern in the stair hall went up. Our kitchen appliances went in.

We'd made good progress on the list of things left to do that we'd compiled last week, but as always a few details remained to be polished off. When I looked around for Norm to ask him how much he thought we still had to do, I found him out back by the garage, hard at work as usual. Nearby, Sam the painter was brushing linseed oil on the decking.

"We've got about a week's work still to do, Bob," Norm told me. Breaking down his projection, he estimated that there was a day's work needed on the garage, half a day on windows, one day upstairs and another downstairs on priming woodwork and finishing up in general — nothing major, just an assortment of loose ends.

A literal and petty-minded person, some hard-nosed attorney for the prosecution, might sneer that we hadn't really made our deadline at all, but in my book we had triumphed. Today I went from the very top of the house, where I discussed sooty matters with one very hot chimney sweep sweltering in his classic costume of top hat and tails, ◄ right on down to the very bottom, the cool, quiet basement. As I looked around me, I was very proud of the group effort that had produced such a transformation. I hoped our example had been educational. Maybe it would even be inspirational.

Please join me in a kind of celebration, as we take a photographic tour of the premises. May I introduce — this new house.

With the bell tower of St. Peter's looking down on us, we crunch over the freshly graveled driveway, past the new fence and the flagstone walk to the front entrance, past the kitchen wing, to the east side of the house. Not a scrap of debris remains anywhere on the premises. Amazing expanses of green lawn and sleek oiled deck stretch uncluttered. On the resurfaced roof of the kitchen wing the profile of the skylight presents itself. The view up from the slope north of the garage is imposing. Our new house looms large over the raked, pruned, and replanted woodland hillside.

Entering the house, we pause for a moment in the front hall and look west across the fresh and gleaming living room, now restored to its original finish and dimensions. We can detect no trace of the jog that once marked the intersection of the new and old parts of the south wall, which is to our left. We look back across the new oak strip floor from the french doors that open into the dining room. There, the restored antique mantel and the new brass chandelier first catch our eyes in the light from the bay window, but the unobtrusive baseboard heating will surely get its full share of appreciation once winter comes again.

Looking east from the dining room through the small arch we opened up, we have a clear vista through the family room and the kitchen to the glass-paned back door and even beyond, for we can catch a glimpse of the garage outside. Before we continue on into the dazzling new kitchen, we take a slight detour into the stair hall to the right, to inspect the fully equipped and newly wallpapered lavatory, one of our major contributions to convenience in our revisions of the original plan of the first floor.

All appliances installed, the closet completed, the last touch of orange laminate finishing the soffits, sun pouring in through the new skylight and windows, our dream kitchen shines bright. Looking at its new incarnation, we can hardly remember it as it once was, dismal and dark and discouraging.

From below we admire the details of the stairway to the second floor, and once up there we repeat the experience with the flight to the third floor. We can peer from the hall into the cheerful bath/laundry on the right.

Still in the hall and turning to face west, we can see simultaneously into the master bedroom to the left and the guest room to the right. We think that the refinished old fir floors look as good as new, and we also like the natural look of the old paneled doors we had stripped. Moving clockwise around the second floor, we encounter a little souvenir from the past, the woodwork detail left in the corner to the right of the window in the northeast bedroom. We get another view into that room through the door to the left in the guest bedroom. Its other door opens back into the hall.

In the master bedroom, we turn back to look toward the hall. At the same time we can see into the master bath through another opening on the right. The sliding doors in the compact new closet arrangement do increase the usable floor space in a room that already has its share of complex traffic patterns. Standing in the master bathroom in front of the large linen closet, we can just see the edge of the bathtub, enclosed by the small partition between us and the doorway out. The window that faces south is on our left.

The most cheerful room on the third floor is in the southwest corner. It's the only one up there that has two dormers. The window on the left, which faces south, was the latecomer, added in a remodeling to provide cross-ventilation and more light. Down in the basement the atmosphere may be less airy and the decor definitely original, but we like to think of the area as our showplace of modern technology. From left to right, we have the new hot water heater, the new gas furnace, and the auxiliary space heater. The last stop on our tour, the basement reminds us that the house is still both new and old. Perhaps — and we like to think it does — it embodies the best of both worlds.

# For Reading and Reference

## General home improvement

The Home Repair and Improvement Series by the Editors of Time-Life Books. The seventeen volumes include *Basic Wiring, Doors and Windows, Floors and Stairways, Heating and Cooling, Paint and Wallpaper, Plumbing, Roofs and Siding,* and *Weatherproofing.*

Bright, James L. *The Home Repair Book.* New York: Doubleday, 1977.

Falcone, Joseph D. *How to Design, Build, Remodel and Maintain Your Home.* New York: Wiley, 1978.

Gladstone, Bernard. *The New York Times Complete Manual of Home Repair.* New York: Times Books, 1978.

Green, Floyd, and Meyer, Susan. *You Can Renovate Your Own Home: A Step-by-Step Guide to Major Interior Improvements.* New York: Doubleday, 1978.

Paulsen, Gary. *The Building a New, Buying an Old, Remodeling a Used, Comprehensive Home & Shelter How-to-Do-It Book.* Englewood Cliffs, N.J.: Prentice-Hall, 1976.

*Reader's Digest Complete Do-It-Yourself Manual.* New York: Norton, 1973.

Stanforth, Deirdre, and Stamm, Martha. *Buying and Renovating a House in the City: A Practical Guide.* New York: Knopf, 1978.

Wing, Charles. *From the Walls In.* Boston: Atlantic–Little, Brown, 1979.

## Old houses

Bullock, Orin M., Jr. *The Restoration Manual.* Norwalk, Conn.: Silvermine Publishers, 1966.

*Guidelines for Rehabilitating Old Buildings: Principles to Consider When Planning Rehabilitation and New Construction Projects in Older Neighborhoods.* Washington, D.C.: U.S. Departments of Housing and Urban Development and the Interior, 1977.

Hotton, Peter. *So You Want to Fix Up an Old House.* Boston: Little, Brown, 1979.

Stephen, George. "Rehabilitating Old Houses," *Information from the National Trust for Historic Preservation.* Washington, D.C.: Preservation Press, 1976.

————. *Remodeling Old Houses, Without Destroying Their Character.* New York: Knopf, 1973.

## City handbooks

Various older cities have published homeowners' guides to rehabilitation, which are useful to residents elsewhere with similar problems. Some of the best are:

*How to Love and Care for Your Old Building in New Bedford,* by Maximilian F. Ferro. New Bedford, Mass.: City of New Bedford, 1977.

*Living With Old Houses.* Portland, Me.: Greater Portland Landmarks, Inc., 1975.

*The Salem Handbook, A Renovation Guide for Homeowners.* Salem, Mass.: Historic Salem, Inc., 1977.

*Rehab Right: How to Rehabilitate Your Oakland House Without Sacrificing Architectural Assets.* Oakland, Cal.: City of Oakland, 1978.

## Architectural history

Anyone interested in this fascinating topic will enjoy these two beautiful volumes:

Cummings, Abbott Lowell. *The Framed Houses of Massachusetts Bay, 1625–1725.* Cambridge, Mass.: The Belknap Press of Harvard University Press, 1979.

*Exterior Decoration: Victorian Colors for Victorian Houses.* A new edition, with an introduction by Samuel J. Dornsife, of the 1885 original. Philadelphia, Pa.: The Athenaeum of Philadelphia, 1975.

## Appraisal

Hoffman, George. *How to Inspect a House.* New York: Dell, 1979.

*Inspection Checklist for Vintage Houses.* Brooklyn, N.Y.: Old-House Journal.

Sherwood, Gerald E. *New Life for Old Dwellings: Appraisal and Rehabilitation.* Washington, D.C.: U.S. Department of Agriculture (Handbook No. 481), 1975.

## Retrofitting

Blandy, Thomas, and Lamoureux, Denis. *All Through the House: A Guide to Home Weatherization.* New York: McGraw-Hill, 1980.

Ackerman, Allan D., et al. *In the Bank — Or Up The Chimney? A Dollars and Cents Guide to Energy-Saving Home Improvements.* Cambridge, Mass.: Abt Associates, 1975.

Drake, George R. *Weatherizing Your Home.* Reston, Va.: Reston, 1978.

Nielsen, Sally E. (ed.). *Insulating the Old House.* Portland, Me.; Greater Portland Landmarks, Inc., 1977.

Smith, Baird. "Conserving Energy in Historic Buildings," *Preservation Brief* 3, and its supplement, "Energy Conservation and Historic Preservation." Washington, D.C.: U.S. Department of the Interior (excerpt from 11593, Vol. 2, No. 3), 1978.

## Construction

Alth, Max. *Do-It-Yourself Roofing and Siding.* New York: Hawthorn, 1979.

Anderson, L. O. *Wood-frame House Construction.* Revised edition. Washington, D.C.: U.S. Department of Agriculture (Handbook No. 73), 1970.

Ball, John E. *Audel's Carpenters and Builders Library.* Four volumes. Indianapolis, Ind.: Audel/Sams, 1977.

Blackburn, Graham. *Illustrated Basic Carpentry.* Boston: Little, Brown, 1977.

Dietz, Albert G. *Dwelling House Construction.* 4th ed. Cambridge, Mass.: M.I.T. Press, 1974.

Wagner, Willis. *Modern Carpentry.* So. Holland, Ill.: Goodheart-Willcox, 1976.

## Tools

*The Tool Catalogue: An Expert Selection of the World's Finest Tools.* By the Editors of Consumer Guide. New York: Harper & Row: 1978.

Jackson, Albert, and Day, David. *Tools and How to Use Them.* New York: Knopf, 1978.

Shuler, Stanley. *The Illustrated Encyclopedia of Carpentry & Woodworking Tools, Terms, & Materials.* Chester, Conn., and New York: Pequot/Random House, 1973.

## Periodicals

*American Preservation: The Magazine for Historic and Neighborhood Preservation.* Bimonthly. Bracy House, 620 East Sixth, Little Rock, Ark. 72202.

*Historic Preservation.* Bimonthly. National Trust for Historic Preservation, 748 Jackson Place N.W., Washington, D.C. 20006.

*The Old-House Journal: Renovation and Maintenance Ideas for the Antique Home.* Monthly. 69A Seventh Ave., Brooklyn, N.Y. 11217.

# Index

thermostats, 92, 113, 115, 124
tiles: carpet, 158; ceramic, 24–25, 76, 136, 153, 158, 232, 238; composition, 24; roof, 177; vinyl, 158
toenailing, 76
tongue-and-groove flooring, 156–157
toolbox, 85
tools: false economies in, 238–239; list for carpentry, 85; list for demolition, 67. *See also specific tools*
top plates, in framing, 74, 75
trash barrels, 66, 67
treads, stair, 218–219
trees, and temperature regulating, 102. *See also* landscaping
Trethewey, Ron (plumbing contractor), 42, 46, 71, 119, 125
trowels, 130, 212
Tucci, Douglass Shand (architectural historian), 214
tuck-pointer, 212

**U**

underlayment: roof, 166; wall, 140
U.S. Department of Housing and Urban Development, *Guidelines . . .* , 27
urea formaldehyde foam, 96
urethane: foam, 96; spray, 105

**V**

vapor barrier, 99–100
Vassallo, Sal (plasterer), 129–133, 145
ventilation, 103, 165
vent system, 117, 119–120
vermiculite, 96
vernacular house, 16
Victorian period: energy conservation in, 102–104; foundation

planting in, 207, 223; maintaining style, 27–28, 54, 95, 142; paint colors, 185, 190; style, 17; windows, 102
vinyl: paper, 100; sheet vs. tile, 158; siding, 27
voltage, 24, 122

**W**

wallboard, 109; Blueboard, 128, 131, 149, 232; foil backing for, 99–100; heat panels, 106; installing, 128–129, 140, 141–142; patching, 140–141; removing, 66; schedule for, 47
wallpaper, 90, 100, 140, 232, 236, 238
walls: evening new and old, 73–74; finishing exterior, 28, 138–139, 142; finishing interior, 128–133, 137–138, 140–142; framing, 71–73, 74–77, 88; load-bearing and demolition, 56, 59–60, 63–64; percentage of costs, 231–232; retaining, 61, 210–214, 220, 225; schedule for work, 46, 47
warping, wood, 80
waste stack, 116
waste system, 116, 117
water: damage to paint, 182; heater, 22, 87, 125; leakage, 23, 24, 30, 161, 162, 163; and preparation for painting, 190; pressure, 24; supply and waste systems, 116–119, 120; vapor, 98–100, 190
water main. *See* main
wax, floor, 156
weather, 31; and exterior painting, 194; and roof damage, 162; and Victorian energy efficiency, 102–103

weatherproofing, 236
weatherstripping, 105
White, Kevin, 179–180
windows, 12, 14, 17; double-glazing, 95, 104, 135; and energy efficiency, 94–95, 101, 102, 104; fixing double-hung, 133–134; framing, 71, 76; installing, 134–135, 145–146, 238; paint buildup on frames, 24; reglazing, 143, 238
windowsill, 71, 146
wind-seal rating, shingles, 175
Wing, Charles, 96, 235
wirecutter, 85
wiring, electrical, 14, 22, 56, 120–123; in demolition, 56, 66; schedule for, 47
wood: deterioration in, 82; dry rot in, 98; fires, and chimney, 106; framing, 78–80; kiln-dried and green, 80–82; old, 66, 83; plywood, 82; preparation of, for painting, 190–192; sizes, 80. *See also* floors; framing; gutters
wood lath, 66, 140
wood preservative, 128, 189
wrenches, 67, 85

**Y**

yard: cleanup, 178, 205, 222–223; maintenance, 222; needs and uses, 220. *See also* landscaping

**Z**

Zarzour, Sam (painter), 186–189, 225, 243
zinc flashing, 167–168
zoning, heat, 113–116, 124
zoning regulations, 51
*Zoster marina* (eelgrass), 95

This book is set in VIP Caledonia, designed in 1938 by W. A. Dwiggins; Serifa Extra Bold; and Beton Bold Condensed.